# EFFECTIVE LEGAL RESEARCH
## 2nd edition

**JOHN KNOWLES**
Law Librarian,
Queen's University Belfast

Previous edition co-authored by
**PHILIP A. THOMAS**
Professor of Socio Legal Studies,
Cardiff Law School,
University of Wales, Cardiff

**SWEET & MAXWELL**

THOMSON REUTERS

Published in 2009 by Thomson Reuters (Legal) Limited
(Registered in Engalnd & Wales, Company No 1679046.
Registered Office and address for service:
100 Avenue Road, London NW3 3PF)
trading as [Sweet & Maxwell]

Typeset by Servis Filmsetting Ltd, Stockport, Cheshire
Printed in Great Britain by Ashford Colour Printers, Gosport

*No natural forests were destroyed to make this product;*
*only farmed timber was used and re-planted.*

A CIP catalogue record for this book is available from the British Library

ISBN 9781847038180

Thomson Reuters and the Thomson Reuters logo are trademarks of Thomson Reuters.
Sweet & Maxwell® is a registered trademark of Thomson Reuters (Legal) Limited.

# Contents

# EFFECTIVE LEGAL RESEARCH

# Acknowledgments

The authors and publishers would like to thank those organisations who have allowed their copyrighted materials to be reproduced as examples throughout this book. All efforts were made to contact the copyright holders and grateful acknowledgment is made to I.C.L.R., TSO, BAILII and Westlaw UK, amongst others for their permissions.

All extracted materials are represented in the format and with the correct content at the time of writing the book and are subject to change.

# Preface

A new law student is faced with a potentially bewildering variety of sources of law. A recent case mentioned in a lecture might be found in a database of law reports, a printed report, or a website providing access to recent court judgments. There might be journal articles or newspaper reports that discuss the case. The text of an Act can be found in a number of different ways, using both online sources and editions of statutes found in a law library. It can be difficult to know where to start. This book aims to help you make effective use of the law resources to which you have access. Online sources are placed alongside traditional print sources in each of the chapters of the book and their use explained, in order that you can make the best possible use of both.

In a sense, this book is a labour-saving device. Use it as a reference throughout your time as a student, or indeed thereafter, should you decide to go into legal practice. Though some of the more detailed coverage is most likely to be of use if you are embarking on a legal research module (or a post-graduate qualification), it is not intended to be a textbook associated with a particular course. It is a reference aid to be consulted whenever you have a problem. Consequently, you might use the book selectively, referring to those sections which are useful at a particular point in your studies, or when recommended to look up a case, statute or issue by a member of the teaching staff.

The book concentrates on the law in England and Wales. Detailed coverage is also given of European human rights law and the law of the European Union. A brief appendix covers online sources of Scots and Northern Ireland law.

The title page of the book reflects the contribution made by Philip A Thomas, as co-author and sole instigator, not only of the first edition of *Effective Legal Research*, but also of the four editions of *Dane & Thomas: How to Use a Law Library*. The coverage of print resources is based, in large part, on the coverage of print materials in *How to Use a Law Library*. The coverage of online sources was largely re-written for the first edition of *Effective Legal Revision* and extensively revised for this one.

# ▶ 1
# Making the most of a law library

## INTRODUCTION

A law library might seem the most traditional of libraries. A university law library contains  ▶ **1.1**
many shelves of heavy bound volumes of statutes and law reports, along with a wide variety of
academic journals and textbooks. Sometimes the law library will be housed in a separate
building; more often it will form one area within a larger library.

Imposing as these print collections can be, however, they constitute only one part of
what a law library offers. The library is also a gateway to online collections of legal materials.
Sometimes the extent of these materials can even surpass what is available in print. To learn
how to research the law efficiently and effectively is to learn how to make use of both the online
and the print collections of a law library.

## THE LIBRARY CATALOGUE

The online library catalogue is your guide to the extent of the print and online materials avail-  ▶ **1.2**
able to you. It will also be supplemented by library web pages which usually provide access to
online services. Online catalogues are easy to use and computers providing catalogue access
will be available throughout the library building. You can also connect to the catalogue from
outside the library using the internet. Find the library catalogue and web pages as soon as you
can and familiarise yourself with the way they work. If you are not already well acquainted with
the law library, make use of library induction talks and seek out guides provided for you, both
in print and on the library website. Remember that librarians are there to support you and so
do not be afraid to ask for help, especially at the start of your course.

## BOOKS

The books held in a university library are usually the best starting point for legal research.  ▶ **1.3**
Making good use of them can save a great deal of wasted effort.

You will find three different kinds of book on the library shelves. Textbooks designed
for undergraduates explain the fundamentals of law in a particular area. These are comple-
mented by research texts (sometimes called monographs) which offer detailed descriptions of
the law and usually a more advanced level of discussion. These often assume the knowledge
set out in undergraduate textbooks. Practitioner texts and loose-leaf updating services, in contrast, aim to provide a detailed, authoritative, statement of the law in a particular area. They

are designed first and foremost for the legal profession. All three types of book can be useful to legal research. Check dates of publication, to ensure that you are using the most recent edition.

Books of all kinds are usually grouped on the shelves according to their subject. The subject dealt with in each book is indicated by numbers, or letters and numbers, which are usually printed on the spine of the book. These symbols indicate the exact subject matter of each volume. They are known as the classification number or classmark and bring together, in one area of the library, all books dealing with the same subject, such as torts, criminal law and constitutional law.

There may be a number of separate sequences in the library. Large books (folios and quartos) and very thin books (pamphlets) may be kept in a separate part of the library. As a result, the size of the book may be important in helping you to find it on the shelves. There will normally be some indication on the catalogue entry for a book, if a book is shelved separately.

## E-BOOKS

**1.4** ▶ It is no longer the case that you are restricted to print volumes when searching for books that might be of value to your research. Significant numbers of books are now available online from most university libraries. These e-books are purchased by your library in much the same way as print volumes and can usually be accessed through the library catalogue. Instead of providing a library location for a book, the catalogue displays a link to an online version of the book's printed text. In many cases complete collections of e-books can be searched from a single dedicated search page. Examples include the ebrary collection of e-books and MyiLibrary. Check library web pages to confirm their availability. Access restrictions will be similar to those for subscription database services (see para.2.8).

It is not usually possible to download the full text of library e-books. Unlike e-books held on hand-held book readers, these books are designed to be read online from a networked computer. Printing is restricted to relatively brief sections of the book.

You will not, unfortunately, find online versions of key student textbooks in the library catalogue. Publishers usually only release e-book versions of research texts to libraries. They also tend to make them available some time (usually at least a year) after the print version. Many legal practitioner texts are however available in current updated versions from LexisNexis Butterworths (para.2.3) and Westlaw UK (para.2.4). These include titles such as *Rayden & Jackson on Divorce and Family Matters* from LexisNexis Butterworths and *Archbold: criminal pleading, evidence and practice* from Westlaw UK.

> **TIPS** • *Use keyword or "keyword in title" searches to find books in the library catalogue. Combine keywords with the author surname if known.*

## SEARCHING THE LIBRARY CATALOGUE

**1.5** ▶ Library catalogues allow you to search for books by the author's name, or the title of the book. It is usually easier and quicker to search by title (ignoring words such as "The" or "A" in the title), or alternatively by a combination of author surname and title. If you do not have the exact title, a "keyword search" enables you to search for words occurring anywhere in the title. In many cases, the initial search page of the library catalogue contains only a single search box. If this is so, enter author surnames and title words in a single search phrase. Further search options can usually be found under an "advanced search" link. These usually include searches by subject area or classification (see para.7.29).

If the library has the book you want, the catalogue entry will give you its full details (e.g. its publisher, the date of publication and the length of the book in pages) and the location of the book on the shelves.

Author searches which display search results as an author index should be used with care. Even if you are sure of the author of the book, you may need to check a number of author entries before you find the right one. Suppose you have a reference to a book written by John Jackson. If you use the author search and enter "Jackson, J" you will see index entries that might feature the following variations of the name (among others):

Jackson, J.A., John Archer, 1929–
Jackson, J.D, John Dugland, 1955–
Jackson, J.E., John Ellwood
Jackson, John, 1887–1958
Jackson, John E.

You need to start with "Jackson, J.A." and work down the list in order to find the right author. In this case, the second author listed is a writer on legal subjects, but a search using "Jackson, John" would have missed the correct entry. The index display would begin with "Jackson, John, 1881–1952".

Another potential cause of confusion is the tendency of law books which have run to a number of editions to be known by the name of the original author, even though that author may no longer be involved in the writing of the book. This is something you will need to take account of when using the catalogue. *Winfield and Jolowicz on Tort*, for example, is in its 17th edition and Winfield has not been involved with the work for many years, but his name is still associated with the book. You will usually find an author entry under Winfield, but there will also be an entry under Rogers, W.V.H. who is the author of the current edition. If you are using a title search you need to search for "Winfield and Jolowicz on Tort", not "Tort", which was the original title of the book.

Many law books have been written jointly by two or more authors. You may be referred for example to Craig and de Burca (*EU Law*) or Clayton and Tomlinson (*The Law of Human Rights*). There will be an entry in the catalogue for both authors, and title searches should be for "EU Law" or "Law of Human Rights".

Sometimes a book does not have an individual as the author. It is published by an organisation or society and the organisation is, in effect, the author. In this case, you will find an entry in the catalogue under the name of the body, e.g. Law Commission, Law Society, Legal Action Group, United Nations.

## Finding and borrowing books

The classification number for a book appears prominently in the library catalogue entry. It is usually combined with letters and numbers based on the author's name which enable you to ▶ 1.6

trace the precise place the book should appear on the shelves. Remember to check also for any indication that the book you wish to find may be shelved in a separate sequence—(pamphlets, large-sized books etc).

If the book is on loan to another reader, the library catalogue will give the current return date for the book. It is usually possible for you to reserve the book using the catalogue, in which case the book will be recalled from its present borrower.

A book may be mis-shelved or missing, or have been removed by library staff for some reason, e.g. re-binding. If you have any problems finding a book, ask a member of the library staff for help.

When you borrow a book from a library issue desk (or use a self-service issue machine), you will be given a return date for the book. Remember that the book could be requested before that date if another reader has reserved it. There will also be fines for late return. These fines can be expensive if the book has been borrowed from a short-loan, reserve, or consultation collection.

## LAW REPORTS AND JOURNALS

**1.7 ▶** In the course of your legal studies you will often need to look at reports of cases which have been heard in courts, both in the UK and abroad. These reports are published in a number of publications called law reports. Amongst the best known series of law reports are the *All England Law Reports*, the *Weekly Law Reports* and the *Law Reports*. These are examined in more detail in Ch.3. There is a standard form of writing references to law reports, and this is explained in para.3.3.

The bound volumes of law reports found on library shelves are usually held in a separate sequence. These volumes are not for loan. In a well-established library, the collections of law reports will be extensive. A single series of these reports, The *Law Reports*, first published in 1864, occupies many metres of shelving in the law library. Although this is the most extensive series, there are many others. In addition to the shelves containing such bound volumes, the library will also have prominently located display shelves for recent, unbound issues of law reports.

Most law reports are also available online and access is provided almost exclusively by database services such as LexisNexis Butterworths and Westlaw UK. These are described in para.2.2. It is worth keeping in mind just how much information these services contain. The *Law Reports* are almost certainly available to you online and they form only one part of a single database within LexisNexis Butterworths and Westlaw UK.

You will find, in addition, that you are referred to articles and case notes in journals (or periodicals). Journals provide commentary on cases and advanced discussion of legal issues. They are published for the most part either weekly, monthly or quarterly (hence the name, periodical). A journal reference should give you the author and title of a journal article, the year, the volume number, an abbreviation for the title of the journal in which the article appeared and the page number of the first page of the article itself, e.g.:

A Roberts "Pre-trial defence rights and the fair use of eyewitness identification procedures" (2008) 71 M.L.R. 331

Law database providers such as LexisNexis Butterworths and Westlaw UK provide access to the full text of journal articles as well as to law reports. However, not all UK journals are available online from these databases. Many other journals can be accessed directly from publishers' websites or through intermediary sites. If your library has a subscription for online access, the full text of articles will be available.

As is the case with law reports, the bound print volumes of printed journals are usually shelved in a separate sequence in the library. There is usually a display area for recent unbound issues similar to the display area for unbound law reports.

## Abbreviations

The tradition adopted by lecturers and authors of referring to journals and law reports only by an abbreviated form of their full title can present a major difficulty for new students. Instead of writing the name of the journal or law report in full, they are invariably shortened to such cryptic abbreviations as:

▶ **1.8**

(2008) 71(9) M.L.R. 331
[2008] 3 W.L.R. 166

This may make it difficult for you to know whether you are looking for a law report or a journal article. To make things even more difficult, library catalogues use the full unabbreviated title of a journal or law report. As a result, abbreviations need to be de-coded before you can use them to check for online or print access. If you are in any doubt as to the nature of a reference, ask a member of the library staff for advice. Many of the references are also confusingly similar, e.g. L.R. can be the abbreviation for both "law report" and "law review". This can be frustrating if you are looking for print volumes in the library. The law reports are shelved together, but separately from the law reviews, which are journals. Consequently, if you are looking along the shelves of bound volumes for a publication, you could find yourself looking in the wrong sequence. A common mistake, for instance, is to assume that a reference to a report of a case in "Crim.L.R." means that you must search amongst the law reports for a series entitled the *Criminal Law Reports*. There is no such series (although there is a series called the *Criminal Appeal Reports*). The reference "Crim.L.R." is to the *Criminal Law Review*, which is a journal shelved with the other journals. It contains both articles and reports of cases.

The meaning of abbreviations can be checked both online and in print and key sources are noted in para.3.5.

## Tracing journals and law reports

It can be difficult to establish which journals and law reports are available online. The library catalogue and web pages may provide an A–Z list of the journals and law reports you can access. If not, you need to search the journals sections of LexisNexis Butterworths and Westlaw UK (assuming these are available), in order to establish whether access to the full text of the journal which interests you is provided by either service (see para.5.2). Links to the websites of publishers providing subscription access may also be provided from the library catalogue. To discover if this is the case, search the catalogue as if you were looking for the print volumes of the journal. The full online text of journals is usually available

▶ **1.9**

for journal articles published after the mid 1990s, in many cases earlier articles are also available.

To find out if the printed volumes of a journal or law report are available in the library, search the library catalogue using the full title of the journal or report, not its abbreviation. The catalogue should allow you to select a separate journal title search, so that you only search for journal entries.

If you are looking for a journal which includes the name of an organisation in its title, you may by unsure of the precise title to use. Is it the *American Bar Association Journal*, for example, or the *Journal of the American Bar Association*? In these cases it is usually possible to search for the journal by the name of the organisation that produces it. If the publication you wish to find has "Bulletin", "Transactions" or "Proceedings" at the start of its title, retain these words when you make your search or use a "keyword in title" search.

## REFERENCE SOURCES

**1.10** ▶  A number of reference sources are available for legal research, both online and in print. The key legal encyclopedia is *Halsbury's Laws of England* (para.7.3), accessed online from LexisNexis Butterworths.

### Dictionaries

**1.11** ▶  Lawyers have a language of their own, which is a mixture of Latin, French and English. There are several small single volume dictionaries of law which may be useful for your research. Some may be available in the library reference section. The library may also have subscriptions for online versions. Examples include the *Oxford Reference Dictionary of Law* (2006) and the *Collins Dictionary of Law* (2006), both available online and in print. Check the library catalogue or reference web pages for online access. The library shelves are also likely to contain more substantial multi-volume law dictionaries such as *Strouds Judicial Dictionary of Words and Phrases*. Standard English dictionaries may also be useful. The multi-volume *Oxford English Dictionary* should be available, in many cases in both online and print versions.

Latin phrases and maxims may cause difficulties for students who have no classical languages. Latin phrases appear in most legal dictionaries and a collection of legal maxims can be found in the various editions and reprints of H. Broom, *A Selection of Legal Maxims*. If you are carrying out research in legal history, you may need J.H. Baker, *Manual of Law French* (1990).

### Tracing people and addresses

**1.12** ▶  The law library reference collection will contain a number of standard directories which can help you find the addresses of courts, legal firms, professional bodies, etc. Solicitors and barristers can be easily traced from the online listing provided by the directory websites. The Waterlow's website (at *www.waterlowlegal.com*) provides access to the lists of solicitors and barristers contained in their *Solicitors' and Barristers' Directory*. The website also contains a careers and development section which includes basic careers advice and information on continuing professional development. If you want to trace a solicitor by area of specialisation, this can be done by using the Law Society website (at *www.lawsociety.org.uk*) which provides access to the listing contained in the Law Society's *Directory of Solicitors and Barristers*. The sections of the *Bar Directory* covering barristers' chambers by location and barristers in private practice can be searched online using the legal hub website from Sweet and Maxwell (at *www.legalhub. co.uk*). The Legal500 website is more selective, providing profiles of leading commercial firms.

Biographical details of prominent members of the legal profession can also be found in *Who's Who*. *Debrett's Correct Form* is also useful in this context, providing advice on the correct form of address when writing to, or addressing, members of the judiciary and other eminent people. Check the library catalogue for online subscription access to both *Who's Who* and *Debrett's*. The addresses of regional legal advice offices are found on the Legal Services Commission website (at *www.legalservices.gov.uk*).

The addresses of many organisations and bodies may be found in the *Directory of British Associations and Associations* and in the companion publication, *Councils, Committees and Boards*. The latter group of organisations in particular can be difficult to trace from general internet searches. The main reference collection in your library will contain many other print sources enabling you to trace people and organisations. Ask library reference staff for advice if you need help.

# ▶ 2
# Using online sources of law

## INTRODUCTION

**2.1 ▶** The start of the century saw a dramatic shift in the scope and availability of information online. At the same time, the use of a web search engine such as Google to find useful information has become second nature for anyone with internet access. Beware, though, of assuming that a web search engine is the only route to online information, especially when undertaking legal research. A great deal of relatively recent case law and legislation, along with important parliamentary and government publications, can be found using a web search engine. The response will also be gratifyingly quick and apparently comprehensive. However, restricting your search to Google will mean that a great deal of useful source material for research will be missed.

To make effective use of online sources of law also requires that you learn how to use the database services already noted in Ch.1. Services such as LexisNexis Butterworths and Westlaw UK are the only sources, for example, that can give you a complete, up-to-date statement of law in force for England and Wales. They, and other subscription services, also contain extensive archives of case law which are not otherwise available online. Just as important, the vast majority of journal articles currently accessible online are only available from database services, or from other subscription websites. All of these information sources—cases, legislation in force and journal articles—are effectively part of the hidden web. This means that unless you have access to subscription sources made available by a library, they will be closed to you.

Searching subscription database services such as LexisNexis Butterworths and Westlaw UK using keywords and indexes also requires a different approach to that used in searching internet search engines. You will need to be more precise in the keywords and phrases you use, but there will be a corresponding gain in the precision of the results obtained. Database searching is described in more detail in para.2.11. The coverage of the database services themselves is noted from para.2.2 onwards.

It would be wrong, however, to suggest that subscription services provide the only important source of law online. The BAILII website, the Statute Law Database and the OPSI legislation pages provide free public access to primary sources and their use should not be ignored. Further information on these sites is provided in para.2.12.

Understanding the way both subscription and non-subscription law sites work will help you get the best from the online sources available to you. You will find them referred to a great deal in the following chapters. Throughout the book the use of an online resource for legal research is outlined first, followed by an outline of how to use the print alternative, if there is one. Remember, there remain advantages to the use of print sources in your legal research (para.2.16).

## SUBSCRIPTION DATABASE SERVICES

▶ **2.2**

Your university library or law school is likely to have subscriptions to at least two of the services provided by the major commercial database providers. These are services which provide access to a package of case law, legislation, and often either index references to journal articles, or the full text of the articles themselves. Practitioner texts may also be included as online books.

These services are web-based and the home page of the service once found looks much like any other web page on the internet; so too will the search and results pages. One difference is that the web pages you see when you are using one of the online subscription services are part of a live interactive session in which you are sending questions and commands to a database and receiving information in response. There will be some form of logging on and exit procedure to start and finish your online session and you may also be "timed out" if you leave a page for a long period of time and then wish to restart. Because you are logged on to a remote service it is also not advisable to use the "forward" and "back" commands of your web browser, as this can mean that the pages you are using become out of step with the server at the other end of your search session. The logging on procedure will also ensure that you are a valid user of the system. Standard logging on and authentication procedures for UK universities are covered in para.2.8.

There are a number of advantages to using these services, beyond their search capabilities, which you might want to take into account. They offer Word-based printing and saving options, for example, which are not available on pubic websites. Documents can also be emailed to your email account. Another feature of these services is the integration of links to law reports and legislation into the text of the document you are reading. This means that if a particular section of an Act is referred to in a law report, it is possible to link directly to that section. More specialist features include the ability to save and re-run searches and receive the results as update emails, or the ability to view current awareness updates in particular subject areas.

For these reasons, it is worth spending time getting to know how subscription services work, even though the need for a logging in procedure can be off-putting. Later chapters of this book will highlight search strategies to use when finding law reports, legislation and journals using LexisNexis Butterworths (para.2.3) and Westlaw UK (para.2.4) in particular.

The database coverage of each of the major subscription services is outlined in the following sections. Understanding the different coverage of the database providers can help you decide where to start your legal research online. Though both LexisNexis Butterworths and Westlaw UK contain comparable legislation databases, for example, the specialist law reports and to a large extent the journals contained in their databases will be different. This is because LexisNexis Butterworths is linked to LexisNexis publishing, while Westlaw UK is linked to Sweet & Maxwell. Other services, such as Lawtel (para.2.5) and Justis (para.2.6) are also able to offer additional services and content not available from either LexisNexis Butterworths or Westlaw UK.

### LexisNexis Butterworths

**2.3 ▶** Since 2007, the LexisNexis Butterworths service has combined access to resources found in earlier versions of LexisNexis Butterworths with access to content derived from the former US-based LexisNexis Professional service. LexisNexis Professional provided access both to UK law resources and to a wide range of international sources of law. All of the former LexisNexis Professional content can now be found in LexisNexis Butterworths.

UK universities usually subscribe to a core set of databases which match, and to some extent supplement, the UK coverage formally available from LexisNexis Professional. This core content can be found in the "Cases", "Legislation" and "Journals" sections of the service. Additional database content may also be added, much of which is focused on specific areas of law.

The "Cases" section of the service includes just over 40 specialist law reports in full text, along with the full text of the *All England Law Reports*, the *Law Reports* (from 1864) and the *All England Law Reports Reprints*, covering 1558 to 1935. Transcripts of judgements made in "unreported cases" (see para.3.19) are available from the mid-1980s onwards. These transcripts are sometimes of particular value, as transcripts of judgments pre-dating 2000 are often difficult to obtain from other sources. LexisNexis Butterworths is also the only subscription source for Northern Ireland case law.

The "Legislation" section of the service provides the full text of Public General Acts in force in England and Wales, a full statutory instruments database for England and Wales, and the full text of Scottish Parliament Acts and statutory instruments.

EU cases and legislation can also be found in the "Cases" and "Legislation" sections of the LexisNexis Butterworths service, though these are currently somewhat confusingly found under shortcuts to "International Cases" and "International Legislation" respectively.

The "Journals" section of the service includes the full text of over 60 law journals, many aimed at an academic audience, some at the legal practioner. Most of the titles are only available online through LexisNexis Butterworths, though some—those published by Oxford University Press in particular—are available online from other sources.

Much of the supplementary content available from LexisNexis Butterworths can be found in the "Commentary" section of the service. The database sources available will depend on the additional subscriptions taken out by your university, but may well include *Halsbury's Laws of England* (para.7.3), the major legal encyclopedia for England and Wales. Specialist titles, which aim to give a comprehensive statement of law in a particular area, may also be found. These include *Harvey on Industrial Relations and Employment Law*, for example, and *Clarke Hall & Morrison on Children*. The *Encyclopaedia of Forms and Precedents* is also likely to be available in most universities as it is of particular value to students undertaking legal practice courses. It can be found in a "Forms and Precedents" section of the service.

The international content of the former LexisNexis Professional databases can be found by exploring the "Sources" section of LexisNexis Butterworths. Sources are listed by country, or can be traced using keyword searches. Substantial databases of US primary law are included, along with the full text of a large number of North American law journals. Primary law and some journals from other jurisdictions can also be found—for the most part from Commonwealth or former Commonwealth countries.

LexisNexis Butterworths also has a companion Nexis (news and business) service,

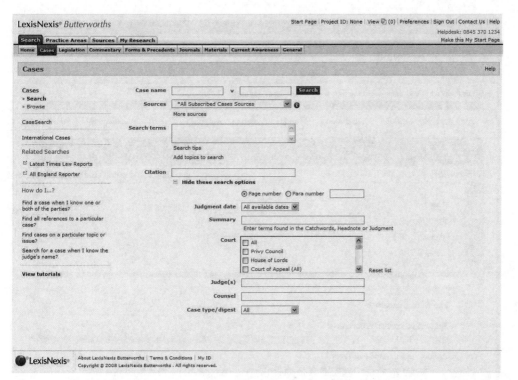

**Fig 2.1**
LexisNexis
Butterworth Cases
search

structured in much the same way as LexisNexis Butterworths. The news content of the service can be of particular benefit for legal research. The full text of all UK national newspapers is included, for the most part from the mid 1980s, along with many regional newspapers. International news sources are also included.

## Westlaw UK

Westlaw UK uses the US-based Westlaw service to provide access to case law, legislation and journal databases provided by Sweet & Maxwell. As with LexisNexis Butterworths, a database of law in force in England and Wales is available, but full text coverage of law reports differs significantly. Like LexisNexis Butterworths, the full text of the *Law Reports* can be found in the cases section of the service, but unlike LexisNexis Butterworths, the full text of the *All England Law Reports* is not included. However the full text of the *Weekly Law Reports* is present, along with the full text of over 30 specialist law reports. The specialist law reports, published by Sweet and Maxwell, are not available online elsewhere.

> **2.4**

The Sweet & Maxwell content also means that Westlaw UK has the most comprehensive case finding database available for case law that applies to England and Wales. Using the indexes and brief case summaries published in print as *Current Law*, the Westlaw UK "Cases" search provides summaries of a wide range of cases, along with citations for each of the law report series that has published a report. Where relevant, brief case histories are also added, allowing the reader to discover, for example, which cases have followed the ruling made in a particular judgment and which cases have considered it. Where the full text of a law report, or

**Fig 2.2**
Westlaw UK Cases
search

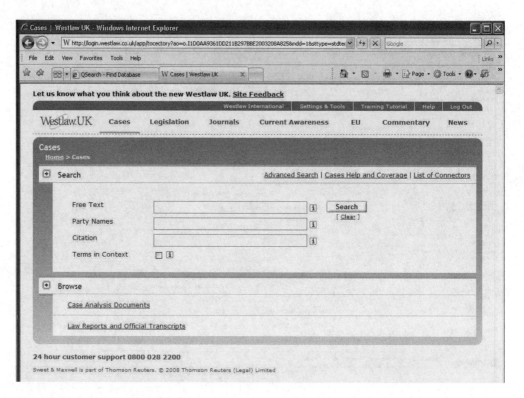

a judgment transcript, is available in the Westlaw UK cases database, a link is made from the summary of the case to the full text.

In a similar way, Westlaw UK's "Legislation" search makes use of indexes and notes published in *Current Law* to provide information on legislation in force which includes commencement and amendment information, along with lists of cases which have cited the legislation where relevant. Links are provided to the relevant sections of statutes and statutory instruments.

Another important feature of Westlaw UK is the extensive journals indexing featured in the journals section of the service, derived from Sweet & Maxwell's *Legal Journals Index*. The *Legal Journals Index* content means that articles published in almost any UK legal journal can be discovered using the journals search (see para.5.6). Links are provided to the full text of articles if they are available within Westlaw UK. Articles published in over 80 different journals are available in full text, most published from the mid-1990s onwards. Journals available in this way include the *Criminal Law Review* and the *Statute Law Review*.

The link with the US-based Westlaw service means that Northern American cases, legislation and journal articles can also be accessed from Westlaw UK using the "Westlaw International" link. A directory of sources gives a full listing of the law resources available. North American coverage is much the same as that provided by LexisNexis Butterworths.

## Lawtel

2.5 ▶ Although aimed primarily at the legal profession, many university libraries provide access to Lawtel. Lawtel is essentially a current awareness digest service which provides brief case reports, usually within a day of a judgment being made. The case reports, which date back to the mid-1980s, are in turn linked to the full text of judgment transcripts as they become available. A number of additional features include a legislation search, which provides update notes on amendments and repeals made to sections of Acts, and an articles index, which provides summaries of articles from over 60 legal and potentially relevant non-legal journals.

The Lawtel service is now a Westlaw UK product, but it has retained its separate role and identity.

### Justis Publishing

Your library may be able to provide access to one or more full text databases from Justis Publishing. These include online versions of the *Law Reports* and the *Weekly Law Reports* in which the text is presented in printer-ready pdf images, reproducing the pages of the original print versions. These may be attractive to libraries which do not have full archives of the original volumes, or to libraries aiming to fully replace print volumes with online versions. Justis also provides separate subscriptions for specialist reports otherwise unavailable online, such as the *Mental Health Reports* and the *Police Law Reports*. These may be available as individual Justis subscriptions. ▶ **2.6**

Two unique legislation databases might also be available from your library. The UK statutes database contains the full unamended text of all Acts of Parliament made in England and Scotland from 1235 onwards, providing convenient access to historic legislation now repealed. The UK Statutory Instruments database provides the full text of statutory instruments made form 1691 onwards.

Your library may in addition have a subscription to the JustCite service. This provides access to an index of cases, legislation and journal articles containing links to the full range of full text sources available online. The service can work particularly well for case law. For each case indexed, a brief digest summary is provided, along with a listing of any later cases which considered the case and any journal articles providing significant discussion. The particular strength of the database is the provision within the index of full text links not just to the free online source of the judgment made in a case (see para.2.12), but also to any reported versions of the case available from LexisNexis Butterworths and Westlaw UK.

Early versions of JustCite were hampered by the authentication problems inherent in linking to subscription databases in a university context (see para.2.8) and the number of law libraries using JustCite is currently limited. However, if available, JustCite may provide a valuable alternative to the Westlaw UK "Cases" search described in detail in para.3.15. In particular, library users may no longer need to switch from Westlaw UK to LexisNexis Butterworths (or Justis) to find the full text of a law report.

### Jordans Publishing

Jordans Publishing provide an alternative online source for the *Law Reports* and the *Weekly Law Reports*. University libraries are relatively unlikely to use these versions. They are more likely to be used by law firms. However, you may find subscriptions to specialist reports from Jordans, these include the *Immigration and Nationality Reports* and the *Education Law Reports*. ▶ **2.7**

## ACCESSING SUBSCRIPTION DATABASE SERVICES

**2.8** ▶ As already noted, subscription database services are web-based. This means that network access requires no more than a computer with an internet connection and a web browser such as Internet Explorer. There is no specialist software that needs to be loaded or mastered.

However, you will only be able to use these services if your university law library or law school has paid a subscription. Typically access is licensed to staff and students of a university, either for a limited number of simultaneous users, or more usually, for unlimited access to any number of users. The licence will have been paid for on an annual basis with the result that no additional charge is made by the database provider for the connection time to the database.

Because subscription services are only available to licensed users, there must also, inevitably, be some method in place to ensure that the person accessing the service is indeed a student or staff member of a particular university. Two approaches are possible. One is based on the recognition of the university network by the service provider, allowing access to the relevant database service. The other approach is to use an authentication system which grants access to individual users as staff and students of a university.

Many databases are set to recognise a university network (using "ip recognition") and this means that no usernames or passwords are needed if you are on the university network. Most online journals work in this way. Other services use an authentication system granting access to individual users, and these always require a username and a password. This enables various personalisation features for the service, including, for example, the ability to save searches, or add shortcuts to favourite resources.

UK universities use Shibboleth, a standard international system, to authenticate usernames and passwords. It is not important to understand how the system operates, but its use by UK universities has the important consequence that access to a service using Shibboleth is only possible using your own university's Shibboleth login page. The most convenient access route is likely to be a web page link provided by your university library or law school to the service you wish to use. The link will direct you initially to the local login page, where you will need to enter the username and password you have been given by your university for database access. The login page may not mention Shibboleth explicitly. Once your username and your password have been entered, you will be re-directed to the welcome page of the service you wish to use.

The Shibboleth system also makes it possible to log in using links provided by the home pages of services such as LexisNexis Butterworths and Westlaw UK. To use these links, you must ensure that you choose options provided for academic users. There will be other login options provided for non-academic users. The login option for academic users will direct you to a long list of universities who are members of the "UK Access Management Federation". Selecting your own university directs your web browser once again to the university's local login page for Shibboleth.

Another consequence of the use of the Shibboleth authentication system, is that you will find that you are only asked for your username and password once in any online session. This means that if you log in first, for example, to a Justis database and then decide to move to Westlaw UK, you will not be asked for a username and password when you link to Westlaw UK. You are already recognised as a user with rights to access the service.

The Shibboleth authentication system works both on and off campus in the same way, so you will not notice any difference if you are accessing a Shibboleth authenticated service from outside your university network. Most universities also have systems that ensure, in addition, that "ip authenticated" resources, those that allow access by recognising your university network, can still be accessed off campus. For these systems to work, it is important that you access resources using links provided by university web pages. Before you link to the resource you wish to use, your university username and password will be requested and you will be allowed access as if you were on the university network.

Either way, all of the database resources paid for by your university should be available to you off campus. By using the correct web page links you can ensure that you are recognised as a valid user of a subscription service whether you are logging in from an off-campus hall of residence, from home, or from the other side of the world.

## Usernames and passwords

In most universities a single username and password combination enables a student to log on to both internal computing resources, such as a university email account, and to subscription services such as Westlaw UK or LexisNexis Butterworths. This is because usernames and passwords are validated locally, using a login page belonging to your own university. As a result your university username and password can be used to access remote subscription services. Both username and password are usually given to you when you first register with the university.

**▶ 2.9**

In some cases a different username and password will be needed for accessing remote services and you will be given separate account details. Your university library or computing service should inform you if you need to use an additional account.

Universities are also working towards the provision of a "single sign on" for all networked services. In a single sign on system, once you have logged on to the university network, you will not be asked again for usernames and passwords, whether you are using email accounts, accessing exam results, or using online subscription services.

## Library portals

In many universities access to online resources is now provided by a library portal. The portal consists of special set of library or university web pages that allow you to search many of the online services to which you have access using a single standard search page. The portal then translates the search into the form required for the database selected. A particular advantage of a library portal is that more than one database can be searched in response to a single query.

**▶ 2.10**

Unfortunately, the way the major subscription law services structure their databases means that they cannot be searched directly from a library portal search page. Instead, the portal simply provides a link to the "native" interface of the service. You will in effect have to leave the portal pages and use the service in the normal way.

However, law services such as Westlaw UK and LexisNexis Butterworths are usually listed in library portals. Even though the usual benefits of portal searching are not available, the portal may provide a convenient access route to the service.

## DATABASE SEARCHING

**2.11** ▶ Although the search pages of services such as Westlaw UK and LexisNexis Butterworths appear as web pages, and even though the results of a search are presented as a sometimes lengthy list of links to further web pages, when you search a subscription database you are not searching a website. The subscription services provide access to databases constructed from the fully indexed raw text of reports, statutes etc. This has consequences for the way these databases are best searched.

> **TIPS** • *Break down your search query into single keywords and two-word phrases. Then combine keywords using "search operators" such as "AND" or "NEAR". Use "w/6" to specify that words should be near each other when using LexisNexis Butteworths or Westlaw UK*

When a database of full text or bibliographic (reference) data is constructed, all uses of a word are automatically indexed and tagged according to their place in the document. Words are indexed as title words, for example, or as names appearing in the "parties" section of a case report. This will enables searches to be restricted to words in the title or names in the parties section or "field" of the database. If a name, e.g. "Hart" is tagged as the name of a party to a case, for example, all cases in which someone called Hart is one of the parties will be listed in the computer index used for party names. If you search for Hart as the party to a case, the name you entered is matched against the database indexes and the relevant documents retrieved. The database index works at this level in much the same way as the index to this book, and the database search software is performing an operation that is equivalent to looking up a word in the index and seeing which pages contain relevant information.

This indexing of words makes so-called "Boolean" searching a powerful way of retrieving information from a database. Two examples might help.

Suppose first, that you wish to search the journals section of Westlaw UK in order to find journal references relevant to the issue of provocation as a defence. You are particularly interested in linking the issue to domestic violence against women. Enter the words:

**Provocation AND domestic violence**

in the "Free Text" area of the search page and click the search button. The search software will now retrieve all index entries that are linked both to the term "provocation" and the term "domestic violence". The significance of the "AND" (one of the "Boolean operators") is that it requests this linking of index entries to be made. The result is a list of references which contain both the word "provocation" and the words "domestic violence". (In many databases you need to use quotation marks to indicate that you wish "domestic violence" to be treated as a phrase).

If you wanted to go further with this search, you might also consider that "domestic violence" is not the only phrase of potential interest that could occur in the title or summary of a journal article. Another significant Boolean operator that can help is "OR" which acts as a request to group the index entries for two different words. Using:

**Battered women OR domestic violence**

will widen the scope to the references found to include those using either the phrase "battered women" or the phrase "domestic violence". As there are articles which use the term "battered women" but not "domestic violence", more references will be found. In this case it would be better to make two searches, one for both "Provocation and domestic violence" and the other for "Provocation and battered women".

Suppose now you wish to find cases that have discussed the way the word "charity" has been interpreted in English law. You have decided to look for judgments in which "charity" has been judicially interpreted and are going to search a full text database of case law, such as that provided by the cases search of either Westlaw UK or LexisNexis Butterworths. Here things can become a little more involved.

An initial consideration might be that because of the complexity of the English language, along with "charity", your keywords might also include, "sense", "usage", or "definition" as well as "interpretation". All these terms should be included in your search (either by repeating searches or using "OR"). Different forms of the same word can also be used. You might want to search for "define", "defines" and "defining" along with "definition" for example. Fortunately most databases allow a truncation symbol which can help, so that "defin!" could cover all of the forms mentioned. Less fortunately, "definite" would also be included in the search, so use truncation with care.

Having thought about your search terms, also make sure that you use the symbol or "search operator" for the database that specifies that your keywords must be found close to each other in the long text of a judgment. Many databases allow "NEAR" to specify a standard proximity, LexisNexis Butterworths uses "w/" so that "w/6" specifies within 6 words.

Putting these considerations together, a "good" search for judgments on the interpretation of charity, might consist of the following string of words, truncated words and search operators. The brackets ensure that all the alternatives are taken together in one search:

**Charit! w/6 (defin\* OR sense OR usage)**

Still other combinations are possible. Though convenient, there is no necessity to make a single complex search in quite this way. Brackets are also not always interpreted in the way you would wish. Simpler searches could be made and a results list built up by saving the results of each search individually.

The important point to remember is that Boolean searches provide a way of refining the accuracy and scope of your search. No single search is necessarily comprehensive. It is advisable to reconsider your search words and re-edit them as you read your search results and find, perhaps, much more than you had anticipated, or, indeed, much less. Be aware of the coverage of the database you are using, and don't be misled into thinking that any search is final or comprehensive.

Constructing searches in this way differs from the approach you would take if you were searching the internet using a search engine. The way in which results are presented is also different. A database usually lists the results containing your search words in reverse chronological order. A search engine lists a series of web links in which the pages carrying most prominently the word or words you used in your search are listed first. The words "AND" and "OR" also have a particular significance for databases which they do not have for search engines. These differences are worth remembering.

## FREE SOURCES OF LAW ON THE INTERNET

The primary sources of law, the judgments made in the courts, and the statue law made by the UK's various legislative bodies, are not the property of legal publishers or subscription database providers. From the mid-1990s onwards, first the House of Lords and then the Court

▶ 2.12

Service of England and Wales, have put the full text of judgments onto their own websites; an example followed in both Scotland and Northern Ireland. During the same period the Office of Public Sector Information (OPSI), in its former guise as HMSO, began to place UK legislation on its own website (para.2.14). The recognition of the problems caused by this proliferation of public primary sources of law, led, in 2000, to the creation of the BAILII website (para.2.15). The site brings together judgment transcripts from the different UK court services, enabling them to be searched from a single website, along with the various sources of UK legislation. A further significant development occurred in 2007, with the launch of the Statute Law Database (para.2.13) by the Ministry of Justice. The database aims to provide the first publicly accessible version of legislation in force in the UK.

It should be noted though, that OPSI, BAILII and the Statute Law Database cannot provide some of the "value added" features provided by the commercial database suppliers. Results cannot be emailed, and printing can be inconvenient. There are also no hypertext links placed within the text of some documents. More importantly, neither are there the added headnotes and case summaries that are found in the commercially published law reports. Despite the Statute Law Database, it remains the case that only the subscription database services can offer a completely current, amended text of legislation in force.

### The Statute Law Database

**2.13** ▶ The UK Statute Law Database (at *www.statutelaw.gov.uk*) provides access to revised versions of UK Acts, including Acts of the Scottish Parliament and the Northern Ireland Assembly. Statutory instruments made since 1991 are included, but these are not revised. Unrevised Local Acts are included for 1991 onwards.

> **TIPS** • *Always look for the "Advanced Search" when searching websites. Limit your search to the kind of document that interests you. Also specify* e.g. *that "All words" must be found in the pages searched.*

Care needs to be taken when using the revised versions of Acts contained in the Statute Law Database. Though the Acts are revised, this does not necessarily mean that they are a statement of law currently in force. Revisions made to Acts of Parliament and to Scottish Acts within the last six years are not included. It is possible to use tables of legislative effects contained in the database to trace recent revising legislation, but the process in not straightforward. Using subscription database services (para.2.2) remains the most effective route to legislation in force.

The position is somewhat better for Northern Ireland primary legislation. Only revisions made within the last three years are excluded. This applies not just to the Acts of the Northern Ireland Assembly contained in the database, but also the Orders in Council and Acts of the former Northern Ireland Parliament. Together these Acts and Orders constitute primary legislation for Northern Ireland. This legislation is not available from subscription database services in any form.

### OPSI

**2.14** ▶ The OPSI website (at www.opsi.gov.uk) provides access to both original and revised texts of UK legislation. The original, unrevised text of Acts of Parliament is available for the period from 1988 onwards. Statutory instruments are available from 1987. Some Acts of Parliament are also available for the period 1837 to 1988 in their unrevised form. Northern

Ireland, Scotland and Wales legislation pages provide access to the full text of devolved legislation.

Only Acts enacted before 1988 are available in revised versions. The text is extracted from the Statute Law Database (para.2.13) and displays legislation as currently in force.

The website can be searched by type of legislation, by year and by keywords. The keyword search engine uses the "relevance ranking" approach familiar to users of search engines such as Google. As a result it is almost always a good idea to go directly to the "Advanced Search" option which allows the search to be restricted to types of legislation. Only unrevised legislation from 1987 onwards is included in the search.

The problems of using the initial keyword search box rapidly become apparent if a search is made for a Northern Ireland Statutory Rule. Using the words "Northern Ireland" with a general search will ensure that the search results highlight legislation in which the words "Northern Ireland" appear most often. The search results are then dominated by the Northern Ireland Act 1998, not of course a Statutory Rule at all.

## BAILII

The BAILII (British and Irish Legal Information Institute) website (at *www.bailii.org*) provides access to a series of databases derived from public sources of law. The site includes judgements drawn from official websites, or in the case of older England and Wales judgments, from official shorthand writers, to provide an extensive database of House of Lords, Court of Appeal and High Court judgments from 1996 onwards. Selected earlier judgments are also included from as early as 1838. The "Case Law Search" is particularly useful in this context, as it allows judgments to be found using law report citations. A wide range of United Kingdom tribunal

**▶ 2.15**

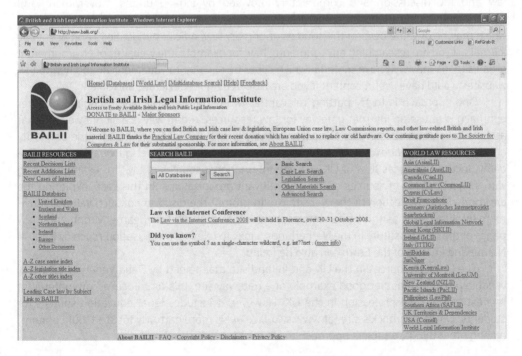

**Fig 2.3**
BAILII home page

decisions can also be found, dating for the most part from 2000. Some earlier decisions are available. The website is, in addition, a valuable source of judgments for Scotland, Northern Ireland and the Republic of Ireland. The site should finally not be overlooked as a potential source of EU and European human rights case law, as it includes judgments of the European Court of Justice from 1954 onwards, and judgments of the European Court of Human Rights from 1960.

The United Kingdom legislation available on the website is drawn both from the Statute Law Database (para.2.13) and the OPSI website (para.2.14). Legislation drawn from the OPSI site includes United Kingdom statutory instruments, Acts and statutory instruments of the Scottish Parliament and Northern Ireland legislation.

The great advantage of the BAILII website is that all of these disparate sources are brought together in a standardised database format, easing searching. The database searching made possible by BAILII is also almost always an improvement on the search facilities available on the home site for the legislation or case law concerned. It is possible to search, for example, using Boolean searching ("AND", "OR" etc) and proximity searches enable the search to specify that keywords should be found close to each other in the full text of case law and legislation. BAILII was launched using systems and approaches developed by AUSTLII (Australasian Legal Information Institute) and this also means that primary sources of law for Commonwealth and former Commonwealth countries can be found from the site.

## INTERNET GATEWAYS

**2.16** ▶ As you develop your legal research, you may well wish to move beyond the primary sources of law and the discussion and commentary provided by legal journals. Government and Parliamentary publications are covered in Ch.5. However, there are many other internet sites which may be of value beyond the sources of primary law, official publications and academic journals. If you are researching environmental law, for example, the websites of environmental organisations may well have material which could be of value to you. Medical and health law websites would have useful content if you are researching medical law, and so on.

One approach is to try putting relevant keywords into a web search engine. Another approach is to use an internet gateway for law resources. A gateway is a single website that acts effectively as a directory for some part of the internet. The lawlinks site from the University of Kent (at *www.kent.ac.uk/lawlinks*) is a good example of an internet gateway with an academic focus. It provides lists of UK, EU and international sources of law, for example, along with subject listings of sources of law and relevant organisations. In this case, exploring the environmental law section of the website would prompt the discovery of such valuable environmental law sites as the Ecolex information service and the European environmental law pages of the Asser Institute in the Netherlands. Links to relevant organisations such as English Nature and Friends of the Earth can also be found.

The Legal Resources in the UK and Ireland site maintained by Delia Venebles (at www.venables.co.uk) is another good example of a gateway site, this time focused on material of interest to the legal profession in the UK. However, it includes legal education sources for students. David Swarbrick's site (at *www.swarb.co.uk*) is more narrowly focused, but contains, among other things, a subject approach to UK case law.

Legal material is also accessible via the more general UK academic listings provided by the Intute service (at *www.intute.ac.uk*). The service provides links to a selection of full text resources evaluated by subject specialists. Law resources can be found in the social sciences section. The websites of many university law schools and law libraries also offer additional starting points for exploring law resources on the internet. The HERO website provides a full listing of UK academic sites (at *www.hero.ac.uk*).

Going beyond UK sources, the "Research the Law" section of the US Findlaw site (at *www.findlaw.com/casecode*) is a valuable starting point for US law. Law.com (at *www.law.com*) and Hieros Gamos (at *www.hg.org*) are focused on the US legal profession. The UK sources already mentioned, especially the lawlinks site, are good starting points for European and international law.

## WHEN TO USE PRINT SOURCES

The reasons for using online sources are compelling. Sources of information which you ▶ 2.17 may not otherwise be able to use will be available to you and you need never suffer the frustration caused by the discovery that the printed volume you sought on the library shelves is in use, missing or mutilated. More importantly, the availability of full text sources online means that sources of law can be searched in a way that simply was not possible when only print indexes were available. However, it should not be assumed that online sources are always better. For some tasks, such as checking a citation when the name and year of a case is already known to you, a print source can be quicker and easier to use. A fast, accurate result can be achieved, for example, by using the *Current Law Case Citator* (see para.3.16). The full text of an Act of Parliament, or a House of Lords judgment, may also run to many pages. The typeface and layout of the printed versions, combined with the ability to scan and skip easily through the text, can make the printed publication much easier both to read and handle; especially when the alternative is a stack of pages gathered from a computer printer. There is also a significant time investment in getting to grips with an online source of information. The peculiarity of individual online services needs to be mastered, as does the search language associated with database searching. Of course, you cannot even begin, unless you have access to a networked computer.

As a library user, you will also be faced with a limited choice of available sources. Just as the book and journal coverage of a library is limited by the funds available, so too is access to online subscription services. Very few libraries have access to anything like the full range of services. Where both print and online services are available, the choice generally depends on the particular resources to hand, the task you have in mind, and, of course, your own personal preferences.

Remember too, that some of the most significant legal resources are still found only in print form. The student textbooks and research monographs which make up much of a library collection are currently available, for the most part, only in print. This is still true of many of the authoritative practitioner texts. Some of the older journal literature in law is still also available only in print, though much is now available online (see para.5.2).

## COMBINING PRINT AND ELECTRONIC SOURCES

**2.18** ▶ It is important to place electronic resources in the wider context of your legal research. Online resources are an important part of the resources available to you, but you need to learn how to make use of these alongside printed resources. It is not simply the case that "online" means "modern" and "paper" means "old fashioned". Bear in mind that a student textbook usually provides your best starting point when you are new to a subject area. If you wish to find out about the impact of the Human Rights Act 1998 on statutory interpretation, for example, you need to clarify the basic issues. This is often best achieved with the help of a recent textbook and some quality time to think about the core issues. You will find no shortage of textbooks in this area. Books published as "cases and materials" will offer a valuable quick reference as they contain extracts from leading cases and statute law. Only after you have looked at the textbook material will it probably make sense to go online using the journals search in Westlaw UK for example. Having studied the available textbook material, you will be ready to search for references to journal articles that have discussed and developed the issues you have identified in your basic preparation. Online access to case law might have its place as you search for judgments that have cited what you now know to be the key cases. Having traced journal articles and cases online, you may finally need to return to print sources and use the library catalogue to locate particular journals or law reports on the library shelves.

To make the best use of law library resources you must learn how to move comfortably between electronic and print sources. The ability to do so will result in better time management and better coverage of the material. The remaining chapters of this book, placing as they do, online resources beside those in print, are designed to enable you to switch research techniques as and when appropriate.

## CD-ROMS

**2.19** ▶ Many of the full-text products of the commercial legal publishers, including the *All England Law Reports*, the *Law Reports* series and UK Statutory Instruments, were first made available in CD-ROM form. The Westlaw UK databases first appeared on CD-ROM as Current Legal Information. In general, university libraries no longer carry major databases in this form, though they can still be useful for small organisations. However, CD-ROMs may be used in the library to provide improved search access to some of the key practitioner texts and loose-leaf updating services (where they save on filing).

If you wish to use a CD-ROM held by your library you have to borrow the disc from an issue or information desk. As the CD-ROM requires particular search software to be loaded onto a computer before it can be used, you will be directed to a particular PC or workstation on which the search software is loaded. Alternatively the CD-ROM may be pre-loaded on a particular computer and you will need to locate the one that holds the CD-ROM database. This may or may not be located within the law library. Where CD-ROMs have been networked by your university, it may be possible for any machine on a university's local network to use the CD-ROM database, though again the particular machine may need to have CD-ROM search software pre-loaded. When in doubt ask for advice from the library staff about what is located where in the library.

# ▶ 3
# Law reports

## INTRODUCTION

Law reports are one of the basic (or "primary") sources of English law. Traditionally, the ▶ **3.1** common law develops through the practical reasoning of the judges. This is based on the particular facts of the case in question, social forces and previous judicial reasoning when it has a bearing on the case being heard. Legal principles stated in earlier decisions are given effect in later cases by the operation of the doctrine of precedent, which is described in detail in most introductory texts to the English legal system. The successful development of the common law depends largely upon the production of reliable law reports which carry not only the facts, issues and decision, but also, most importantly, the legal principles upon which the judgment is made. Currently, the senior judiciary spend most of their court time considering the scope and application of particular Acts of Parliament.

A law report re-prints the full text of a judgment, i.e. the statement of facts and judicial reasoning made by judges in a case and adds additional material. This consists of a summary of the legal issues, lists of other cases cited, legislation referred to, and other key features of the case (see para.3.6).

Only a very small proportion of cases decided by the courts is reported in the law reports. Just because a case is widely reported in the media, it does not follow that it will appear in a law report. A case is selected for reporting if it raises a point of legal significance. Judgments made in appeal cases which are not reported, though publicly available, are referred to as "unreported judgments". Unreported judgments can nonetheless be cited in court cases where it is felt that relevant legal issues are raised. Typescript transcripts of judgments and judgments held on online databases have been referred to in court cases for some time.

Since 2000 these "unreported" judgments have been made available on the websites of the courts themselves, and in a variety of other non-subscription sites (para.3.19). House of Lords judgments have been available on the Parliament website since 1996. As a result, almost all the judgments published in law reports in recent years are also available free online. However, despite this, the element of selection provided by the law reports, and the additional explanatory material included, has meant that law reports continue to be the major primary source of case law in the English legal system. Throughout your legal study you will make constant use of law reports, occasionally supplemented by unreported judgments, usually those made in significant recent cases which have not yet been reported. It is worth remembering, though, that if you do not have access to a particular recent law report, the judgment made in the case reported is almost certainly available online. For the great majority of 19th and 20th century cases, you will have to rely on law reports.

## THE HISTORY OF LAW REPORTS

**3.2 ▶** Law reports have existed, in one form or another, since the reign of Edward I. These very early law reports are known as the *Year Books*. If you wish to see a copy, reprints of a number of these *Year Books* are available in the series of publications published by the Selden Society, in the Rolls Series and in facsimile reprints issued by Professional Books.

After the Year Books had ceased, collections of law reports published privately by individuals began to appear. These reports, the first of which were published in 1571, were normally referred to by the name of the reporter or compiler. For this reason, they are collectively referred to as the *Nominate Reports* and they vary considerably in accuracy and reliability. Few libraries will have a complete collection of these old reports and if you do obtain a copy, you may find that the antiquated print makes it difficult to read. Fortunately, the great majority of these *Nominate Reports* can be found in at least one of three reprint series: the *English Reports*, the *Revised Reports* and the *All England Law Reports Reprint* series. The most comprehensive of the three series is the *English Reports*, which is examined in detail later in the chapter (para.3.12).

In 1865, a body called the Incorporated Council of Law Reporting commenced publication of the Law Reports, a single series of reports covering all the major courts. These reports were rapidly accepted by the legal profession as the most authoritative version of law reports and, as a result, most of the earlier series published by individuals ceased publication in 1865 or soon after. Judgments in the Law Reports have been checked by the relevant judges before publication and are cited in court in preference to any other series. The *Law Reports* series is described in more detail in para.3.10.

Today, there are over 50 different series of law reports for England and Wales. The *Weekly Law Reports* and the *All England Law Reports*, like the *Law Reports*, cover a wide range of topics and are aimed at the lawyer in general practice. There are also a large number of law reports which cover a specialised area of the law, such as the *Criminal Appeal Reports* and the *Road Traffic Reports*.

A case may be reported in more than one series of law reports. For example, a short report may appear in *The Times* newspaper (under the heading "Law Report") a day or so after the judgment is given. A summary or a full report may be published in some of the weekly legal journals, such as the *New Law Journal* and the *Solicitors Journal*, or a case note may discuss the significance of the new judgment. Several months later, the case may be published in one or both of the two general series of law reports which appear weekly, the *All England Law Reports* and the *Weekly Law Reports*, and in specialist law reports and journals (e.g. *Tax Cases*, the *Criminal Law Review*). Some time later, a final, authoritative version checked by the judges concerned may be published in the Law Reports. Thus, if your library does not hold the series of law reports given in the reference you have, it is worth checking whether the case is reported elsewhere (see para.3.14).

# CITATION OF LAW REPORTS

Lawyers often use abbreviations when referring to the sources where a report of a case can be found. These can appear confusing at first, but constant use will rapidly make you familiar with the meaning of most of the abbreviations used. References to cases (called citations) are structured as shown in the following example:

▶ 3.3

> *Giles v Thompson*[1] [1993][2] 2[3] W.L.R.[4] 908[5].

In this example, the case of *Giles v Thompson* will be found in the 1993 volumes of the *Weekly Law Reports* (abbreviated to W.L.R.). There are three volumes of the *Weekly Law Reports* containing the cases reported in 1993. The case referred to will be found in the second volume, at p.908.

If you wish to draw attention to a particular phrase or section in the judgment, you should write out the citation for the case, followed by "at" and the page number where the section or phrase is printed, hence:

> *Giles v Thompson* [1993] 2 W.L.R. 908 at 910.

Since 2001 reports published by Sweet & Maxwell have been cited using a case number rather than a page number. For example: *Nestlé v Mars* [2005] 3 C.M.L.R. 12

This refers to case n.12 of volume 3 of the *Common Market Law Reports*. The report begins on p.259 of volume 3.

Although designed to help someone find a report in a printed volume, law report citations are also valuable aids to finding cases online. This quickly becomes apparent if you try searching without the aid of a full citation including year, volume number, abbreviation and page number. Though cases can often be found quite easily using party names if the names themselves are relatively uncommon, things can soon become problematic. What if the case is a family case and the party names are simply "X v Y"? What if the party names are unproblematic, but you are not sure which of the possible cases are being referred to? There are a number different cases, for example, where the parties are *"Douglas v Hello"*.

Suppose you have a citation, e.g. [2008] 3 All E.R. 1. Look for the citation search box in one of the major online sources of case law, e.g LexisNexis Butterworths (para.2.3), an appropriate source in this instance, as it contains the full text of the *All England Law Reports*, or Westlaw UK (para.2.4). Then enter the year, volume number, abbreviation and page number of a citation exactly as they have been given, i.e. "[2008] 3 All E.R. 1".

Searching in this way means that you only find the case being referred to and no other. Citation searches are effective even if the particular law report cited is not available in the online service you have used. Westlaw UK does not for example contain text of the *All England*

---

1   the names of the parties involved in the case;
2   the year in which the case is reported. Square brackets indicate that the date is an essential part of the citation. Some series of law reports number the volumes serially from year to year, so the reference is sufficient even if the year is omitted. Round brackets are used if the date is not essential but merely an aid;
3   the volume number, i.e. the second volume published in 1993. Where only one volume is published in a year, the volume number is omitted unless it is essential for finding the correct volume;
4   the abbreviation for the name of the law report or journal;
5   the page number on which the case begins.

report cited, *R. (on the application of Gentle) v Prime Minister*. However, the search does find the same case as reported in the *Weekly Law Reports*. Law Report citations can also be used to find judgments using the case law search featured in the BAILII website.

If you have been given a "neutral citation" for a case (see para.3.4 below), these can be used in exactly the same way as law report citations to find recent judgments and reports.

### Neutral citations

**3.4** ▶ In 2001 the High Court and Court of Appeal adopted a neutral, or common, form of citation for all cases. These "neutral" citations do not distinguish between print and online media and are independent of any of the published law reports. This form of citation has been adopted in order to make it easier to cite and to trace unreported judgments. The neutral form of citation can be seen in the following example:

> *R. (Ebrahim) v Feltham Magistrates Court* [2001] EWHC Admin 130.

EWHC Admin is the standard abbreviation for the High Court (Administrative Division) for England and Wales. The number 130, placed without brackets after EWHC Admin, tells you that the judgment is judgment number 130 for 2001.

Other abbreviations are EWCA Civ for the Court of Appeal (Civil Division) and EWCA Crim for the Court of Appeal (Criminal Division).

Rather than give page references, these citations use numbers in square brackets which indicate the paragraph of a judgment, e.g.

> *R. (Ebrahim) v Feltham Magistrates Court* [2001] EWHC Admin 130 at [40]–[42].

When judgments are given in the High Court or Court of Appeal the neutral form of citation is always given at least once, ahead of any other citations. *R. (Ebrahim) v Feltham Magistrates Court* has been reported in the *All England Law Reports*, so the case would be cited as follows:

> *R. (Ebrahim) v Feltham Magistrates Court* [2001] EWHC Admin 130 at [40]–[43];
> [2001] All E.R. 831 at 841.

The House of Lords adopted a similar form of neutral citation in 2001. The 2001 case *Johnson (AP) v Unisys Ltd*, for example, is cited using the neutral system as:

> *Johnson (AP) v Unisys Ltd* [2001] UKHL 13.

UKHL is the abbreviation for the House of Lords and the number 13, placed without brackets after UKHL, tells you that the judgment is judgment number 13 for 2001. Any numbers in square brackets at the end of the citation represent paragraph numbers, as they do for Court of Appeal and High Court cases.

## HOW TO FIND THE MEANING OF ABBREVIATIONS

**3.5** ▶ A variety of different reference sources enable you to check the meaning of abbreviations. The most extensive is the Cardiff Index to Legal Abbreviations (at *www.legalabbrevs.cardiff. ac.uk*). If you are faced with an abbreviation for a law report or journal which you do not recognise, the website's abbreviations search finds matching law publications using a database compiled from a wide range of legal abbreviations. Either exact or close matches can be sought, making it possible to search for the meaning of an abbreviation even if you are not sure of the initial letter. A particular advantage of an online index is the ability it provides to search for the preferred abbreviation of a journal or law report. This can be useful if you have noted the full title of a law report or journal, but are unsure how to abbreviate it for citation purposes.

The *Current Law Monthly Digest* provides a convenient print source for current UK abbreviations. A list of abbreviations of reports and journals cited in *Current Law* (para.3.16) can be found near the front of each issue. *The Digest* (para.3.17) prints a list of abbreviations near the front of Vol.1(1) which can help with older abbreviations. Most law library reference shelves also have Raistrick's *Index to Legal Citations and Abbreviations*. Some of the most commonly used abbreviations are listed in Appendix 2 of this book.

## FORMAT OF LAW REPORTS

Page 28 gives a typical example of the first page of a law report. The citation is *Cleveland Petroleum Co. Ltd v Dartstone Ltd and Another* [1969] 1 All E.R. 201. Several key points in the illustration are numbered. ▌ **3.6**

1.  The names of the parties. In a civil case, the name of the plaintiff (the person bringing the action) comes first, followed by the name of the defendant. The small letter "v" between the names is an abbreviation of the Latin "versus" but when speaking of a civil case, you say "and" not "versus". A criminal case, on the other hand, might appear as *R. v Smith*. R. is the abbreviated form for the Latin words Rex (king) or Regina (queen). The charge against Smith, the accused, is brought on behalf of the Crown and this case would be said as "the Crown against Smith".
2.  The name of the court in which the case was heard, the names of the judges (M.R.: Master of the Rolls; L.JJ.: Lords Justices) and the date on which the case was heard.
3.  A summary of the main legal issues of the case. You are advised not to rely on this, as it is not necessarily complete or accurate.
4.  The headnote, which is a brief statement of the case and the nature of the claim (in a civil case) or the charge (in a criminal case). Again, do not rely on the publisher's précis but instead read the case.
5.  The court's ruling is stated, with a summary of reasons.
6.  In certain reports, e.g. the *All England Law Reports*, the major legal points are cross-referenced to *Halsbury's Laws* and *The Digest*.
7.  A list of cases which were referred to during the hearing.
8.  A summary of the history of the previous proceedings of the case. The final sentence explains where in the report you can find the details of the facts of the case.
9.  The names of the counsel (the barristers) who appeared for the parties. Q.C.s (Queen's Counsel) are senior counsel.
10. The start of the judgment given by Lord Denning M.R.

**Fig 3.1**    *First page of a Law Report from the All England Reports. The illustration is taken from the online version available from LexisNexis Butterworths.*

[1969] 1 All ER 201

# Cleveland Petroleum Co Ltd v Dartstone Ltd and Another [1]

COURT OF APPEAL, CIVIL DIVISION

LORD DENNING MR, RUSSELL AND SALMON LJJ[2]
26 NOVEMBER 1968

*Trade—Restraint of trade—Agreement—Petrol filling station—Solus agreement—Lease by garage owner to petrol supplier—Underlease to company to operate service station—Covenant in underlease for exclusive sale of supplier's products—Assignment of underlease by licence granted by supplier—Interim injunction to restrain breach of covenant.*

[3]

S the owner in fee simple of a garage, leased the premises to the plaintiffs for 25 years from 1 July 1960. The plaintiffs granted an underlease to COSS by which COSS covenanted, inter alia, to carry on the business of a petrol filling station at all times and not to sell or distribute motor fuels other than those supplied by the plaintiffs. After several assignments the underlease was assigned to the defendants who undertook to observe and perform the covenants. The defendants thereupon challenged the validity of the ties. The plaintiffs issued a writ claiming an injunction restraining the defendants from breaking this covenant. The plaintiffs obtained an interim injunction against which the defendants appealed.

[4]

**Held**—The appeal would be dismissed, the tie was valid and not an unreasonable restraint of trade because the defendants, not having been in possession previously, took possession of the premises under a lease and entered into a restrictive covenant knowing about such covenant, and thereby bound themselves to it (see p 203, letters *c*, *f* and *g*, post).
Dicta in *Esso Petroleum Co Ltd v Harper's Garage* (Stourport) ([1967] 1 All ER at pp 707, 714, and 724, 725) applied.      [5]
Appeal dismissed.

**Notes**
As to agreements in restraint of trade, see 38 *Halsbury's Laws* (3rd Edn) 20, para 13; and for cases on the subject, see 45 *Digest* (Repl) 443–449, *271–297*.[6]

#### Case referred to in judgment
   -*Esso Petroleum Co Ltd v Harper's Garage (Stourport)* [1967] 1 All ER 699, [1968] AC 269, [1967] 2 WLR 871, *Digest* (Repl) Supp. [7]

### Interlocutory Appeal
This was an appeal by the defendants, Dartstone and James Arthur Gregory, from an order of Eveleigh J, dated 1 November 1968, granting an interim injunction restraining the defendants from acting in breach of a covenant contained in an underlease made on 1 July 1960 between the plaintiffs, Cleveland Petroleum Co and County Oak Service Station and assigned to the defendants on 30 August 1968. The facts are set out in the judgment of Lord Denning MR. [8]

*Raymond Walton QC and M C B Buckley for the defendants.* [9]
*A P Leggatt for the plaintiffs.*

### 26 November 1968. The following judgments were delivered.
**LORD DENNING MR.** [10]

This case concerns a garage and petrol station called County Oak service station, at Crawley in Sussex. Mr Sainsbury was the owner in fee simple. On 1 July 1960, there were three separate transactions: First, Mr Sainsbury granted a lease.

# RECENT LAW REPORTS

The law is constantly changing, with new cases being reported daily. Therefore be prepared to consult recent reports. This is essential if you are to remain aware of new developments in the law. The most up-to-date reports are found in the some of the national newspapers. *The Times*, the *Financial Times*, the *Daily Telegraph*, *The Independent* and *The Guardian* all regularly publish law reports. These newspaper reports appear ahead of the major law report series, but, unlike them, do not reproduce the full text of judgments. This need not be a problem. If you wish to see the full text of judgments, these are available from a number of websites (para.3.19).

    It is not necessary, however, to scan the print issues of the newspapers themselves to see recent newspaper reports. Recent reports can be found on *The Times* website for example (at www.timesonline.co.uk), in the business section. The full text of a wide range of UK newspapers is also available from an online subscription news service such as Nexis.

▶ 3.7

## Finding recent law reports online

Recent law reports, such as those found in the *All England Law Reports*, the *Weekly Law Reports* and the various specialist series are straightforward to find if you have a citation, as noted in para.3.3. The major online services also offer the possibility of browsing through the most recent issues of a particular law report online, in much the same way as you might browse through recent unbound printed issues (see para.3.9). LexisNexis Butterworths (para.2.3), Westlaw UK (para.2.4) and Justis Publishing (para.2.5) all have "browse" options on their case search pages which allow you first to select a particular law report series and then page through recent issues viewing the contents in page order. Bear in mind though, that unlike newspaper reports, even the online versions of these reports usually appear some weeks or months after the judgment date.

    The most important thing to remember when using online services to find these reports, is that no one service can provide access to all the major law report series. The *All England Law Reports*, for example, remain the most widely cited report series for recent cases, as they are widely available throughout the legal profession in print and aim at a general coverage of England and Wales case law. However, the full text of the reports is only available from LexisNexis Butterworths. The full text of reports published in the *Weekly Law Reports* in contrast is available from Westlaw UK and from Justis, but not from LexisNexis Butterworths.

    Specialist reports are also rarely found in more than one online service, which can be nuisance as many new cases appearing in these reports cannot be found elsewhere. A property case may only be reported in *Property, Planning and Compensation Reports*; a family case may only be reported in the *Family Law Reports*. The relevant report might be found in either Westlaw UK, Justis, or LexisNexis Butterworths, so be prepared to check all available sources. If you wish to browse for recent reports there is no alternative other than to check the lists of reports available in the browse option of the cases search and select specialist reports of interest.

▶ 3.8

## Finding recent law reports in print

If you wish to find a report of a case in the printed All *England Law Reports* or the *Weekly Law Reports* (or indeed most other series of law reports), which has been published in the last few

▶ 3.9

months, you will not find a bound volume on the shelves but a series of paper covered parts, or issues. However, your reference (citation) will make it appear that you are looking for a bound volume. So how do you locate the report? You will find, at the top of the front cover of each unbound issue, the date of this issue, the part (or issue) number, and the year, volume and page numbers covered by this issue, e.g.:

[2008] 4 All E.R. 351–444 Part 5, October 22, 2008

This indicates that this issue (pt.5) will eventually form pp 351–444 of the fourth bound volume of the *All England Law Reports* for 2008. Also on the front cover appears a list of all the cases reported in that part, showing the page number on which each report begins.

Many other law reports are published in a number of parts during the current year. At the end of the year, these are replaced by a bound volume or volumes. Every part will indicate on its cover the volume and pages in the bound volume where it will finally appear.

The *Weekly Law Reports* is a series (which commenced in 1953) that you will make use of frequently. The arrangement of its weekly print issues is rather confusing. Three bound volumes are produced each year, and each weekly issue contains some cases which will eventually appear in Volume 1 of the bound volumes for that year, and some cases which will subsequently appear in either Vol. 2 or Vol. 3. The front cover of each issue shows the contents

**Fig 3.2**
'Westlaw UK cover page'

[2008] 1 WLR 2057–2096
[2008] 3 WLR 825–891          10 October 2008          **Part 36**

# THE WEEKLY LAW REPORTS

**Editor** CLIVE SCOWEN *Barrister*

ICLR

THE INCORPORATED COUNCIL OF **LAW REPORTING**
FOR ENGLAND & WALES

### INDEX

| | | | Vol | Page |
|---|---|---|---|---|
| **ADOPTION** | Prospective adopters seeking parental responsibility orders in order to take child overseas for adoption — Whether statutory requirements complied with **In re G (A Child) (Adoption: Placement outside Jurisdiction)** | CA | 3 | 853 |
| **HIGH COURT** | Issue as to beneficial ownership of assets arising both in tax appeals and in High Court proceedings — Whether within exclusive jurisdiction of special commissioners **Stow v Stow** | Warren J | 3 | 827 |
| **HIGH COURT** | Reconsideration of Asylum and Immigration Tribunal decision refused by High Court judge — Whether High Court having jurisdiction to set aside judge's decision **R (AM (Cameroon)) v Asylum and Immigration Tribunal** | CA | 1 | 2062 |
| **HUMAN RIGHTS** | Sark Law receiving Royal Assent on advice of defendants — Whether defendants breaching claimants' Convention rights **R (Barclay) v Lord Chancellor and Secretary of State for Justice** | Wyn Williams J | 3 | 867 |
| **LOCAL GOVERNMENT** | Local authority deciding person with accommodation available in Uganda not homeless — Relevance of reasonableness of expectation that person should occupy it **Maloba v Waltham Forest London Borough Council (Law Society intervening)** | CA | 1 | 2079 |
| **PRISONS** | Secretary of State's power to decide whether long-term prisoner serving determinate sentence to be released on licence — Whether compatible with Convention rights **R (Black) v Secretary of State for Justice** | CA | 3 | 845 |

Cases in Volume 1 are those not intended to be included in The Law Reports and the volume in which these pages will eventually appear. For example on the front cover shown above is printed:

> Part 36
> October 10, 2008
> [2008] 1 W.L.R. 2057–2096
> [2008] 3 W.L.R. 825–891

Part 36 therefore contains pp 2057–2096 of what will eventually form Vol.1 of the *Weekly Law Reports* for 2008 and pp 825–891 of Vol.3. A sheet of green paper is inserted in the issue to mark the division between the pages destined for Volume 1 and those forming part of Vol. 3. A list of all the cases included in the part is printed on the front cover, and the volume and page number for each case is shown. You may wonder why the publishers (the Incorporated Council of Law Reporting, who also publish the *Law Reports*) have chosen this method of publishing the issues. The reason is that the cases in Vols 2 and 3 will be republished, after being checked by the judges and with a summary of counsel's arguments, in the *Law Reports*. Those cases appearing in Vol.1, however, will not reappear in the Law Reports.

The latest issue of each journal and law reports series is usually displayed in a separate area of the library. The remainder of the issues for the current year may also be filed in this area, or they may be in a box on the shelves alongside the bound volumes.

## THE LAW REPORTS SERIES

The publication known as the *Law Reports*, which commenced publication in 1865, was origi- **3.10** nally published in 11 series, each covering a different court. The rationalisation of the court structure since that time has reduced this to four series. These are:

> Appeal Cases (abbreviated to A.C.);
> Chancery Division (Ch.);
> Queen's Bench Division (Q.B.);
> Family Division (Fam.).

This is the order in which the bound volumes are usually arranged on the library shelves. Paper-covered parts are issued monthly and are replaced by bound volumes at the end of the year. The monthly issues of the Chancery Division and Family Division, however, are published within the same paper-covered part, although they are bound as separate series.

The location on the shelves of the various earlier series often reflects their relationship to the present four series, for example, the historical predecessors of the present Queen's Bench Division (called the King's Bench Division when a King is on the throne) were the Court for Crown Cases Reserved, the Court of Common Pleas and the Court of Exchequer. These are therefore usually shelved before the Queen's Bench Division reports (because they are its predecessors) but after the Appeal Cases and Chancery Division reports. The same arrangement is applied with the other three current series (i.e. reports of the predecessors of the present courts are filed at the beginning of each series).

Fig 3.3

### *Law Reports*

#### TABLE OF THE LAW REPORTS

The mode of citation is given in brackets. In the first, second and third columns, dots ( . . . ) are put where the number of the volume would appear in the citation. In the fourth column square brackets([ ]) are put where the year would appear in the citation.

| 1866–1875 | 1875–1880 | 1881–1890 | 1891–present |
|---|---|---|---|
| House of Lords. English and Irish Appeals (L.R. … H.L.) | | | |
| House of Lords. Scotch and Divorce Appeals (L.R. … H.L.Sc. or L.R. … H.L.Sc. and Div.) | Appeal Cases (…App.Cas.) | Appeal Cases (…App.Cas.) | Appeal Cases ([ ]) A.C.) |
| Privy Council Appeals (L.R. … P.C.) | | | |
| Chancery Appeal Cases (L.R. … Ch. or Ch. App.) | Chancery Division (…Ch.D.) | Chancery Division (…Ch.D.) | Chancery Division ([ ]) Ch.) |
| Equity Cases (L.R. … Eq.) | | | |
| Crown Cases Reserved (L.R. … C.C., or, … C.C.R.) | Queen's Bench Division (…Q.B.D.) | | |
| Queen's Bench Cases* (L.R. … Q.B.) | | Queen's Bench Division (…Q.B.D.) | Queen's (or King's) Bench Division ([ ] Q.B. or K.B.)† |
| Common Pleas Cases (L.R. … C.P.) | Common Pleas Division (…C.P.D.) | | |
| Exchequer Cases‡ (L.R. … Ex.) | Exchequer Division (…Ex.D.) | | |
| Admiralty and Ecclesiastical Cases (L.R. … A. & E.) | Probate Division (…P.D.) | Probate Division (…P.D.) | Probate Division ([ ]P.) Since 1972 Family Division ([ ]Fam.) |
| Probate and Divorce Cases (L.R. … P. & D.) | | | |

* Note that there is also a series called Queen's Bench Reports in the old reports (113–118 E.R.).
† After 1907 this includes cases in the Court of Criminal Appeal. later the Court of Appeal. in place of the previous Court for Crown Cases Reserved.
‡ Note that there is also a series called Exchequer Reports in the old reports (154–156 E.R.).

(Reproduced from G. Williams, *Learning the Law* (12th ed.), p. 40.)

The figure on page 32 shows the way in which the complete series of *Law Reports* are arranged on the shelves in most libraries. The abbreviations used to denote each series are shown, and also the dates during which each series appeared.

Citations for the *Law Reports* have varied over the years as the system of numbering the reports changed. Until 1891, for example, each volume in the various series had its own individual number, running sequentially through the years. The date in the citation is therefore in round brackets, to show it is not essential to the reference. For the Law Reports after 1891, however, the date is in square brackets, since the year must be quoted in order to locate the correct volume. The other slight complication in the citation of the Law Reports is the use of the abbreviation L.R. (for Law Reports) which is placed before the volume number in citation of *Law Reports* before 1875, e.g. *Rylands v Fletcher* (1868) L.R. 3 H.L. 330.

The figure on page 32 also clarifies the use of abbreviations and brackets for the Law Reports. It is worth noting, however, that the abbreviation H.L. stands for Law Reports: English and Irish Appeal Cases and not, as you might guess, Law Reports: House of Lords.

The Law Reports are available online from Westlaw UK (para.2.4), LexisNexis Butterworths (para.2.3), Justis (para.2.6) and Jordans Publishing (para.2.7).

## Older Law Reports

▶ **3.11**

We have concentrated upon the modern series of law reports because these are the reports which you will be using most frequently. However, from time to time you will need to look at older cases, that is, those reported in the first half of the nineteenth century or even several centuries earlier. Reports of older cases can be found in several series: the *English Reports*, *Revised Reports*, the *Law Journal Reports*, the *Law Times Reports* and the *All England Law Reports Reprint* series. We shall now look at some of these series in more detail.

The reports published privately by individuals (and known as the *Nominate Reports*) ceased publication around 1865, when the Law Reports were first published. If the date of the case you want is before 1865, you are most likely to find it in a series known as the *English Reports*. The *English Reports* reprinted the original *Nominate Reports* in a uniform series of volumes, annotating the reprinted text with the page and volume numbers of the original reports.

Many libraries have the *English Reports* in print form. An increasing number also provide access to the full text of the reports online, either from Justis Publishing (para.2.6), or the HeinOnline journal archive. Searching for cases using either source is straightforward if you have the names of parties, the citation of the original report, or the citation for the report as it appeared in the *English Reports*. The text of the reports can be confusing though if you are not aware of the way in which the *English Reports* are organised in print. The chart to the *English Reports* reproduced in the following section shows how citations to the original nominate reports, with their standard abbreviations, are related to volumes in the *English Reports*.

## How to use the English Reports

▶ **3.12**

If you know the name of the case, look it up in the alphabetical index of the names of cases, printed in Vols 177–178 of the *English Reports*. Beside the name of the case is printed the abbreviation for the name of the original nominate reporter, and the volume and page in his reports

**Fig 3.4**    **Table of Cases in the English Reports**

| 424   DAN | Index of Cases | | |
|---|---|---|---|
| Ⓐ | Ⓑ | | Ⓒ |
| → Daniel *v.* North, 11 East, 372 | | | **103** 1047 |
| ——*v.* Phillips, 4 T. R. 499 | | | **100** 1141 |
| ——*v.* Pit, Peake Add. Cas. 238 | | | **170** 257 |
| ——*v.* Pit, 6 Esp. 74 | | | **170** 834 |
| ——*v.* Purbeck, W. Kel. 97 | | | **25** 510 |
| ——*v.* Purkis, W. Kel. 97 | | | **25** 510 |
| ——*v.* Purkurst, 2 Barn. K. B. 214, 220 | **94** | **457,** | **461** |
| ——*v.* Russell, 14 Ves. Jun. 393; 2 Ves. Jun. Supp. 376 | **33** 572; | **34** | 1139 |
| ——*v.* Skipwith, 2 Bro. C. C. 155 | | | **29** 89 |
| ——*v.* Sterlin, 1 Freeman, 50 | | | **89** 39 |
| ——*v.* Thompson, 15 East, 78 | | | **104** 774 |
| ——*v.* Trotman, 1 Moo. N. S. 123 | | | **15** 649 |
| ——*v.* Turpin, 1 Keble, 124 | | | **83** 852 |
| ——*v.* Ubley, Jones, W. 137 | | | **82** 73 |
| ——*v.* Uply, Latch, 9, 39, 134 | **82** 248, | **264,** | **312** |
| ——*v.* Upton, Noy, 80 | | | **74** 1047 |
| ——*v.* Waddington, Cro. Jac. 377 | | | **79** 322 |
| ——*v.* Waddington, 3 Bulstrode, 130 | | | **81** 111 |
| ——*v.* Warren, 2 Y. & C. C. C. 290 | | | **63** 127 |
| ——*v.* Wilkin, 7 Ex. 429 | | | **155** 1016 |
| ——*v.* Wilkin, 8 Ex. 156 | | | **155** 1300 |
| ——*v.* Wilson, 5 T. R. I. | | | **101** 1 |
| Daniel's Case, 2 Dy. 133 b | | | **73** 291 |
| ——Trust, *In re*, 18 Beav. 309 | | | **52** 122 |

where the case appeared. The number printed in bold type next to this is the volume number in the *English Reports* where the case will be found, and this is followed by the page number in that volume:

*Daniel v North*6[a]    11 East, 372[b]    **103**[c] 1047

You will see that Vol.103 of the *English Reports* has the volumes and names of the *Nominate Reports* which are to be found in that volume printed on the spine. Page 1047 appears in its normal position at the top outer corner of the page whilst the volume and page number of the original report are printed at the inner margin.

Sometimes you may only have a citation (reference) to the original nominate report, e.g. 3 Car. & P. (Carrington and Payne); 2 Barn. & Ald. (Barnewall and Alderson). This reference is often printed in an abbreviated form. You do not know the name of the case, so you are unable to look it up in the index to the *English Reports*. Let us suppose, for example, that you have come across a reference to (1809) 11 East 372. Because the date is before 1865, you

[a]  name of the case;
[b]  volume, name of the original reporter, page number in the original report, i.e. the original report of this case appeared in Volume 11 of *East's Reports* p.372;
[c]  the reprint of the report appears in Volume 103 of the *English Reports* at p.1047.

**Chart to the English Reports**                                                                 Fig 3.5

Table of English Reports

| Old Reports. | Volume in English Reports. | Abbreviations. | Period Covered (approximate). | Series. |
|---|---|---|---|---|
| Dow & Clark, 1 & 2 | 6 | Dow & Cl. | 1827–1832 | H.L. |
| Dowling & Ryland | 171 | Dowl. & Ry. N.P. | 1822–1823 | N.P. |
| Drewry, 1–3 | 61 | } Drew. | 1852–1859 | V.C. |
| Drewry 4 | 62 | | | |
| Drewry & Smale, 1 & 2 | 62 | { Drew & Sm. or Dr. & Sm. } | 1860–1865 | V.C. |
| Dyer, 1–3 | 73 | Dy. | 1513–1582 | K.B. |
| East, 1–6 | 102 | | | |
| East, 7–11 | 103 | } East. | 1801–1812 | K.B. |
| East, 12–16 | 104 | | | |
| Eden, 1 & 2 | 28 | Eden. | 1757–1766 | Ch. |
| Edwards | 165 | Edw. | 1808–1812 | { Ecc. Adm. P. & D. |
| Ellis & Blackburn, 1–3 | 118 | | | |
| Ellis & Blackburn, 4–7 | 119 | } El. & Bl. | 1851–1858 | K.B. |
| Ellis & Blackburn, 8 | 120 | | | |
| Ellis, Blackburn & Ellis | 120 | El. Bl. & El. | 1858 | K.B. |
| Ellis & Ellis, 1 | 120 | } El. & El. | 1858–1861 | K.B. |
| Ellis & Ellis, 2 & 3 | 121 | | | |
| Eq. Cases Abridged, 1 | 21 | } Eq. Ca. Abr. | 1667–1744 | Ch. |
| Eq. Cases Abridged, 2 | 22 | | | |
| Espinasse, 1–6 | 170 | Esp. | 1793–1807 | N.P. |

know that it is likely to be found in the *English Reports*; but you do not know the name of the case. How do you find it? If the name of the report has been abbreviated, e.g. 3 Car. & P., you will need to look in Raistrick's *Index to Legal Citations and Abbreviations* or one of the similar reference works (see para.3–5) to find the meaning of the abbreviation. You then turn to the *Chart to the English Reports*. This may be displayed near the *English Reports*, or it may be a slim volume shelved with the *English Reports* themselves. The Chart contains an alphabetical list of the names of all the reporters whose work has been reprinted in the *English Reports*, showing which volume their work appears in. The Chart indicates that Vols 7 to 11 of *East's Reports* are reprinted in Vol.103 of the *English Reports*. If you open Vol.103 at random, you will see that, at the top of each page (at the inner margin) the volume and page numbers of the original report are printed. Find the volume and page reference which most nearly corresponds to your reference. There is no entry at the top of the page for Vol.11 of *East's Reports*, p.372, but there is an entry, at the top inner margin, for p.371. If you look at the figure on p.24, you will see the heading "11 East 371" at the top of the page. There are also numbers printed, in square brackets, in the body of the text. These indicate when the page numbers in the original report changed. For instance, in the original Vol.11 of *East's Reports*, p.371 began with the words "practice, but a specific notice of trial at Monmouth . . .". Page 372 began with the case of *Daniel v North*.

**Fig 3.6**

before; but they could not agree on the person to be substituted, and therefore the original appointment stood as before.

Per Curiam. Rule absolute.

AMBROSE *against* REES.   Wednesday, June 14th, 1809.   Notice having been given for the trial of a cause at Monmouth, which arose in Glamorganshire, as being in fact the next English county since the st. 27 H. 8, c. 26, s. 4, though Hereford be the common place of trial; the Court refused to set aside the verdict as for a mis-trial, on motion; the question being open on the record.

Marryat opposed a rule for setting aside the verdict obtained in this cause, upon the ground of an irregularity in the trial.   The venue was laid in Glamorganshire, and the cause was tried at Monmouth, as the next English county where the King's writ of venire runs (*b*); but it was objected that it ought to have been tried at Hereford, according to the general custom that all causes in which the venue is laid in any county in South Wales should be tried at Hereford.   But the rule being that the cause should be tried in the next English county, and Monmouth being in fact the next English county to Glamorganshire, and more conveniently situated for the trial of the cause, there seems no solid ground for impeaching the validity of the trial; though the practice relied on is easily accounted for by the consideration that Monmouthshire was originally a Welch county, and till it became an English county in the 27th year of Hen. 8, Herefordshire was in fact the next English county to Glamorgan.   And there is no reason for setting aside this verdict on the ground of surprize; for the defendant had not merely a notice of trial in the next English county, generally, which might have misled him by the notoriety of the **[371]** practice, but a specific notice of trial at Monmouth, to which he made no objection at the time.

Abbott, in support of the rule, relied on the known practice which had always prevailed, as well since as before the Statute 27 H. 8; and referred to *Morgan* v. *Morgan* (*a*), where the question arose in 1656, upon an ejectment for lands in Breknockshire, which was tried at Monmouth; and afterwards judgment was arrested, on the ground of a mis-trial, as it ought to have been tried in Herefordshire; for that Monmouthshire was but made an English county by statute within time of memory; and that trials in the next English county of issues arising in Wales have been time out of mind and at the common law; so that a place newly made an English county cannot have such a trial.   And he observed, that if this trial were good, all the judgments in causes out of Glamorganshire tried at Hereford have been erroneous.

Lord Ellenborough C.J. If the question appear on the record, then the defendant cannot apply in this summary manner.   And as he did not object at the time, we shall not relieve him upon motion.

Per Curiam. Rule discharged.

**[372]**   DANIEL *against* NORTH.   Wednesday, June 14th, 1809.   Where lights had been put out and enjoyed without interruption for above 20 years during the occupation of the opposite premises by a tenant; that will not conclude the landlord of such opposite premises, without evidence of his knowledge of the fact, which is the foundation of presuming a grant against him; and consequently will not conclude a succeeding tenant who was in possession under such landlord from building up against such encroaching lights.

[Considered and applied, *Wheaton* v. *Maple* [1893], 3 Ch. 57; *Roberts* v. *James*, 1903, 89 L. T. 286.   For *Rugby Charity* v. *Merryweather*, 11 East, 375, n., see *Woodyer* v. *Hadden*, 1813, 5 Taunt. 138; *Wood* v. *Veal*, 1822, 5 B. & Ald. 457; *Vernon* v. *St. James's, Westminster*, 1880, 16 Ch. D. 457; *Bourke* v. *Davis*, 1889, 44 Ch. D. 123.]

The plaintiff declared in case, upon his seisin in fee of a certain messuage or dwelling-house in Stockport, on one side of which there is and was and of right ought to be six windows; and stated that the defendant wrongfully erected a wall 60 feet high and 50 in length near the said house and windows, and obstructed the light and

---

(*b*) Vide 1 Term Rep. 313.                           (*a*) Hard. 66.

**Other older law reports**

If the *English Reports* are not available in your library, you may find the case you need reprinted in the *Revised Reports*. The *Revised Reports* has similar coverage to the *English Reports* but is not as comprehensive.

▶ 3.13

The *All England Law Reports Reprint* series is another useful source for old cases between 1558 and 1935. The cases are reprinted from the reports which originally appeared in the *Law Times Reports*, which commenced in 1843, and from earlier reports. The *Reprint* series contains some 5,000 cases selected principally upon the criterion that they have been referred to in the *All England Law Reports* and in *Halsbury's Laws of England*. Online access to the full text of the *Reprint* series is available from LexisNexis Butterworths (para.2.3). The *Reprint* cases can be searched alongside more modern cases, or searches restricted to *Reprint* cases only. There is an index volume to the printed series containing an alphabetical list of cases and a subject index of the cases included in the reprint.

Two other series of nineteenth century cases are also referred to regularly: the *Law Journal Reports* and the *Law Times Reports*. The *Law Journal Reports* cover the period 1823–1949. They can be complicated to use because usually two volumes were published each year, both bearing the same volume number. In one volume were printed the cases heard in common law courts, while in the other were printed equity cases. You will need to check both volumes, unless you know whether the case you want is equity or common law. To add to the difficulty, the volume numbering and the method of citation changed during the course of its publication. The first nine volumes (1823–1831) are known as the Old Series (L.J.O.S.). References to the New Series (1833–1949) omit the letters N.S. Citations give the abbreviation for the court in which the case was heard. It is therefore necessary to decide if the court was a court of common law or equity, so that you consult the correct volume. For example, the reference 16 L.J.Q.B. 274 is a reference to Volume 16 of the *Law Journal* (New Series) in the common law volumes (since Queen's Bench was a court of common law), at p.274 of the reports of Queen's Bench. Volume 16 contains law reports from several different courts. Each court's reports have a separate sequence of page numbers. You are looking for p.274 in the sequence of Queen's Bench reports.

The *Law Times Reports* (L.T.) cover the period 1859–1947. Prior to this, the reports were published as part of the journal entitled *Law Times* and these are cited as the *Law Times, Old Series* (L.T.O.S.) which ran from 1843–1860. You may find this Old Series is shelved with the Journals, not with the law reports.

## HOW TO FIND A REPORTED CASE WHEN YOU ONLY KNOW ITS NAME

We will now turn to some of the problems frequently encountered by students and show how these are solved. Often you know the name of a case but you have no idea where the case was reported; or else the reference which you have been given has proved to be inaccurate. How can you find out where a report of the case appears?

▶ 3.14

The easiest way of tracing a case is to use the Westlaw UK "Cases" search (para.3.15), especially if you think your case was probably decided in or after 1947. Only brief entries are available for earlier cases. *The Digest* (para.3.15) can help find older cases. In addition, most series of law reports have their own indexes to cases. The JustCite service from Justis Publishing (para.2.6), if available, is an effective alternative to the Westlaw UK cases search. It provides much the same information on cases as Westlaw UK, with the additional advantage that links are provided to the appropriate location of the online text of the reports and judgments cited. The Westlaw UK Cases search can only link to the full text of reports and judgments available within Westlaw UK.

### How to use the Westlaw UK Cases Search

**3.15 ▶** The Westlaw UK "Cases" search enables you to trace a case when you only have the name of one, or possibly both, of the parties. The search uses a database which contains information on all reported England and Wales cases since 1947, taken from the print volumes of *Current Law*, along with keywords and citations for earlier cases where they have been cited by *Current Law*. In addition, the database links directly to cases reported in the *Law Reports* from 1864 onwards.

To use the search, select the "Cases" tab on the Westlaw UK home page and enter the case names you have in the "Party Names" search box. If both party names are known the "v" citation convention can be used to retrieve all cases featuring the two names e.g.

> **TIPS** • *The full name of both parties does not need to be entered when searching for a case using party names. Enter the most distinctive elements, e.g. "Factortame", not "Secretary for State for Transport Ex p. "Factortame".*

*"Douglas v Hello"*

A results list showing brief details of matching cases is then displayed. A number of separate cases have been reported for *"Douglas v Hello"* and the results list will include, for example:

> *Douglas v Hello! Ltd (no.1)*

The "no.1" in brackets has been added to distinguish this case from a number of subsequent related cases, e.g. *Douglas v Hello! Ltd (no.9)*. You may need to check to ensure that you are looking at the right case.

As noted in para.3.3, cases which use initials for party names to protect anonymity can cause particular problems. A search for "R v A", for example, finds literally hundreds of potential matches in the cases database. A citation becomes essential unless the case name has been extended to include further identification, e.g. *R v A (Complainant's Sexual History)*. The full phrase in brackets can be added to ensure that a match is found for the particular case you are looking for. If you are fairly sure of the keywords likely to be used in a case, an alternative is to use the "Subject/Keyword" search which can be found under "Advanced Search".

Selecting the "Case Analysis" link for a case from the brief details provided in your search results displays a page of information headed by a list of citations for the case. As already noted, a significant case is likely to be reported in a number of law reports, so that *R. (on the application of Al-Jedda) v Secretary of State for Defence*, for example, has been reported, among other places, in the *Law Reports*, as [2008] 1 A.C. 332, and in the *UK Human Rights Reports* as [2008] U.K.H.R.R. 244. The neutral citation for the case is also included, [2007] UKHL 58. This is not a citation to a law report (see para.3.4).

If the full text of the law report is available from the Westlaw UK, the relevant citation will be shown as a hyperlink. This opens a reproduction of the law report text within Westlaw UK. Asterisked numbers placed within the screen text mark the start of the printed pages and

Fig 3.7

# R. (ON THE APPLICATION OF AL-JEDDA) V SECRETARY OF STATE FOR DEFENCE

### House of Lords

### 12 December 2007

## CASE ANALYSIS

### Where Reported

[2007] UKHL 58; [2008] 1 A.C. 332; [2008] 2 W.L.R. 31; [2008] 3 All E.R. 28; [2008] H.R.L.R. 13; [2008] U.K.H.R.R. 244; 24 B.H.R.C. 569; (2008) 152(1) S.J.L.B. 22; Times, December 13, 2007; Official Transcript

### Case Digest

**Subject:** Human rights

**Keywords:** Armed forces; Choice of law; Detention; False imprisonment; Iraq; Right to liberty and security; United Nations resolutions

**Summary:** Right to liberty and security; Detention; Appellant held in custody by British forces in Iraq; Lawfulness of detention

**Abstract:** The appellant (J), who since October 2004 had been held in custody by British troops at detention facilities in Iraq, appealed against a decision ([2006] EWCA Civ 327, [2007] Q.B. 621) that his detention did not infringe his rights under the European Convention on Human Rights 1950 Art.5(1) . J had been detained on the ground that his internment was necessary for imperative reasons of security. He was suspected of being a member of a terrorist group involved in weapons smuggling and explosive attacks in Iraq. The issues were (i) whether J's detention was, by reason of the relevant United Nations Security Council Resolutions, attributable to the United Nations and therefore outside the scope of the Convention; (ii) whether the United Kingdom became subject to an "obligation" within the meaning of the United Nations Charter Art.103 to detain J and, if so, whether and to what extent such obligation displaced or qualified J's rights under Art.5(1) of the Convention; (iii) whether English common law or Iraqi law applied to J's detention. Appeal dismissed. (Lord Rodger dissenting on the first issue) (1) J's detention was not attributable to the UN. The multinationçal force in Iraq had not been established at the UN's behest, had not been mandated to operate under UN auspices and was not a subsidiary organ of the UN. There had been no delegation of UN power in Iraq. Further, it could not realistically be said that the United States and UK forces were under the effective command and control of the UN, or that UK forces were under such command and control when they detained J, Behrami v France (Admissibility) (71412/01) 22 B.H.R.C. 477 ECHR distinguished. (2) J had asserted that Art.103 of the United Nations Charter was not engaged, as the relevant UN Security Council Resolutions, read in the light of the Charter, at most authorised the UK to take action to detain him but did not "oblige" it to do so. That argument was unsound for several reasons. Firstly, during the period when the UK was an occupying power, it was obliged to take necessary steps to protect the safety of the public and its own safety. If the occupying power deemed it necessary to detain a enable precise quotations to the print volumes be traced. Where cases cited within the report are available from Westlaw UK, citations are again shown as hyperlinks.

The "Official Transcript" placed at the end of the law report citations can be helpful if Westlaw UK does not have the full text of a law report online. However, if your library has a subscription to LexisNexis Butterworths (para.2.3), or to Justis (para.2.4), it makes sense to search those services for a full law report, once a citation has been confirmed.

The Westlaw UK "Cases" search also provides a significant amount of additional information about a case which can be of value even if the full text or a report or judgment is not available.

Summaries are provided for all of the cases reported after 1947. In addition a "Case History" section of the case analysis page shows a list of cases which have followed, for example, the decision made by the case in question, or been "distinguished" from it. See para.7.18 for more on tracing the judicial history of the case. The case analysis page also lists citations for journal articles which have commented on the case.

### How to use the Current Law Case Citators

**3.16** ▶ The print volumes of the *Current Law Case Citator* each have an alphabetical list of the names of cases which have been published or quoted in court between the dates specified on the spine. If you have an idea of the approximate date, and easy access to the Citator volumes, they provide a quick and easy way to trace a citation. The Citator is published in a number of parts:

1. The *Current Law Case Citator* bound volumes covering cases which were reported or cited in court in the years noted on the Spine, e.g. 1947–1976, 1991–2001, 2002–2004.
2. A paperback issue of the *Current Law Case Citator* including references to cases reported or cited since the last bound volume and before the end of the preceding year.
3. The *Current Law Monthly Digest*. To find cases reported in the current year, look in the Table of Cases in the most recent issue of the *Monthly Digest*. The December issue of the previous year's *Monthly Digest* can be used to find cases in that year, if the cumulative supplement has not yet been published.

The different parts of the Citator may at first seem confusing. It is best to look through the Citators in chronological order, as above, in order to ensure that you have looked in all the relevant issues.

You may find your library has copies of the *Scottish Current Law Case Citator* for the periods 1948–1976 and 1977–1988. Despite its name, the Scottish version does contain all the English cases but, in addition, it lists Scottish cases in a separate alphabetical sequence at the back of the volume. The two publications have now merged and the *Current Law Case Citator* volumes since 1989 have included Scottish cases. Part 1 of the Citator lists all the English cases, while the Scottish cases are listed in Pt.2. Make sure you look for your case in the right section!

In each of the Citators, the cases are listed in alphabetical order. Cases which start with a single letter, e.g. *S. v Cox*, are at the beginning of that letter of the alphabet; criminal cases starting with R. v are at the beginning of the letter R section. If the title of the case is *Re Smith*, or *Ex p. Smith*, look under Smith. When you have traced the case you require, you will find an entry similar to the following:

> Biles *v* Caesar [1957] 1 W.L.R. 156; 101 S.J. 108; [1957] 1 All E.R. 151;
> [101 S.J. 141; 21 Conv. 169], C.A. . . . .. *Digested*, 57/1943: *Followed*, 59/1834:
> *Applied*, 68/2181; 69/2037

The entry for *Biles v Caesar* in the 1947–76 volume shown here gives you a complete "life history" of the case for the years covered by the volume. Like the Westlaw UK Case Locator database (para.3–15) it shows you where and when the case was originally reported and where you can find journal articles commenting on the case; there are also citations relevant to its subsequent judicial history (see para.7.18).

The entry for *Biles v Caesar* gives the following information:

(1) After the name of the case (*Biles v Caesar*) there is a list of three places where you can find a full report of the cases:
    (a) [1957] 1 W.L.R. 156–for the year 1957 in the first of the three volumes of the *Weekly Law Reports* at p.156;
    (b) (1957) 101 S.J. 108–for the year 1957 in volume 101 of the *Solicitors Journal* at p.108 (this, as the name suggests, is a journal, shelved with other journals);
    (c) [1957] 1 All E.R. 151–for the year 1958 in the first volume of the *All England Law Reports* at p.151.
(2) The entries which are enclosed in square brackets in the printed volume—[101 S.J. 141; 21 Conv. 169]—are references to articles or comments in law journals where the case is discussed in some detail. If you select Vol.101 of the Solicitors Journal, or Vol.21 of *The Conveyancer*, you see articles discussing the case of *Biles v Caesar*.
(3) The C.A. after the references to the case tells us that it is a Court of Appeal Decision. If the decision of the court of first instance was reported, references to these reports would have been included after the C.A.
(4) The word Digested followed by the figures 57/1943 indicates that you will find a digest (a summary) of the case in the 1957 volume of the *Current Law Year Book* (see para.7–13). Every item in the 1957 volume has its own individual number; you will find that item 1943 is a summary of the facts and decisions in the case of *Biles v Caesar*.

You may also wish to know whether the decision given in a particular case has been subsequently approved, i.e. whether the case has been quoted with approval by another judge in a later case. By 1976, when the print *Citator* volume was published, the case of *Biles v Caesar* has been quoted in three other cases—in 1959, when the decision was followed, and in 1968 and 1969 when the courts applied the decision in the *Biles* case to two other cases, following the doctrine of precedent. You can find the names of the cases in which *Biles* was referred to by looking in the 1959 Current Law Year Book, at item 1834, and in the 1968 and 1969 Year Books, at the item numbers given.

If you are using the *Citator* and, as in the above example, you find a reference to your case in the *Citator* for 1947 to 1976, it is still advisable to check through the more recent *Citators* to find the present status of the judgment. You can find out whether since 1976, for example, the case has been taken to a higher court or the decision has been approved or overruled in other judgments.

### How to trace a case in The Digest

**3.17** Older English and Scottish cases can most easily be traced using *The Digest* (formerly known as the *English and Empire Digest*), as can many cases heard in Irish, European and Commonwealth courts. *The Digest* consists of the main work (around 70 volumes), several *Continuation Volumes*, a *Cumulative Supplement*, a *Consolidated Table of Cases* and a *Consolidated Index*. *The Digest* is in its third edition which is called the *Green Band Reissue* because of the green stripe on the spine. All of the Green Band Reissue volumes have been updated and reprinted at least once. They are now in their 2nd or 3rd re-issue and the re-issue is stated on the spine. The date of reissue of any volume is printed on the title page inside the front cover.

To trace a particular case in *The Digest*, go first to the four-volume *Consolidated Table of Cases*. This contains an alphabetical list of the cases summarised in *The Digest* and gives a reference to the volume in which the case can be found. Page 43 shows the entry in the *Consolidated Table of Cases* for the case of *Bell v Twentyman*. This case is included in Vols 19(1), 35(3) and 36(1) of *The Digest*, since it is relevant to the law of easements, negligence and nuisance. At the front of each of these volumes, there is another Table of Cases which refers you to the case number (or page number in older volumes—see the heading at the top of the column) where you can find a summary of the case and a list of citations where the full report can be found. If, for example, you wished to find a summary of the negligence aspects of the case of *Bell v Twentyman*, you would now look up the name of the case in the Table of Cases at the front of Vol.35(3). Alongside the name of the case is the number 378, which refers you to case number 378 in that volume. The entry is shown on page 44. The case number is given in bold, followed by a summary of the case and references to where the full text of the report can be found. The case of *Bell v Twentyman* was reported in a number of series. To find the meaning of the abbreviations used, look in the list of abbreviations in the *Cumulative Supplement*. The *Consolidated Table of Cases* is updated and reprinted every two years. To find the latest cases, you will need to look in the annual *Cumulative Supplement*. There is a Table of Cases at the front of the volume, which indicates where in the *Cumulative Supplement* a summary of the case can be found. For more information on *The Digest*, refer to para.7.14.

### Tracing a case through the indexes in law reports

**3.18** In addition to the *Current Law Case Citators* and *The Digest*, there are a number of indexes to the cases in individual series of law reports. For instance, the *All England Law Reports* has published a volume containing a list of all the cases in the *All England Law Reports Reprint* series (see para.3.13), which covers selected cases between 1558 and 1935. In addition, there are three volumes containing the *Consolidated Tables and Index 1936–1992*. Volume 1 contains a list of all the cases included in the *All England Law Reports* between these dates. The reference

Fig 3.8

Bell v Jarvis (Sheriff) (1850) (CAN) **42(1) Shrffs**
Bell v Johnson (1861) **22(2) Evid**
Bell v Johnston Bros Ltd (1917) (CAN) **35(4) Negl**
Bell v Jutting (1817) **1(3) Agcy; 29(1) Insce**
Bell v Keesing (1888) (NZ) **3(1) Arbn; 7(3) Bldg Conts**
Bell v Kennedy (1868) **11(2) Confl**
Bell v Klein (No 3) (1955) **18 Discy**
Bell v Klein (No 5) (1955) (CAN) **22(2) Evid**
Bell v Krohn (1931) (CAN) **1(4) Agcy**
Bell v Kymer (1814) **43(2) Ship**
Bell v Lafferty (1894) (CAN) **7(1) B of Sale**
Bell v Lee (1883) (CAN) **37(2) Powers**
Bell v Lever Bros Ltd (1932) **20(1) Empt; 34(2) Mistake; 37(1) Pldg**
Bell v Light (1867) (CAN) **27(1) H & W**
Bell v London & North Western Ry Co (1852) **8(3) Chos**
Bell v London & South Western Bank (1874) **7(3) Bldg Soc**
Bell v Long (1928) (CAN) **21(2) Exon**
Bell v Lothiansure Ltd (in liq) (1990) (SCOT) **29(2) Insce**
Bell v Love (1883) **34(1) Mines**
Bell v McCubbin (1989) **2 Agric**
Bell v McDougall (1882) (CAN) **4(3) Bkpcy**
Bell v McKindsey (1865) (CAN) **17(1) Deeds**
Bell v McLean (1868) (CAN) **42(1) Shrffs**
Bell v Maklin (1887) (CAN) **40(2) S Land**
Bell v Manning (1865) (CAN) **6 B of Exch**
Bell v Mansfield (1893) (AUS) **42(1) Ship**
Bell v Marsh (1903) **21(2) Estpl**
Bell v Marsh (1951) (CAN) **19(1) Esmt**
Bell v Matthewman (1920) (CAN) **23(1) Exors**
Bell v Midland Ry Co (1861) **17(2) Damgs; 19(1) Esmt; 36(1) Nuis**
Bell v Miller (1862) (CAN) **3(2) Arbn**
Bell v Miller (1877) (AUS) **29(1) Insce; 29(2) Insce**
Bell v Milner (1957) (CAN) **9(2) Coys**
Bell v Moffat (1880) (CAN) **6 B of Exch**
Bell v Montreal Trust Co (1956) (CAN) **45 Stats**
Bell v Murray (1833) (SCOT) **27(3) H & W**
Bell v Nangle (1841) (IR) **17(1) Deeds**
Bell v Nash (1994) (CAN) **44(1) Solrs**
Bell v National Forest Products Ltd, Luttin, Porter (1964) (CAN) **26(1) Guar**
Bell v National Provincial Bank of England Ltd (1904) **27(5) Inc T**
Bell v Nevin (1866) **36(2) Prtnrs**
Bell v New Zealand Rugby Football Union (1931) (NZ) **12(2) Contr**
Bell v Nicholls, Ex p Richards (1919) (CAN) **21(2) Exon**
Bell v Nixon (1816) **29(1) Insce**
Bell v North Staffordshire Ry Co (1879) **37(3) Prac & Proc**
Bell v Northern Constitution Ltd (1943) (NI) **32(1) Libel**
Bell v Northwood (1886) (CAN) **45 Sp Pfce**
Bell v Norwich (Bp) (1565) **19(2) Eccl**
Bell v Oakley (1814) **18 Distr**
Bell v Ogilvie (1863) (SCOT) **44(1) Solrs**
Bell v Ontario Human Rights Commission and McKay (1971) **16 Cr Pract**
Bell v Ontario Human Rights Commission and McKay (1971) (CAN) **1(1) Admin L**
Bell v Ottawa Trust & Deposit Co (1897) (CAN) **5(1) Bkpcy**
Bell v Park (1914) (IR) **52 Wills**
Bell v Parke (1860) (IR) **32(1) Libel**
Bell v Patent (1903) (CAN) **33 Mags**
Bell v Peter Brown & Co (a firm) (1990) **32(2) Limit of A; 44(1) Solrs**
Bell v Petry (1897) (NZ) **27(1) H & W**
Bell v Phyn (1802) **36(2) Prtnrs; 52 Wills**

Bell v Pitt (1956) (AUS) **19(1) Esmt**
Bell v Plumbly (1900) **46(1) Stk Exch**
Bell v Port of London Assce Co (1850) **22(2) Evid**
Bell v Portland Shire (1876) (AUS) **1(2) Admin L**
Bell v Postlethwaite (1855) **3(2) Arbn**
Bell v Puller (1810) **43(1) Ship**
Bell v Quebec Corpn (1879) **49(2) Water**
Bell v Raisbeck (1844) **23(1) Exors**
Bell v Riddell (1882) (CAN) **27(1) H & W**
Bell v Riddell (1884) (CAN) **12(2) Contr**
Bell v Robinson (1824) **18 Distr; 25 Fam Arr**
Bell v Robinson (1909) (CAN) **5(2) Bkpcy**
Bell v Rogers (1914) **6 B of Exch**
Bell v Rokeby (1905) (CAN) **1(4) Agcy**
Bell v Ross (1885) (CAN) **5(1) Bkpcy**
Bell v Rowe (1901) (AUS) **12(2) Contr**
Bell v Roy Estate (1993) (CAN) **50 Wills**
Bell v Ry Comr (1861) (AUS) **2 Animals**
Bell v Sarvis (1903) (CAN) **50 Wills; 51 Wills**
Bell v Schultz (1912) (CAN) **39(3) S Goods; 46(2) Tort**
Bell v Scott (1922) (AUS) **40(2) S Land**
Bell v Secretary of State for Defence (1986) **16 Cr Pract; 39(2) Royal F**
Bell v Shuttleworth (1841) **6 B of Exch; 12(3) Contr; 26(1) Guar; 30 Jdgmts**
Bell v Simpson (1857) **4(2) Bkpcy**
Bell v Skelton (1831) **23(2) Exors**
Bell v Smith (1826) **22(2) Evid**
Bell v Spelliscy (1932) (CAN) **23(1) Exors**
Bell v Spereman (1726) **38(3) Recrs**
Bell v Stanley Industrial Consultants Ltd (1996) (CAN) **20(1) Empt**
Bell v Stewart (1842) (IR) **6 B of Exch**
Bell v Stocker (1882) **27(1) H & W**
Bell v Stockton etc Tramway Co (1887) **39(1) R Traf**
Bell v Stone (1798) **32(1) Libel**
Bell v Sunderland Bldg Soc (1883) **35(2) Mtge**
Bell v Tainthorp (1834) **30 Juries**
Bell v Tape (1837) (IR) **11(3) Const L**
Bell v Taylor (1836) **44(2) Solrs**
Bell v Thatcher (1675) **32(1) Libel**
Bell v Thompson (1934) (AUS) **2 Animals**
Bell v Tilden Car Rental Inc (1997) (CAN) **35(3) Negl**
Bell v Timiswood (1812) **23(1) Exors**
Bell v Toronto Transportation Commission (1926) (CAN) **18 Discy**
Bell v Travco Hotels Ltd (1953) **29(1) Inns**
Bell v Turner (1874) **22(2) Evid**
Bell v Turner (1877) **48(2) Trusts**
Bell v Twentyman (1841) **19(1) Esmt; 35(3) Negl; 36(1) Nuis**
Bell v Union Bank (1923) (NZ) **3(3) Bank**
Bell v Walker & Debrett (1785) **13(1) Coprt**
Bell v Wardell (1740) **17(1) Custom; 46(1) Time**
Bell v Welch (1850) **12(1) Contr; 26(1) Guar**
Bell v Wermore (1880) (CAN) **21(2) Exon**
Bell v Westmount Town (1899) (CAN) **8(3) Comwlth**
Bell v Wetmore (1880) (CAN) **17(2) Damgs; 27(2) H & W**
Bell v White (1857) (CAN) **7(1) Bounds**
Bell v Whitehead (1839) **13(1) Coprt**
Bell v Wilson (1865) **17(1) Deeds; 34(1) Mines**
Bell v Wilson (1866) **34(1) Mines**
Bell v Wilson (1900) (CAN) **32(1) Libel**
Bell v Windsor & Annapolis Ry Co (1892) (CAN) **8(1) Car**
Bell v Wright (1895) (CAN) **44(2) Solrs**
Bell v Wyndham (1865) **25 Fish**
Bell v Young (1855) **4(1) Bkpcy**
Bell (or Young or Farrell) v Arnott (1857) (SCOT) **3(1) Arbn**

**Fig 3.9**

*Example Page from The Digest, Vol. 35(3), 3rd Reissue*

1 GENERAL PRINCIPLES OF THE LAW OF NEGLIGENCE          Case **384**

goods by order, delivered them at a booking-office, with the customer's address, and booked them, to be forwarded to him, not specifying any particular conveyance, and no particular mode of transmission having been pointed out by the customer.

*Quaere*: whether the consignor could maintain an action against the office-keeper for a negligent loss of the goods while under his charge.

*Gilbart v Dale* (1836) 5 Ad & El 543; 2 Har & W 383; 1 Nev & PKB 22; 6 LJKB 3; 111 ER 1270

ANNOTATION **Apld** Mid Ry v Bromley (1856) 17 CB 372

**378 No negligence without duty**

In case for an injury to plaintiff's reversionary interest by defendant's obstruction of a water-course on his land and thereby sending water upon and under the house and land in the occupation of plaintiff's tenant, defendant pleaded, that the obstruction was caused by the neglect of plaintiff's tenant to repair a wall on the demised land, that in consequence it fell into the watercourse, and caused the damage, and that within a reasonable time after defendant had notice he removed it: *Held* to be a bad plea, it not showing any obligation on the tenant to repair the wall merely as terre-tenant. *Quaere*: whether it would have been good if it had.

*Bell v Twentyman* (1841) 1 QB 766; 1 Gal & Dav 223; 10 LJQ B 278; 6 Jur 366; 113 ER 1324

ANNOTATION **Distd** Taylor v Stendall (1845) 5 LTOS 214

**379 No negligence without duty**

A declaration in case stated, by way of inducement, that plaintiff was possessed of a dwelling-house as tenant to defendant, and that defendant, at the request of plaintiff, promised to fit up a cellar for a wine cellar, with brick and stone bins; and then charged that it became the duty of defendant to use due care in fitting up the same, but that he did not, and that the slabs gave way, and broke plaintiff's wine bottles. It was proved that defendant did fit up a wine cellar with brick and stone bins; but that plaintiff afterwards required more bins to be made, and defendant consented to have the partitions carried up to the roof of the cellar. The workmen, however, by plaintiff's directions, erected the new partitions upon the centre of the slabs which covered the bins first made, and the slabs then gave way. It was proved that those slabs would have been strong enough to bear the weight of empty bottles; but some of the witnesses thought not that of full bottles: *Held* under these circumstances no breach of duty was shown, defendant having only undertaken to fit up a wine cellar with brick and stone bins, and not one of any particular character.

*Richardson v Berkeley* (1847) 10 LTOS 203

**380 No negligence without duty**

The declaration stated that defendants were possessed of a mooring anchor, which was kept by them fixed in a known part of a navigable river, covered by ordinary tides, that the anchor had become removed into, and remained in, another part of the river covered by ordinary tides, not indicated, whereof defendants had notice, and although they had the means and power of refixing and securing the anchor, and indicating it, they neglected so to do, whereby plaintiffs' vessel, whilst sailing in a part of the river ordinarily used by ships, ran foul of and struck against the anchor, and was thereby damaged, etc: *Held* bad, for not showing that defendants were privy to the removal of the anchor, or that it was their duty to refix it and to indicate it.

*Hancock v York, Newcastle & Berwick Ry Co* (1850) 10 CB 348; 14 LTOS 467; 138 ER 140

**381 No negligence without duty**

Negligence creates no cause of action unless it expresses a breach of a duty (*Erle, CJ*).

*Dutton v Powles* (1862) 2 B & S 191; 31 LJQB 191; 6 LT 224; 8 Jur NS 970; 10 WR 408; 1 Mar LC 209; 121 ER 1043, Ex Ch

**382 No negligence without duty**

Plaintiff, a carman, being sent by his employer to defendants for some goods, was directed by a servant of defendants to go to the counting house. In proceeding along a dark passage of defendants in the direction pointed out, plaintiff fell down a staircase, and was injured: *Held* defendants were not guilty of any negligence; for if the passage was so dark that plaintiff could not see his way, he ought not to have proceeded; and if, on the other hand, there was sufficient light, he ought to have avoided the danger.

*Wilkinson v Fairrie* (1862) 1 H & C 633; 32 LJ Ex 73; 7 LT 599; 9 Jur NS 280; 158 ER 1038

ANNOTATIONS **Apld** Lewis v Ronald (1909) 101 LT 534 **Consd** Campbell v Shelbourne Hotel Ltd [1939] 2 KB 534

**383 No negligence without duty**

*Skelton v London & North Western Ry Co* no 828 post

**384 No negligence without duty**

Plaintiffs, merchants at Valparaiso, received through defendants a telegram purporting to come from London and addressed to them, ordering a large shipment of barley. No such message was ever in fact sent to plaintiffs. The misdelivery of the message was caused by the negligence of defendants, and occasioned heavy loss, to plaintiffs, in consequence of a fall in the market price of barley. In an action to recover the amount of this loss: *Held* there was no duty owing by defendants to plaintiffs in the matter, either by contract or law, and therefore no action would lie.

given is to the year, volume and page number. Cases reported since 1992 appear in the annual cumulative *Tables and Index*, updated quarterly by the *Current Tables and Index*.

If you know that the case you are looking for is old, you can turn to the index in Volumes 177 and 178 of the *English Reports*, and this will tell you if the case is printed in the *English Reports* (see para.3.12). Several other series of law reports also publish indexes and these can be useful if you know that a case is reported in a particular series but you have not got an exact reference.

The indexes to the *Law Reports* are very useful for all but the most recent cases. From 1865 to 1949, a series of *Law Reports: Digests* were published. These contain summaries of the cases reported in the *Law Reports*, in subject order, and a list of cases is usually included. From 1950 this has been published as the *Law Reports Consolidated Index* (lettered on the spine Law Reports Index), usually referred to as the *Red Index*. Four bound volumes, each covering cases in a 10–year period, have been published for the period 1951–1990. An annual paper back *Red Index* is published, containing cases indexed to the end of the previous year. This is supplemented by the *Pink Index*, which is issued at intervals during the year and lists all the cases published during the current year. The main arrangement of all the indexes is by subject, but there are two alphabetical lists. The list of Cases Reported, at the front of each volume, covers recently reported cases, whilst the separate list of Cases Judicially Considered, at the back of the volume, gives information on older cases which have been mentioned in court during the period covered by the index. In addition to cases published in the *Law Reports* and the *Weekly Law Reports*, the Red and Pink indexes also include cases published, in the *All England Law Reports*, the *Criminal Appeal Reports*, the *Lloyd's Law Reports*, the *Local Government Reports*, the *Industrial Cases Reports*, and the *Road Traffic Reports* and *Tax Cases*.

## Recent Unreported Judgments

Transcripts of judgments made in the Court of Appeal have been added to LexisNexis data-bases since the 1980s. However, recent judgments have become much more widely available since the late 1990s as courts have added judgment texts to their websites. Transcripts of judgments made in a very wide range of cases are now available on the internet, sometimes within hours of the judgment being handed down. Perhaps the most useful aspect of this development is the opportunity this gives you to find the text of very recent judgments. Where cases have provoked coverage in the newspapers and other media, the availability of judg-ments on the internet makes it possible to examine the legal issues by going directly to the full text.

▶ 3.19

The House of Lords led the move towards the publication of judgments on the internet, and has made its own judgments available on the Parliament website (at www.parliament.uk) since 1996. As these are the judgments of the court of final appeal, they are the most influential recent judgments available online. The judgments are found in the "Judicial Work" section of the Parliament website under "Judgments". The most recent judgments are listed first as they appear, followed by alphabetical lists of judgments grouped according to the year in which they were made. The "Advanced Search" on the Parliament website allows a search to be restricted so that only the judgments on the website are searched. Keywords, exact phrases or dates can then be added to retrieve particular judgments. The Privy Council has made judgments of its Judicial

Committee available (at *www.privy-council.org.uk*) since 1999. (The Privy Council complements the role of the House of Lords as the court of final appeal for some Commonwealth Countries, the Channel Islands, Isle of Man and UK overseas territories.)

The volume of recent judgments greatly increased in the late 1990s when the Court Service began adding judgments to its website. Now re-titled Her Majesty's Court Service, the Service not longer makes judgments directly available on its website (at *www.hmcourts-service. gov.uk*). Instead, anyone seeking a judgment is referred to the BAILII or Casetrack sites (see para.3.20 below).

### How to find recent judgments

**3.20** ▶ If you are looking for an extremely recent House of Lords judgment, perhaps one made the previous day, it makes sense to look for the judgment on the Parliament website as noted in para.3–19. However, the wider coverage of the BAILII website makes it the most useful starting point for recent judgments. Most UK universities also provide access to the Casetrack service, which provides access to a rapidly updated database of judgments. Some universities subscribe, in addition, to Lawtel, which combines summaries of judgments with access to the full text.

The BAILII website (at *www.bailii.org*) provides a convenient way of finding all recent UK judgments as they bring together judgments from Her Majesty's Court Service, the House of Lords and the Privy Council. Judgments from Scotland and Northern Ireland courts are also included. BAILII databases are listed by jurisdiction. Courts are then listed within each jurisdiction. Judgments can be viewed either alphabetically or by year and month by selecting the link for a particular court. Select "England and Wales", for example, and "Court of Appeal (Civil Division) Decisions" to see the relevant judgments. Select "United Kingdom" to see House of Lords and Privy Council judgments.

However, unless you are looking for a relatively recent judgment, the BAILII "Case Law Search" provides the most effective means of finding judgments on the website. A link is provided from the BAILII home page to the full search screen. Searches can be made by case name or citation using the search screen, and all UK jurisdictions searched in a single operation. More general keyword or "exact phrase" searches are also possible. If you wish to restrict a search to a particular court this can be done by selecting the court using the tick boxes placed below the main search area.

The Casetrack service (at *www.casetrack.com*) provides direct access to Smith Bernal transcripts of judgments made in the Court of Appeal, the Administrative Court and the High Court, along with searchable links to House of Lords and Privy Council judgments. Again, Scotland and Northern Ireland judgments are included. As Smith Bernal is the official reporter to the Court of Appeal and the Administrative Court, judgments from these courts can be made available very quickly, sometimes within hours of being handed down. As a result judgments not yet available on BAILII may be available from Casetrack. The database can be searched by case name, date and keyword. Searches can also be restricted to subject areas. Access to the database is limited to registered users, so you will need to request a username and a password from your law library (Casetrack does not use either the Shibboleth authentication system generally used by UK universites, or the older Athens authentication system—see para.2.8).

As the UK's leading current awareness service for law, Lawtel (para.2.5) provides another effective way of searching for recent judgments, though by no means all university law libraries subscribe. The range of judgments available is again wide, and judgments are loaded onto Lawtel databases as soon as they become available. The brief summaries of judgments provided by Lawtel are a particular advantage, making it possible to quickly grasp the key points of a case.

It should be emphasised, however, that the greatest benefit of the availability of judgments online, lies in the opportunity it gives the student to find recent judgments which are already known to be of legal significance. The ability to search through large numbers of judgments is not in itself a particular benefit to the law student. Some of the judgments will be reported later, but many will not. About a third of Court of Appeal cases will be reported. As noted in the introduction to this chapter, the aim of law reporting is to make available those cases that raise a point of legal significance. It is unusual for cases which raise a significant legal issue to go unreported.

> **TIPS** • *Use the "neutral citation" (3–4) if known when searching for recent judgments, e.g. [2005] UKHL 35. (The citation can be used with paragraph numbers in square brackets when quoting from a judgment.)*

## SUMMARY: HOW TO FIND A CASE

1. If the date is unknown:
   use the Westlaw UK "Cases" search, or the *Current Law Case Citator*, or
   *The Digest Consolidated Table of Cases*, and *Cumulative Supplement*.
2. If the case is thought to be very old, look in:
   *The Digest Consolidated Table of Cases*,
   the index to the *English Reports* (or search the *English Reports* online from Justis Publishing or HeinOnline),
   the index to the *All England Law Reports Reprint* (or search the *Reprint* online using LexisNexis Butterworths).
3. If the case is thought to be very recent and unreported, use one of the databases described in para.3.19 and para.3.20.
4. If the case is thought to be recent, and reported, use:
   the Westlaw UK "Cases" search,
   or the *Current Law Monthly Digest*; the indexes of the *Law Reports*, the *Weekly Law Reports* and the *All England Law Reports* provide further print alternatives.
5. If you know that the case has been reported in one of the leading series, but your reference is incomplete:
   search for the case online (see para.7.8), or look in the printed index to the series if there is one.

## HOW TO TRACE JOURNAL ARTICLES AND COMMENTARIES ON A CASE

You may want to find journal articles written about a case, or trace comments on a recent court decision. Such articles and comments usually explain the significance of the case and

▶ **3.21**

relate it to other relevant decisions. Sometimes writers who disagree with a decision made in a case may suggest that the case provides a justification for a substantive change in the law.

If you have used the Westlaw UK "Cases" search to find a case (para.3.15), or the *Current Law Case Citator* (para.3.16), you may already have been alerted to the existence of journal articles providing comment and analysis. Brief journal citations appear at the end of the "Case Analysis" entry for a case provided by Westlaw UK. These will be linked to the full text of the article if it is available within Westlaw UK. In the *Current Law Case Citator*, journal articles appear in square brackets after citations for law reports.

Not all cases attract comment in journals. Significant cases may be referenced many times. *Douglas v Hello! Ltd* (no.1) has been discussed to date in over 80 journal articles. Some of the articles will be very brief, others extensive, running to many pages. Case Comment from legal journals may appear before a case is fully reported; more extensive academic discussions may be available relatively soon after a case is reported. The case *R (on the application of Al-Jedda) v Secretary of State for Defence* mentioned in para.3.15 was reported in 2008. Three relatively substantial articles appeared soon after it was reported. The citation:

E.J.I.L. 2008, 19(3), 509–531

refers to an article published in the *European Journal of International Law* which discussed the case. An earlier case comment appeared in 2007, soon after the judgment was made. It is cited as:

S.J. 2007, 151(47), 1570

which refers to comment published in Vol.51, issue 47 of the *Solicitors Journal* on p.1570.

Sources explaining the meaning of abbreviations are noted in para.3.5. These can be useful if you need to check a library catalogue to see if a university library holds a particular journal (para.1–9).

However, the Westlaw UK "Cases" search and the *Current Law Case Citator* provide only the briefest information about a journal article. This can be a problem if you wish to assess the potential value of the article. More information can be found using the Westlaw UK "Journals" search, or the Lawtel "Articles Index". Both services provide brief summaries of articles indexed.

To search for articles on a case using the Westlaw UK "Journals" search, first select the "Advanced Search" from the "Journals" search page. The citation for the case which interests you (or the party names) can then be entered in the relevant search box. Brief details of any potentially relevant journal articles are displayed once the search has been made, along with link under "Documents" to the summary of the article found in the *Legal Journals Index* (see para.5.6). This will not necessarily be the same list of articles as that found in the "Case Analysis" for the case, as indexing for the *Legal Journals Index* is carried out separately. The article summaries can be very brief, especially for older articles, but are usually more than sufficient as an aid to assessing the focus and nature of an article. The summary for the *European Journal of International Law* article cited above, states, for example, that it:

> "Discusses, with reference to leading case law, the scope of state responsibility for human rights violations conducted by national military forces when those military

forces are operating under a United Nations resolution but not under direct United Nations control."

The keywords associated with the *Legal Journals Index* entry can also be useful. If the full text of an article is available, a "Full Text Article" link is displayed alongside the "Legal Journals Index" link.

The Article Index contained in the Lawtel service (para.2.6) provides an effective online alternative to the journals search on Westlaw UK. Although fewer articles are indexed than is the case for Westlaw UK, the summaries provided are somewhat more extensive. Articles are indexed from 1988. To search for case comment on Lawtel, select the "Articles Index" tab on the home page, then "Focused Search". Case names can be entered in the "Case Law Cited" box. A search on *"Douglas v Hello"* finds slightly fewer articles than the equivalent search in Westlaw UK.

If you are simply looking for any comment on a recent case likely to be of general interest, a more direct approach can be adopted. If you know the date of a case, the relevant issue of weekly journals such as the *New Law Journal* or the *Solicitors Journal* can be checked on the library shelves. These always carry notes and comments on recent cases. Key specialist journals such as *Public Law* and the *Criminal Law Review* can be used in a similar way. Again, these journals always carry notes and comments on recent cases.

> **TIPS** ● *Use both the Westlaw UK "Cases" search (look for the "Case Analysis") and the "Journals" "Advanced Search" when tracing journal articles on a case. Different articles can be listed.*

## HOW TO FIND UPDATES ON RECENT CASES

A number of online services provide brief summaries of new cases. These enable the legal profession to identify the key features of recent judgments that might be of interest. Cases can be reviewed quickly, without the need to read through the judgments. The brief summaries provided by these services may sometimes be the only text available that notes the content of a judgment.

**▶ 3.22**

Updating services are provided by the *All England Reporter* section of the LexisNexis Butterworths service (para.2.3), the W.L.R. Daily service, Lawtel (para.2.5), and the Westlaw UK "Cases" search (para.3.15). These are explained below. The value of the print issues of the *Current Law Monthly Digest* is also noted. These provide update summaries of reported cases.

The *All England Reporter* from LexisNexis Butterworths is one of the most wide-ranging sources for summaries of new judgments; most appearing soon after the judgment is made. Some of the judgments will later be reported in the *All England Law Reports*, but many will not. The cases that will be reported later are marked with an asterisk against the case name.

To access the *Reporter* database, first select "Cases" from the LexisNexis Butterworths home page, then "Browse". Select the *Reporter* database to display a list of cases. The most recent are shown first. Judgments can also be viewed by legal practice area ("Banking", "Civil Procedure" etc). Although relatively brief, the summaries provided give the key facts for each case. Subject keywords are also added.

A summary can be cited using the *All England Reporter* reference number and the month of the judgment, e.g.:

*R v Thomas* [2008] All E.R. (D) 88 (Sep)

A more selective alternative to the *All England Reporter* database is provided by the Incorporated Council for Law Reporting. Its W.L.R. Daily service (at *www.lawreports.co.uk*) provides digests of cases that will later be reported in the *Weekly Law Reports*. This has the distinct advantage of ensuring that the cases summarised on the database raise questions of legal significance. The site is also a non-subscription site, guaranteeing access to the database content. The summaries provided are reasonably extensive and a full list of keywords is provided. Once a case has been reported in the *Weekly Law Reports* the entry is removed from W.L.R. Daily. Cases can be viewed by week, or by court and subject matter. If the latter option is selected, case names and keywords can be viewed by major subject heading (e.g. "Arbitration", "Audit", "Children"). The summaries can be cited using a W.L.R. Daily reference number as follows:

*R v B and Others* [2008] W.L.R. (D) 296

Not all libraries provide access to Lawtel, but Lawtel's "Case Law" search provides another rapidly updated source of summaries of judgments. An advantage of the Case Law search is that the case report summaries provided are always linked to the full text of judgments. A similar result can be achieved using the Westlaw UK "Cases" search. Select the "Advanced Search" from the case search page, then set one of the standard date limits, e.g. "28 days" and click to search. Brief details of recent cases are displayed along with links to summaries contained in the "Case Analysis" page. Subject keywords (e.g. "Privacy") can also be entered to find new reported cases of interest in a particular subject area.

Though these services are highly effective, the availability of online summaries of recent judgments can nonetheless be a mixed blessing, especially when the database providing the summaries is as wide-ranging as Lawtel's Case Law service or the *All England Reporter*. Though the specialist practitioner, or legal academic, may be able to sift through case summaries and decide which raise legal issues of significance, this is not easily accomplished by the law student. Finding information and interpreting it are two separate tasks involving different skills and levels of expertise.

Updates on recent reported cases, though less immediate, are more likely to yield new cases that might be important. The *Current Law Monthly Digest* prints summaries of cases under major subject headings (along with notes of journal articles and new legislation). A Cumulative Table of Cases in each monthly issue enables cases to be traced by name for the current year. The relevant month and entry item num ber is noted against each case.

## EUROPEAN HUMAN RIGHTS CASE LAW

3.23 ▶ The Human Rights Act 1998 incorporated into UK law the principles of the European Convention for the Protection of Human Rights and Fundamental Freedoms. Although the Convention had been of potential relevance to the law of the UK before the Human Rights Act, the Act requires that courts take Convention case law into account in all cases where it might be considered relevant, greatly increasing its importance to UK domestic law. As a result, knowing how to find and cite European Convention case law has become an essential skill for students of UK law.

**Fig 3.10**
'First page of an ECHR judgment'

CONSEIL
DE L'EUROPE

COUNCIL
OF EUROPE

# COUR EUROPÉENNE DES DROITS DE L'HOMME
# EUROPEAN COURT OF HUMAN RIGHTS

**FOURTH SECTION**

**CASE OF BOYLE V. THE UNITED KINGDOM**

*(Application no. 55434/00)*

**JUDGMENT**

**STRASBOURG**

**8 JANUARY 2008**

**FINAL**

*08/04/2008*

*This judgment will become final in the circumstances set out in Article 44 § 2 of the Convention. It may be subject to editorial revision.*

The European Convention is a treaty agreed by the member states of the Council of Europe—not to be confused with the European Union, though many of its 46 member states are also members of the EU. The UK ratified the Treaty in 1951 and it came into force in 1953. The Convention established both the European Court of Human Rights and the European Commission of Human Rights and both bodies have played a role in the creation of Convention case law. The role of the European Commission is now subsumed into that of the European Court.

European Convention case law consists of both judgments and decisions. Judgments are made by the full sessions of the European Court of Human Rights, sitting in Strasbourg. Decisions are admissibility decisions which determine whether a case should proceed to a full hearing of the European Court. Before 1998 admissibility decisions were made by the European Commission of Human Rights. Decisions are now made by a committee of the European Court of Human Rights itself. Both judgments and decisions are relevant to the interpretation of the European Convention and must be taken into account under the Human Rights Act 1998.

All applications to the European Court of Human Rights are given an application number consisting of five digits plus two digits for the year the application was lodged. Where a case is unreported, this application number can be used to cite both judgments and decisions, e.g.:

*Boyle v the United Kingdom* no.55434/00, January 8, 2008

specifies the judgment made in the case;

*Boyle v the United Kingdom* (dec.), no.55434/00, October 28, 2005

specifies the decision made in the same case.

An abbreviation such as ECHR or ECtHR is often added where it may not be obvious that a European Court case is being cited. The citation format noted for judgments follows the Council of Europe's specification. The practice of UK publishers does not always follow the Council of Europe specification.

## Tracing European Convention case law

3.24 ▶ The full text of European Convention case law can be found on the European Court of Human Rights website (at *www.echr.coe.int*). Judgments and decisions are held in the HUDOC database, part of the European Court of Human Rights Portal. The database contains all judgments made by the European Court of Human Rights since 1959 and all admissibility decisions made since 1986. Some decisions are also available for the period 1955 to 1986.

If you have the application number for a case, use the full number in the "Application Number" search box of the HUDOC database, to retrieve a link to the full text (e.g. "44875/98"). Tick boxes allow judgments, decisions or both to be selected for searching. Resolutions of the Committee of Ministers of the Council of Europe are also included, though these are not often cited in legal discussion.

If you do not have the application number for a case, the name of the case can be entered under "Case Title" (e.g. "B.B." or "Hobbs"), along with the respondent state (e.g. "United Kingdom"). The use of abbreviations in case titles and the need to have an exact case name can cause problems. It may be necessary to try likely subject keywords in the "Text" box to find a case.

Though the HUDOC database is the official online source for European Court of Human Rights case law, judgments (though not decisions) from the Court are also available from the BAILII database (para.2.15). The judgments are listed by year and can be found under the "Europe" heading on the BAILII home page (at *www.bailii.org*). Particular judgments can also be located using the BAILII "Case Law" search. Tick the "European Court of Human Rights" box below the search area to limit the search to the relevant case law. Party names can be used in the "Case name" search, but be careful to enter the names exactly as cited by the Court (e.g *"X, Y and Z v the United Kingdom"*). Application numbers need to be entered in the "Exact phrase" search box.

BAILII also adds a citation following the UK neutral citation module. The Boyle judgment cited in para.3.23 is cited in BAILII as [2008] E.C.H.R. 15.

## Printed judgments and decisions

Judgments made before 1996 were published by Carl Heymanns Verlag in *Series A* of the Publications of the Court. Each judgment has a number within the series, so that a full citation is as follows:

▶ **3.25**

> *Soering v the United Kingdom*, judgment of July 7, 1989, Series A no.161

References to pages or paragraph numbers may follow (e.g. pp 40–41; para.or § 65).

The text of individual judgments was also printed by the Council of Europe and distributed to libraries up until 1997. Some law libraries which do not hold the *Series A* text of a judgment may have retained these individually printed transcripts. Confusingly, they have their own numbering system. This is not used in citation.

From 1996 onwards selected judgments and decisions have been published (again by Heymanns Verlag) as *Reports of Judgments and Decisions*, and cited e.g. as:

> *Robins v the United Kingdom*, judgment of September 23, 1997, Reports 1997–V

Pages and paragraph numbers may again be added to the citation.

Decisions made between 1974 and 1995 were published by the Council of Europe as *Decisions and Reports* (DR). These are cited as follows:

> *Hewitt and Harman v the United Kingdom* (1989) 67 DR 88

Here, 67 specifies the volume number and 88 the first page of the report. Only a few law libraries hold the full *Decisions and Reports* series, which can be a problem as the HUDOC database does not contain all decisions made before 1986. Decisions made between 1960 and 1974 were published by the Council of Europe as *Collection of Decisions of the European Commission on Human Rights* (C.D.). These are rarely cited.

## Other sources of European human rights Law

Most of the human rights cases cited in UK courts have been reported in either the *European Human Rights Reports* (E.H.R.R.) or *Butterworths Human Rights Cases* (B.H.R.C.). Digests are also available in the *European Human Rights Law Review* (E.H.R.L.R.). These are commercial publications available both in print and online. The full text of the *European Human Rights Reports* and the *European Human Rights Law Review* are available online from Westlaw UK (para.2.5). *Butterworths Human Rights Cases* is available online from LexisNexis Butterworths

▶ **3.26**

(para.2.3). Citations from these publications use the standard format for UK law reports and journals. As with other Sweet & Maxwell law reports, the *European Human Rights Reports* from 2001 onwards are referenced using a case number rather than a page number, e.g.

> *Boyle v United Kingdom* (2008) 47 E.H.R.R. 19

Here the reference is to case 19 of the 2008 reports volume. Summaries and extracts of reports are also included in the *European Human Rights Reports,* and these are referenced as e.g.:

> *Brinks v Netherlands* (2005) 41 E.H.R.R. SE5

Some admissibility decisions are reported in a separate section of the E.H.R.R. and are cited as E.H.R.R. C.D.

Although the *European Human Rights Reports* concentrates on European Convention case law, *Butterworths Human Rights Cases* is more wide ranging, including cases from other common law countries which may be of relevance to the human rights law of the UK. Cases might be reported from the Constitutional Court of South Africa for example, or the United States Supreme Court. These appear alongside reports of UK cases.

Textbooks on UK human rights law also refer to cases from the Court of Justice of the European Union (para.8.13) where these concern European Convention principles.

Summaries of European Court of Human Rights cases have also been published in book form. Vincent Berger's *Case Law of the European Court of Human Rights* for example was published in three volumes and covers the period 1960 to 1993. Peter Kempees' *Systematic Guide to the Case Law of the European Court of Human Rights* covers the period 1960 to 1998 in four volumes, arranging summaries according to the relevant article or articles of the European Convention within each volume.

> **TIPS** • *Use Westlaw UK and LexisNexis Butterworths to search for ECHR cases reported in UK law reports. These are the cases most often cited in UK legal discussion. All ECHR judgments can be found on the BAILII website.*

The *Human Rights Information Bulletin*, produced by the Council of Europe, provides extensive summaries of recent judgments along with information on cases currently pending. Current issues can be found in the publications section of the Council of Europe website (at *www.coe.int*), along with back issues from no.41 1997. The European Court of Human Rights has issued Case-law information notes since 1999 which contain brief summaries of judgments arranged by Convention article. These can be found in the "Case-Law" section of the website (at *www.echr.coe.int*).

## TRIBUNALS

**3.27** ▶ The establishment of the welfare state led to the creation of a large number of tribunals. They were set up to resolve disputes over entitlement to welfare benefits. Subsequently, other areas, such as problems between landlords and tenants, and between employer and employees because of unfair dismissal, became subject to resolution through tribunals. Tribunals can be extremely busy, hearing many thousands of cases each year, but only a small number of cases are eventually reported in the law reports. Some law reports, such as the *Industrial Cases*

*Reports* and *Immigration Appeals*, carry reports of appeals from the tribunal to an appeal court, but the vast majority of cases heard by tribunals are not reported. However, relatively recent decisions from a wide range of tribunals can by found on the BAILII website (at *www.bailii.org*). These include, for example, decisions of the Employment Appeal Tribunal (from 1999) and the Financial Services and Markets Tribunal (from 2003). The full listing can be found under the "United Kingdom" heading. The full text of judgments can then be found. Where Tribunals also put the text of judgments made on their own websites, these can usually be traced from the relevant page of the BAILII website. For reported and unreported decisions of the Social Security and Child Support Commissioners, see para.3.28. Unreported decisions of tribunals can be cited using unique appeal numbers, e.g. Appeal no.UKEAT/0321/08 for an Employment Appeal Tribunal case.

## Social welfare law

The most important decisions taken by the Social Security and Child Support Commissioners ▶ **3.28** are found on the Commissioners' website (at *www.osscsc.gov.uk*). To find them, select "Decisions" from the home page. The website includes decisions from 1991 to date, and "high-lighted" decisions for the last 12 months. Highlighted decisions are decisions the Commissioners consider to be of particular interest or importance. The website also includes a subject index of reported decisions for the period from 2001 onwards.

Between 1976 and 1990, bound volumes of decisions were published by HMSO, the last appearing in 1993 as *Reported Decisions of the Social Security Commissioner* Vol.13. 1989–1990. Reported decisions between 1948 and 1976 were published in the seven volumes of the *Reported Decisions of the Commissioner under the Social Security and National Insurance (Industrial Injuries) Acts*, known as the *Blue Books* because of their colour.

The form of citation for Commissioners' decisions differs from that used in conventional law reports and references to cases do not include the names of parties. All reported cases since 1950 bear the prefix R, followed, in brackets, by an abbreviation for the series. For example, the prefix R(U) indicates a Commissioner's decision on unemployment benefit, and R(P) a decision on entitlement to pensions. Within each series, reports are cited by the report number and the year: R(U) 7/62 indicates a reported unemployment benefit decision, case no.7 of 1962. The following abbreviations are in use:

| | |
|---|---|
| R(A) | Attendance allowance |
| R(CS) | Child Support |
| R(DLA) | Disability Living Allowance |
| R(DWA) | Disability Working Allowance |
| R(F) | Family allowances and child benefit |
| R(FC) | Family Credit |
| R(FIS) | Family Income Supplement |
| R(G) | General—miscellaneous (maternity benefit, widow's benefit, death grant, etc.) |
| R(I) | Industrial injuries |
| R(IS) | Income Support |
| R(M) | Mobility allowance |

| R(P) | Retirement pensions |
| R(S) | Sickness and invalidity Benefit |
| R(SB) | Supplementary benefit |
| R(SSP) | Statutory Sick Pay |
| R(U) | Unemployment benefit |

Unpublished decisions are prefaced by C instead of R. For example, CP3/81 is a reference to an unpublished 1981 Commissioner's decision on pensions and CSB 15/82 is an unreported decision on supplementary benefits. The year in "starred" cases (1987–2001) is given in full, e.g. CDLA 1347/1999.

Reported cases from 1948–50 had a different method of citation. They were prefixed by C, followed by a letter (not enclosed in brackets) representing the area of law covered. Thus, CI denotes an early decision on industrial injuries. Scottish or Welsh cases were prefixed with CS and CW respectively. The cases were numbered in sequence. However, only a minority were printed, which has resulted in gaps in the numerical sequence. For example, CWI 17/49 is followed by CWI 20/49. Cases numbered 18 or 19 of 1949 are unreported. The abbreviation (KL) after the citation is an indication that the case has been reported, whilst the suffix (K) denotes a decision of limited value.

Decisions on a particular subject can be traced using *Neligan: Social Security Case Law: Digest of Commissioner's Decisions*. The Digest is available from the Department of Work and Pensions website (at *www.dwp.gov.uk*). To find the publication, use the website's search engine and search for "Neligan". *Neligan* summarises the majority of the reported decisions, under appropriate subject headings. Appendix 3 of the work provides a list of decision numbers which allow you to trace the summary of a particular case should the full report of the Commissioner's decision be unavailable. A general subject index is also provided.

### Reported decisions of other tribunals

**3.29** ▶ The wide range of tribunals makes a complete guide to reported decisions impossible within the available space. What follows is selective.

Immigration appeals are covered by *Immigration Appeals*, published by TSO. Also available from TSO are the *VAT and Duties Tribunals Reports*.

Many Lands Tribunal cases appear in the *Property, Planning and Compensation Reports* and in the *Estates Gazette* and the *Estates Gazette Law Reports*. The latter series also covers leasehold valuation tribunals. Barry Rose published a series of volumes entitled *Lands Tribunal Cases*.

Most reported cases, in subjects other than welfare law, appear in standard series of law reports and are conventionally cited. *Current Law* contains references to many tribunal decisions, under appropriate subject headings, and provides a summary for each one. Looseleaf encyclopedias frequently refer to both published and unpublished decisions in the appropriate subject.

The *Industrial Tribunal Reports*, published until 1978, now form part of the *Industrial Cases Reports*. These contain many cases heard by the Employment Appeal Tribunal and many E.A.T. decisions also appear in the Industrial Relations Law Reports.

# ▶ 4
# Legislation

## INTRODUCTION

When a Bill (para.6.6) has been approved by both Houses of Parliament and has received the Royal Assent, it becomes an Act of Parliament. The Act is made available on the Office of Public Sector Information (OPSI) website (at *www.opsi.gov.uk/legislation*) and the first printed version is published by TSO, usually within a few days of receiving the Royal Assent.

▶ **4.1**

There are two types of Acts. Public General Acts deal with public policy and apply to the whole population, or a substantial part of it. Local and Personal Acts, on the other hand, affect only a particular area of the country, or a named organisation or group of individuals. This chapter will concentrate on Public General Acts, which you are more likely to use regularly. Local and Personal Acts will, however, be examined in para.4.25.

## THE STRUCTURE OF AN ACT

A copy of the Ragwort Control Act 2003 is reproduced below. This is an unusually short Act, as most Acts are many pages in length. All Acts are structured in the same way, although some of the parts described below are not included in every Act.

▶ **4.2**

The parts of an Act (see the illustration) are:

1. Short title;
2. Official citation (see para.4.3);
3. Long title. This may give some indication of the purpose and content of the Act;
4. Date of Royal Assent;
5. Enacting formula. This is a standard form of words indicating that the Act has been approved by Parliament;
6. Main body of the Act. This is divided into sections, which are further divided into subsections and paragraphs. When referring to a section, it is usual to abbreviate it to "s." Subsections are written in round brackets. You would therefore write section 2, subsection 1 as s.2(1);
7. Date of commencement. A specific date may be set for the Act to come into force. Alternatively, the Act may give a Minister of the Crown the power to bring it into force at a later date. This will be done through a commencement order, which is a form of delegated legislation. If there is no commencement section at the end of an Act, it comes into force on the date of the Royal Assent;

**Fig 4.1**
facing section if
possible

# Ragwort Control Act 2003 [1]

## 2003 Chapter 40 [2]

An Act to amend the Weeds Act 1959 in relation to ragwort; and for connected purposes.[3]

[4] [20th November 2003]

BE IT ENACTED by the Queen's most Excellent Majesty, by and with the advice and consent of the Lords Spiritual and Temporal, and Commons, in this present Parliament assembled, and by the authority of the same, as follows:- [5]

## 1 Control of ragwort

After section 1 of the Weeds Act 1959 (c. 54) there is inserted-

## "1A
## Code of practice: ragwort [6]

(1) The Minister may make a code of practice for the purpose of providing guidance on how to prevent the spread of ragwort (senecio jacobaea L.).

(2) Before making the code the Minister must consult such persons as he considers appropriate.

(3) The Minister must lay a copy of the code before Parliament.

(4) The Minister may revise the code; and subsections (2) and (3) apply to the revised code.

(5) The code is to be admissible in evidence.

(6) If the code appears to a court to be relevant to any question arising in proceedings it is to be taken into account in determining that question."

## 2 Wales

(1) The reference to the Weeds Act 1959 in Schedule 1 to the National Assembly for Wales (Transfer of Functions) Order 1999 (S.I. 1999/672) is to be treated as referring to that Act as amended by this Act.

(2) Subsection (1) does not affect the power to make further Orders varying or omitting that reference.

## 3 Short title, commencement and extent

(1) This Act may be cited as the Ragwort Control Act 2003.

(2) This Act comes into force at the end of the period of three months beginning with the day on which it is passed.[7]

(3) This Act extends to England and Wales only.[8]

8. Extent. Acts of Parliament usually apply to the whole of the United Kingdom, unless specified otherwise in an extent section.

Schedules and tables are sometimes included at the end of an Act. They may contain detailed provisions not included elsewhere in the Act or may summarise and clarify the effect of the Act. They help to prevent the main body of an Act becoming too cluttered with detail and are used in the same way as appendices in a book. Until 2001 the text of an Act also included helpful marginal notes, explaining the contents of a section.

## Citation of statutes

Statutes (or Acts) are commonly referred to by a shortened version of their title (the short title) ▶ **4.3** and the year of publication, e.g. the Theft Act 1968. Every Act published in a year is given its own individual number and Acts may also be cited by the year in which they were passed and the Act (or chapter) number. Thus the Theft Act was the 60th Act passed in 1968 and is cited as 1968, c. 60. "Chapter" is abbreviated to "c." when written, but it is spoken in full.

The present system of citing statutes by their year and chapter number began in 1963. Before that date, the system was more complicated. Prior to 1963, statutes were referred to by the year of the monarch's reign (the "regnal year") and the chapter number. For example, a citation 3 Edw. 7, c. 36 is a reference to the Motor Car Act 1903, which was the 36th Act passed in the third year of the reign of Edward VII.

A session of Parliament normally commences in the autumn and continues through into the summer of the following year. A "regnal year" is reckoned from the date of the sovereign's accession to the throne and a session of Parliament may therefore cover more than one regnal year. In the case of Queen Elizabeth II, who came to the throne in February, the first part of a Parliamentary session, from the autumn until February, falls into one regnal year, whilst the latter part of the session of Parliament falls into a different regnal year. Statutes passed before February bear a different regnal year to those passed after the anniversary of her accession to the throne. Two examples make this clearer:

1. The Children and Young Persons Act 1956 received the Royal Assent in March 1956, when the Queen had just entered the fifth year of her reign. It was the 24th Act to receive the Royal Assent during the Parliament which commenced sitting in the autumn of the fourth year of her reign, and which continued in session during the early part of the fifth year of her reign. The Act is therefore cited as 4 & 5 Eliz. 2, c. 24.
2. By contrast, the Air Corporations Act 1956 was passed during the following session of Parliament and it received the Royal Assent in December 1956, when the Queen was still in the fifth year of her reign. Since, at that time, there could be no certainty that the Queen would still be on the throne in two months' time or that Parliament would still be in session in February, when she would be entering the sixth year of her reign, the statute was cited as 5 Eliz. 2, c. 3 (i.e. the third Act passed in the Parliament held in the fifth year of the reign). When the Queen subsequently survived to enter her sixth year, the statute would henceforth be referred to as 5 & 6 Eliz. 2, c. 3.

Both these Acts are to be found in the 1956 volumes of the statutes, which contain all the Acts passed during that year, regardless of the session of Parliament in which they were passed.

Until 1939, the volumes of the statutes contained all the Acts passed in a particular session of Parliament. After that date, the annual volumes contain all the statutes passed in a calendar year. This can give rise to some confusion. For instance, the volume for 1937 contains the statutes passed in the parliamentary session which extended from November 1936 to October 1937. Thus, some Acts which actually bear the date 1936 are included in the 1937 volume. The volume for 1938 includes some statutes passed in December 1937 (which one might normally expect to find in the 1937 volume). The simple rule with older Acts is: if it is not in the volume you expect to find it in, look in the volumes on either side of it!

### Citation of the names of monarchs and their regnal years

**4.4 ▶** The names of the monarchs are abbreviated as follows:

| | |
|---|---|
| Anne | Ann. |
| Charles | Car., Chas. or Cha. |
| Edward | Edw. or Ed. |
| Elizabeth | Eliz. |
| George | Geo. |
| Henry | Hen. |
| James | Ja., Jac. or Jas. |
| Mary | Mar. or M. |
| Philip and Mary | Ph. & M. or Phil. & Mar. |
| Richard | Ric. or Rich. |
| Victoria | Vict. |
| William | Will., Wm. or Gul. |
| William and Mary | Wm. & M., Will. & Mar. or Gul. & Mar. |

A list of the regnal year of monarchs showing the equivalent calendar year is found in *Sweet & Maxwell's Guide to Law Reports and Statutes* (4th ed.), pp.21–33; and at the back of *Osborn's Concise Law Dictionary*.

## MODERN STATUTES

**4.5 ▶** Acts of Parliament are published in print in the red-bound volumes of the Public General Acts & Measures. They also appear online on the OPSI website (at *www.opsi.gov.uk*), which now contains the original text of all Acts from 1988 onwards, along with a selection of earlier Acts for the period. These are the official sources of statutes (para.4.6). However, a number of alternative sources for statutes are also available. Which source to use may not be obvious. The following considerations can help ensure that you choose an appropriate source for modern statute law.

First, you should consider whether you need to consult the current amended text of an Act. Is it important that you are consulting law in force? If so, you should consider using one of the sources introduced in para.4.12. These include subscription services such as Westlaw UK (para.4.14) or LexisNexis Butterworths (para.4.13), also the print volumes of *Halsbury's Statutes of England* (para.4.16). The Statute Law Database (para.4.15) might also be considered as a free online source of law in force. Unfortunately, updating for the database is currently incomplete. This may improve, if, as intended, responsibility for the database moves from the Ministry of Justice to OPSI.

If it is important to see the full text of legislation as originally enacted, then turn to the sources noted in the following sections.

Having decided this, it is useful to consider whether you need to consult a particular section of an Act, or the Act as a whole; online sources are usually best if you wish to find a particular section of an Act (especially if you already have the relevant section number). This could be done using one of the subscription sources of law in force noted above, or a free public source of legislation as enacted. This might be the OPSI website (para.4.6) or the BAILII website (para.4.8).

If you wish to gain an understanding of an important piece of legislation taken as a whole, it is worth turning to print editions. Important legislation can be extensive, making it difficult to read and review an entire Act on screen. Your library is likely to have the print volumes of both *Public General Acts & Measures* (para.4.6) and *Current Law Statutes* (para.4.11). These are sources of statutes as originally enacted. *Halsbury's Statutes of England* (para.4.16) is the only print source for statutes in force.

An additional advantage of some print editions is the inclusion of often extensive annotations, which can help direct your understanding of legislation. Both *Current Law Statutes* and *Halsbury's Statutes of England* provide annotations. These are not available in the online databases.

There are also books devoted to particular key Acts of Parliament. These can be particularly helpful as they combine detailed comment with a reprinted version of the Act itself. Relevant secondary legislation is usually included. Extracts of Parliamentary Debates and government white papers might also found. *Blackstone's Guide to the Human Rights Act 1998* (4th edition 2007) and *The Criminal Justice and Immigration Act 2008: a practitioner's guide* (Ward and Bettinson 2008) are examples of such works.

### Official sources of statutes as originally enacted

The OPSI website lists Public General Acts on its legislation pages (at *www.opsi.gov.uk/legislation*). There are also links to Northern Ireland, Scotland and Wales legislation. Acts are listed on the page by year of enactment, both alphabetically and chronologically (i.e. in chapter number order). Selecting the title of an Act displays the full text with hyperlinks from the list of sections near the start of most Acts to the relevant section. In most cases a number of sections of the web page version of an Act are reproduced in long web pages, making printing cumbersome. However almost all the Acts are also available in a PDF file print version which reproduces the pages of the bound volumes. All Acts passed by Parliament from 1988 onwards can be found on the site.

&#9655; **4.6**

Acts are also printed individually as they appear. At the end of each year bound annual volumes are then published as the official *Public General Acts & Measures* of 2008, 2009 etc. This series of volumes has been published since 1831 (originally under the title *Public General Acts*). There are now a number of volumes for each year. At the front of the annual volumes there is a list of all the Acts passed during the year, in alphabetical order, showing where they are to be found in the bound volumes. There is also a list in chapter number order giving the same information. The General Synod Measures of the Church of England are printed in full at the back of the annual volumes of the *Public General Acts*. A list of Local and Personal Acts published during the year is also printed in the annual volume, although the texts are not included. Most law libraries keep both individually printed Acts for the current year and the bound volumes.

### Alternative sources for the official text of statutes

**4.7** ▶ The BAILII website (para.4.8) reproduces the full text of the post 1987 statutes available on the OPSI website. The layout of the BAILII website, along with its more straightforward keyword searching, means that the site can be easier to use than the OPSI site. However the mixture of unamended and amended legislation on the BAILII site noted below can make it confusing to use. In addition, there are no PDF print versions of Acts.

Complete historical coverage online of UK statutes as originally enacted is only offered by Justis UK Statutes (para.4.9). This is a subscription service and not all law libraries can provide access. There are also two current print series which reprint the text of statutes as originally enacted. *Law Reports: Statutes* (para.4.10) reproduces the *Public General Acts & Measures* text in a smaller, more easily handled, format. *Current Law Statutes* (para.4.11) prints the same text with additional annotations. Most law libraries will have one or both of these print series.

### BAILII United Kingdom Statutes

**4.8** ▶ Statutes can be found on the BAILII website (at *www.bailii.org*), under the "United Kingdom" heading. The original, unamended versions of Acts are available from 1988 onwards, along with earlier statutes derived from the Statute Law Database (para.4.15). Links to the relevant statute in the Statute Law Database are provided in all cases, enabling the update status to be checked. Nonetheless, the mixture of recent unamended statutes and earlier amended versions can be confusing. Bear in mind also, that the Statute Law Database is not currently up-to-date in its incorporation of amendments.

Acts can be found by year of enactment and also alphabetically, using a single A–Z listing for all of the Acts on the site. If you are unsure of the year of an Act, this makes the BAILII site a little easier to use than the OPSI alternative. However, each Act is reproduced on the site as a single continuous web page. You need to be sure that you want the entire text of an Act before you click to print. Or better still, go to the printable PDF file version of an Act on the OPSI website. As is the case in the OPSI website, the section names in the list of sections near the start of most Acts are hyperlinked to the relevant section. Northern Ireland, Scotland and Wales legislation is also available.

### Justis UK Statutes

**4.9** ▶ The Justis UK Statutes service is the only complete source of United Kingdom statute law available online, containing the full text of all Acts of Parliament from 1235 onwards. It is one of a number of Justis subscription services (see para.2.6), so you need to check if your law library can provide access. Though the text of statutes is presented as enacted, a particular feature of the database is the ability it provides to trace the path of amendment and repeal from one statute to another. For each statute, any amending legislation is presented as a family tree, with the relevant links leading you from statute to statute. Justis UK Statutes is the best source available for tracing the historical development of statute law. As with other subscription services, Acts are presented section by section, making printing easier than is the case with the BAILII or OPSI websites. PDF facsimiles of Acts as they were originally published are also included.

## Law Reports: Statutes

The Incorporated Council of Law Reporting publishes a series called *Law Reports: Statutes* alongside the *Law Reports* and the *Weekly Law Reports*. The unbound parts issued through the year share the same Royal Octavo page size and publishing format. Each contains the reprinted text of one or more Acts, though there may be some delay between an Act receiving the Royal Assent and its appearance in *Law Reports: Statutes*. At the end of the year annual volumes are printed which replace the loose parts. The page size of the reprint can make the bound volume appreciably easier to manipulate than the large folio volumes of *Public General Acts & Measures*. As a result some law libraries hold the reprint series as well as *Public General Acts & Measures*.

▌**4.10**

## Current Law Statutes Annotated

*Current Law Statutes Annotated* reprints the full text of all Public General Acts soon after they receive the Royal Assent. They are printed in booklet form on blue paper and are filed into a looseleaf Service File in chapter number order. The blue paper denotes that the Act is a reprint of the Queen's Printer copy. Some months later, the Act printed on blue paper is replaced by the annotated version which is printed on white paper. At the front of the Service File are alphabetical and chronological lists of all the Acts included. If the Act you want to look at is in italic type in the contents list, it means that it has not yet been published in this series.

▌**4.11**

The annotations give a detailed account of the background to the Act, including references to discussions on the Bill in the Houses of Parliament as reported in *Hansard*. They also include a summary of the contents of the Act, as well as definitions and explanations of the meaning of individual sections of the Act. The annotations are in smaller print to avoid confusion with the Act itself. Although the annotations have no official standing, they are extremely useful. The author is often a leading authority on the subject matter.

The information in the Service File is reissued during the year in bound volumes. *Current Law Statutes Annotated* covers all Public General Acts since 1948, when the series commenced publication. Private Acts have been included since 1993. The series has been known as *Current Law Statutes Annotated* since 2005. For most of its publication history it has been known simply as *Current Law Statutes*, apart from a brief period between 1991 and 1993 when it was also titled *Current Law Statutes Annotated*.

## SOURCES OF STATUTES AS CURRENTLY IN FORCE

The LexisNexis Butterworths "Legislation" search (para.4.13), the Legislation search from Westlaw UK (para.4.14) and the Statute Law Database (para.4.15) all provide online access to statutes as currently in force. The volumes of *Halsbury's Statutes of England* (para.4.16) provide a print alternative. Though both LexisNexis Butterworths and Westlaw UK are subscription sources, they are likely to be available in most UK universities. The Statute Law Database is a free online resource. However, as noted in para.4.5, delays in updating the legislation

▌**4.12**

**Fig 4.2**
Section 4A of the
Dangerous Dogs Act
1991 (reproduced
from the Westlaw
UK)

## Dangerous Dogs Act 1991 c. 65

*This version in force from:* **June 8, 1997 to present**

**(version 1 of 1)**

[

## 4A.— Contingent destruction orders.

(1) Where—
- (a) a person is convicted of an offence under section 1 above or an aggravated offence under section 3(1) or (3) above;
- (b) the court does not order the destruction of the dog under section 4(1)(a) above; and
- (c) in the case of an offence under section 1 above, the dog is subject to the prohibition in section 1(3) above.

the court shall order that, unless the dog is exempted from that prohibition within the requisite period, the dog shall be destroyed.

(2) Where an order is made under subsection (1) above in respect of a dog, and the dog is not exempted from the prohibition in section 1(3) above within the requisite period, the court may extend that period.

(3) Subject to subsection (2) above, the requisite period for the purposes of such an order is the period of two months beginning with the date of the order.

(4) Where a person is convicted of an offence under section 3(1) or (3) above, the court may order that, unless the owner of the dog keeps it under proper control, the dog shall be destroyed.

(5) An order under subsection (4) above—
- (a) may specify the measures to be taken for keeping the dog under proper control, whether by muzzling, keeping on a lead, excluding it from specified places or otherwise; and
- (b) if it appears to the court that the dog is a male and would be less dangerous if neutered, may require it to be neutered.

(6) Subsections (2) to (4) of section 4 above shall apply in relation to an order under subsection (1) or (4) above as they apply in relation to an order under subsection (1)(a) of that section.

][1]

1. Added by Dangerous Dogs (Amendment) Act 1997 c. 53 s.2 (June 8, 1997)

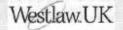

contained in the Statute Law Database mean that it is not currently a complete statement of law in force, though this may change. While this remains the case, LexisNexis Butterworths and Westlaw UK are preferable alternatives for statutes currently in force.

It is important to keep in mind the difference between the amended text of legislation provided by these sources and the unamended text of statutes as originally enacted provided by the sources noted in para.4.6 and para.4.7. A simple example might help.

If you look for the text of the Dangerous Dogs Act 1991 using any source of law in force, you will find that some of the text is printed between square brackets. This is text "inserted" under the provisions of another, later, Act; in this case the Dangerous Dogs (Amendment) Act 1997. This is one of the many Acts whose sole purpose is to revise the provisions of an earlier Act. Sometimes complete new sections are added. These have letters attached to their numbers in order to retain the numbering of the original Act. The text of the Dangerous Dogs Act 1991, for example, now contains a section "4A" inserted by the later amending Act (see the illustration above). This new section makes a significant change to the law on the destruction of dangerous dogs. Note that the amended Dangerous Dogs Act 1991 is still the Act to turn to find the relevant legislation on dangerous dogs. It is not superseded by the later Act.

Sections or subsections of an Act can also be "deleted" by later amending legislation. The brief statement in subs.5(4) of the Dangerous Dogs Act has been deleted in this way. This is shown by the presence of three dots against the subsection. For some Acts, only a single section or part of a section remains in force. This is true of the oldest Acts still in force. Examples can be found if you search for the various Treason Acts in databases of law in force; the earliest one still partly in force dates from 1351.

When using online sources of statutes in force to find legislation, it is also important to check that you have the correct title and year for an Act, including the relevant year. There is only one Human Rights Act for example, but many Education Acts. If you type "Education Act" into the title search of either LexisNexis Butterworths or Westlaw UK and search for statutes, the result will be an extremely long results list that displays sections from different Acts (there are just under 7,000 sections in total). Databases of legislation in force treat sections of Acts as discrete database items. If you search using just the title words of an Act, your results list contains all the sections of Acts indexed under those words. As a result, searching on "Education Act" means you find all the sections of all the Education Acts.

Sections of Acts are the basic units of databases of legislation, because in most legal discussion, it is particular sections of Acts that need to be referred to, not the Act as a whole. Making sections the basic database unit also means that links can be created, for example, that take you directly from a reference to legislation in a judgment, to the full text of a section of an Act in a legislation database. The text of law reports available online from LexisNexis Butterworths and Westlaw UK is linked to legislation in precisely this way. It is sections of Acts, rather than whole Acts, that can be emailed, printed or saved using these databases (though Westlaw UK provides a partial exception to this—see para.4.14). Notes of amending legislation and relevant secondary legislation are also placed at the end of each section of an Act, not at the end of the Act as a whole.

> **TIPS** • *Always enter the exact title of legislation (including the year) when searching databases of legislation in force. Check the title using other sources (e.g. print indexes and textbooks) if you are not sure.*

### LexisNexis Butterworths Legislation search

**4.13** ▶ UK Statutes can be found using the "Legislation" search page in LexisNexis Butterworths. As secondary legislation is included in the search, it can help to use a tick box to restrict the search to Acts only. A "Sources" box can also be used to restrict the search specifically to "UK Parliament Acts", or to select other available legislation sources, e.g. Scottish Parliament Acts.

Enter the title of the Act you wish to find in the title search box, adding the year, if known. It helps greatly to have both an exact title and the year of an act, as noted in para.4.11. If you only have incomplete details, and more than one Act matches the title keywords entered, check the "Results Groups" displayed in the left hand column of the search results. The full titles and dates of the Acts matching the details you have entered are listed in the "Results Groups" section, allowing individual Acts to be selected. Sections are then only displayed for that Act.

The "Find out more" box displayed with the text of each section of an Act is a particular strength of the LexisNexis Butterworths service. The "Find related commentary" link, for example, links directly to any references to the section that might be found in *Halsbury's Laws of England* (para.7.3). Other links include "Is it in force", which displays commencement information for the section, and "Find related cases". The link for the *Halsbury's Statutes Citator* displays a hyperlinked list of any amending legislation for the section.

### Westlaw UK Legislation search

**4.14** ▶ Statutes can be searched by title directly from the Westlaw UK home page. More search options are available from the "Legislation" search. These include the possibility of searching for "historic versions" of Acts. These are versions of an Act at a particular, specified, point in time. This can be helpful, for example, if you are studying the decision made in a particular case and wish to consult legislation in force at that time. Historic versions can found for the period from 1991 onwards. Use the "Advanced Search" within "Legislation" to specify the in force date you wish to use.

To find Acts as currently in force, use the Legislation title search box, including the year on the Act in the title if known. If you do not have the year of an Act, all Acts matching your title words are displayed. Once a particular Act is selected the sections of the Act are displayed as individual screen pages. If you wish to view or print an entire Act, the "PDF of entire Act" link found alongside the standard print, save and email options, opens a new window containing a PDF file which prints the current version of an Act in much the same format as the original HSMO version.

A screen column alongside the results display for a particular Act contains an "Overview Document" showing commencement information, amendments and repeals. A "General Materials" section in the same column shows related legislation, cases and journal articles. The use of this information is explained further in para.4.18.

### The Statute Law Database

**4.15** ▶ To find a statute in the Statute Law Database, enter the title and year of the Act in the "Quick Search" area of homepage (at *www.statutelaw.gov.uk*). A web page of matching legislation is displayed. The "Advanced Search" adds the ability to search for the version of an Act in force at a specified date (from 1991 onwards). Searches can also be restricted by "Geographical Extent", so that only legislation applicable to Scotland, or Northern Ireland, for example is found. Alternatively, a menu choice within "Quick Search" makes it possible to search only for Scottish

Parliament Acts, for example, or Northern Ireland Orders. The Database displays each section of an Act or Order as a separate web page.

As the Statute Law Database is not currently an up-to-date statement of law in force, it is important to check the "Update status of legislation" link displayed with each Act and also on the Statute Law Database homepage. It provides a clear statement of the current position. It is possible to use the "Table of legislative effects" available on the website to check for recent amendments to an Act, but the process is cumbersome. First, the year and chapter number of the Act which interests you needs to be entered in the relevant search boxes. Then a year of affecting legislation needs to be entered. The table which results from the search lists the section of the original Act affected by a change and notes the nature of the change, e.g. "text amended". However only the year, chapter number and relevant section of the legislation making the change, is listed. You will need to search for the affecting legislation itself to obtain, e.g. the wording of an amendment. LexisNexis Butterworths and Westlaw UK are to be preferred as a source of legislation in force if available.

## Halsbury's Statutes of England

*Halsbury's Statutes* differs from the other annotated series of statutes available in print. These reproduce Acts as they were originally printed. The purpose of *Halsbury's Statutes* is to provide the correct and amended text of all legislation in force, whatever the date of Royal Assent. It includes all Public General Acts in force in England and Wales, although the texts of some Acts of limited importance are not printed. The text of each Act is accompanied by notes which provide, for example, details of amendments and relevant case law.

▶ 4.16

The bulk of *Halsbury's Statutes* consists of 50 volumes, arranged alphabetically by subject. Hence, Vol.1 contains the Acts dealing with admiralty, agency and agriculture, whilst Vol.2 contains the law of allotments and smallholdings, animals, arbitration and so on. The current volumes are re-issues of the fourth edition of Halsbury's Statutes first published between 1985 and 1992. Legislation post-dating the main volumes appears in the *Current Statutes Service* binders. The annual *Cumulative Supplement* summarises and explains the effect of new Acts, statutory instruments and case law on existing legislation and this in turn is kept up to date by a looseleaf *Noter-Up* service.

If you know the name of an Act, the easiest way to find it in *Halsbury's Statutes* is by looking in the Alphabetical List of Statutes in the front of the annual paper-covered *Consolidated Index* volume. An example page from the Alphabetical List is shown on page 69. The entry tells you the volume number (in bold type) and the page number in *Halsbury's Statutes* where you will find the full text of the Act. If the volume number in the Alphabetical List of Statutes is followed by (S), you will find the Act printed in the looseleaf *Current Statutes Service* under the volume and page number given. Some Acts are not printed in full in one place, but are divided up, each portion of the Act being printed under the most appropriate subject title. If you want to look at the complete text of an Act which has been split up this way, it may be easier to find the Act in one of the other publications outlined above.

If you want to find the text of a very recent Act, look in the Alphabetical List of Statutes which appears in the first volume of the *Current Statutes Service* under the heading "Contents". The entries give the volume number and page where the text of the Act will be found in the *Current Statutes Service* binders.

Once you have located your Act, either in the main volumes or in the *Current Statutes Service* binders, you will find the official text of the Act. Following each section there are the notes, in smaller type, giving the meaning of words or phrases used, referring to cases on the interpretation of that section and providing details of any amendments which have been made to the text of the Act since it was first passed. You will also find references to statutory instruments which have been passed under the authority granted by that Act. At the beginning of each Act, you are informed when it became law and provided with a summary of the main provisions of the Act. An example page from Volume 48 of Halsbury's Statutes is shown on page 70.

It is important to check that the information on the Act is still up to date (i.e. it has not been amended or repealed). To do this, you will need to consult both the *Cumulative Supplement* and the looseleaf *Noter-up* service.

Let us take an example to see how this works. Suppose you want to know whether there have been changes to the Trade Marks Act 1994 since it was passed. You have looked in the Alphabetical List of Statutes (see p.69) and found the relevant part of the text of the Act in Vol.48 (see p.70). To find out if this Act has been amended since Vol.48 was published, turn first to the *Cumulative Supplement* and look at the entries for Vol.48. The *Cumulative Supplement* lists, volume by and page by page, changes which have occurred in the law since each of the main volumes was published. There are a number of entries showing changes to the Trade Marks Act 1994. These include amending legislation and new statutory instruments issued under authority granted by the Act.

The information in the Cumulative Supplement is up to date to the end of the preceding year. For more recent changes to the Act, you should consult the looseleaf *Noter-up* service under the appropriate volume and page number. This will tell you of any changes in the law in the last few months.

## SUMMARY: FINDING UP-TO-DATE INFORMATION ON AN ACT USING HALSBURY'S STATUTES

1. Look for the name of the Act in the Alphabetical List of Statutes in the paper-covered Consolidated Index volume. This will refer you to the appropriate volume (in bold type) and page number. An (S) following the volume number refers you to the Current Statutes Service.

2. If the Act is very recent, consult the Alphabetical List of Statutes at the front of Vol.1 of the Current Statutes Service.

3. Look up the Act in the appropriate volume, or the Current Statutes Service, and note the volume number and the page which contains the relevant information.

4. Look to see if there is an entry for your volume and page number in the Cumulative Supplement. If there is an entry, there has been a change in the law. Whether or not there is a relevant entry in the Cumulative Supplement, you should now turn to the Noter-up service (see below).

5. Finally, look for any entries for your volume and page number in the Noter-up service. Read this information (if there is any) in conjunction with the information in the main volume and the Cumulative Supplement.

Third Parties (Rights Against Insurers) Act 1930 ........ **4**, 843  
Timeshare Act 1992 ........ **11(1)**, 402  
Tithe Act 1536 ........ **14**, 41  
Tithe Act 1832 ........ **14**, 77  
Tithe Act 1836 ........ **14**, 86  
Tithe Act 1839 ........ **14**, 130  
Tithe Act 1860 ........ **14**, 194  
Tithe Act 1936 ........ **14**, 357  
Tithe Act 1951 ........ **14**, 440  
Tithe Annuities Apportionment Act 1921 ........ **14**, 302  
Tithes and Offerings (1548) ........ **14**, 45  
Titles Deprivation Act 1917 ........ **33(1)**, 7  
Tobacco Advertising and Promotion Act 2002 ........ **47**, 783  
Tobacco Products Duty Act 1979 ........ **13**, 435  
Tokyo Convention Act 1967 ........ **4**, 104  
Tonga Act 1970 ........ **7**, 1329  
Torts (Interference with Goods) Act 1977 ........ **45**, 1829  
Tourism (Overseas Promotion) (Scotland) Act 1984 ........ **47**, 455  
Tourism (Overseas Promotion) (Wales) Act 1992 ........ **47**, 512  
Town and Country Amenities Act 1974 ........ **46**, 38  
Town and Country Planning Act 1954 ........ **9**, 154  
Town and Country Planning Act 1959—  
ss 22–24, 26, 29, 30, 57, 59, Sch 4 ........ **25(1)**, 150  
ss 45, 57, 59 ........ **9**, 182  
Town and Country Planning Act 1990 ........ **46**, 314  
Town and Country Planning (Costs of Inquiries etc) Act 1995 ........ **46**, 1172  
Town and Country Planning (Scotland) Act 1997 ........ **46**, 1183  
Town Development Act 1952 ........ **46**, 16  
Town Gardens Protection Act 1863 ........ **32**, 20  
Town Police Clauses Act 1847—  
ss 1–4, 21, 23–29, 37, 38, 40–66, 68 ........ **38**, 46  
ss 1–4, 31 ........ **35**, 42  
ss 1–4, 35, 36 ........ **12(1)**, 98  
Town Police Clauses Act 1889 ........ **38**, 100  
Towns Improvement Clauses Act 1847 ........ **35**, 36  
Trade Descriptions Act 1968 ........ **39**, 33  
Trade Marks Act 1994 ........ **48**, 105  
Trade Union and Labour Relations (Consolidation) Act 1992 ........ **16**, 203  
Trade Union Reform and Employment Rights Act 1993 ........ **16**, 624  
Trading Representations (Disabled Persons) Act 1958 ........ **47**, 75  
Trading Representations (Disabled Persons) Amendment Act 1972 ........ **47**, 147  
Trading Schemes Act 1996 ........ **47**, 529  
Trading Stamps Act 1964 ........ **47**, 95  
Trading with the Enemy Act 1939 ........ **50**, 432  
Traffic Calming Act 1992 ........ **20**, 1014  
Traffic Management Act 2004—  
ss 1–12, 14–31, 72–100, Schs 7–12 ........ **38**, 1797  
ss 32–39, 40(1), 41(2), (3), 42, 43(1), (3), 45–47, 49–51, 52(2)–(7), 53, 54, 55(2), 57(2), 58, 60, 61, 63, 64(2)–(5), 65, 66, 68, 70(1), (4), 71, 96, 97, 99, 100 ........ **20**, 1064  
Tramways Act 1870 ........ **36**, 119  
Transport Act 1962 ........ **36**, 208  
Transport Act 1968—  
ss 9, 9A, 10–16, 20, 22, 23, 23A, 31, 34, 37, 95–103, 157–160, 162–164, 166, Schs 5, 11, Sch 17, Pt I, Pt II, paras 1, 5, 9 ........ **38**, 180  
ss 38, 41–44, 46–53, 55–57A, 104–115, 123, 134–137, 141, 142, 144, 156–160, 163, 164, 166, Schs 2, 4, 12, 13, 16, 17 ........ **36**, 390  
ss 116–119, 121, 122, 157, 158, 159, 166 ........ **20**, 281  
Transport Act 1978 ........ **36**, 484  
Transport Act 1980—  
ss 32, 42, 43, 64, 69, 70, Sch 9, Pts I, II, IV ........ **38**, 314  
ss 32, 43, 45, 46, 49–60, 68–70, Schs 6, 8, 9 ........ **36**, 490  
Transport Act 1981—  
ss 5–18, 40–43, Schs 2–5, Sch 12, Pts I, II ........ **34**, 366  
ss 35, 40(1), (4), 41–43, Sch 12, Pt III ........ **38**, 404

**Fig 4.3**
'Example Page from the Alphabetical List of Statutes in Halsbury's Consolidated Index'

**Fig 4.4**
'Example Page from
Halsbury's Statutes,
Volume 48'

## 43 Renewal of registration

(1) The registration of a trade mark may be renewed at the request of the proprietor, subject to payment of a renewal fee.

(2) Provision shall be made by rules for the registrar to inform the proprietor of a registered trade mark, before the expiry of the registration, of the date of expiry and the manner in which the registration may be renewed.

(3) A request for renewal must be made, and the renewal fee paid, before the expiry of the registration.

Failing this, the request may be made and the fee paid within such further period (of not less than six months) as may be prescribed, in which case an additional renewal fee must also be paid within that period.

(4) Renewal shall take effect from the expiry of the previous registration.

(5) If the registration is not renewed in accordance with the above provisions, the registrar shall remove the trade mark from the register.

Provision may be made by rules for the restoration of the registration of a trade mark which has been removed from the register, subject to such conditions (if any) as may be prescribed.

(6) The renewal or restoration of the registration of a trade mark shall be published in the prescribed manner.

---

**NOTES**

**Sub-s (1): May be renewed.** It was stated in Chapter 4, para 4.31 of the White Paper "Reform of Trade Marks Law" (Cm 1203) (September 1990) that the Government did not intend to introduce an arrangement requiring the proprietor of a registered trade mark to furnish proof of use in order to renew the registration.

**At the request of the proprietor.** As to acts done by authorised agents, see s 82 post.

**Renewal fee.** As to the payment of fees in respect of applications and registration, etc under this Act, see s 79 post.

See also the second paragraph of the note "Application fee; class fees" to s 32 ante.

**Sub-s (2): Rules.** The Secretary of State may make rules for the purposes of any provision of this Act authorising the making of rules with respect to any matter; see s 78(1)(a) post. See further the note "Rules under this section" below.

**Expiry of the registration.** As to the duration of registration, see s 42 ante.

**Sub-s (3): Months.** See the note to s 25 ante.

**Prescribed.** Ie prescribed by rules made by the Secretary of State; see s 78(1)(b) post. See further the note "Rules under this section" below.

**Sub-s (5): Shall remove the trade mark from the register.** As to the register of trade marks, see ss 63–65 post. As to appeals from decisions of the registrar (including acts of the registrar in exercise of a discretion), see ss 76, 77 post.

**Rules under this section.** Trade Marks Rules 2000, SI 2000/136.

As to the power of the Secretary of State to make rules, generally, under this Act, see s 78 post.

**Transitional provisions.** See s 105, Sch 3, para 15(2), (3) post.

**Definitions.**

| | |
|---|---|
| "publish": s 103(1) | "the registrar": s 62 |
| "the register": s 63(1) | "registration": s 63(1) |
| "registered trade mark": s 63(1) | "trade mark": s 1. |

---

## 44 Alteration of registered trade mark

(1) A registered trade mark shall not be altered in the register, during the period of registration or on renewal.

(2) Nevertheless, the registrar may, at the request of the proprietor, allow the alteration of a registered trade mark where the mark includes the proprietor's name or address and the alteration is limited to alteration of that name or address and does not substantially affect the identity of the mark.

(3) Provision shall be made by rules for the publication of any such alteration and the making of objections by any person claiming to be affected by it.

Remember the stages:

> main volume;
> Cumulative Supplement;
> Noter-up service;

and consult them in that order.

## TRACING COMMENCEMENTS, AMENDMENTS AND RELEVANT CASE LAW

The full provisions of an Act do not necessarily all come into force on the same day. The dates of commencement for some sections may differ from those of others. As a result, it is sometimes important to check the commencement date of an individual section of an Act in order to discover the day on which that section came into force, or is due to come into force.  ▶ **4.17**

The Westlaw UK "Legislation" search (para.4.18) and the statute law pages of the *Current Law Legislation Citator* (para.4.19) provide the most useful means of tracking both commencement dates, amendments and repeals. Both sources have the additional advantage that they draw on the extensive indexing of cases and journal articles which supports both Westlaw UK and the print citator volumes of *Current Law*. However, *Is it in Force?* provides a useful alternative, both in print and online from LexisNexis Butterworths if you wish to check commencement dates for legislation. Details of amending legislation can be found using *Halsbury's Statute Citator*.

*Is it in Force?* can be found online in the "Commentary" section of the LexisNexis Butterworths service as *Halsbury's Is it in Force?* and in print as a single annual volume associated with *Halsbury's Statutes of England* (para.4.16). Both sources list commencement dates for statutes passed since 1980 by year and then alphabetically by title. Commencement dates are noted by section if there is no single date of commencement for the Act. The online version of *Is it in Force?* has the advantage that commencement dates are added as Acts receive the Royal Assent. The print volume only lists Acts previous to the year of publication. Updates are available in the *Noter Up* service binder of *Halsbury's Statutes*. The *Cumulative Supplement* and *Noter Up* services of *Halsbury's Statutes* also enable you to find out if a statute has been repealed or amended.

If you are interested in a specific section of an Act, the *Is it in Force?* content is more usefully obtained online by first searching for the relevant section using the LexisNexis Butterworths "Legislation" search (para.4.13). The "Find out more" box associated with that section then provides access, not only to the relevant information contained in *Is it in Force?*, but also to information on amendments provided by *Halsbury's Statutes Citator*.

Lawtel (para.2.5), if available, provides an additional online means of checking commencement dates of law in force, along with details of repeals and amendments. Lawtel's "Legislation" search provides a "Statutory Status Table" for an Act which lays out amendments and commencements section by section.

It might also be important to legal research to gain an understanding of the way an Act has been amended. This necessitates an understanding of the particular impact of one Act on another. This is complicated by the fact that not all amendments are made using amendment

Acts such as the Dangerous Dogs (Amendment) Act 1997. Changes can be much harder to track. How has the Criminal Justice and Immigration Act 2008, for example, affected the provisions of the Police and Justice Act 2006? Online sources of the full text of law in force (para.4.12) could be used to discover this information, but displaying the text of a series of sections of Acts and checking amendments could prove tedious. Fortunately, the "Table of legislative effects" which forms part of the Statute Law Database (para.4.15) can be used to specify the year and chapter number of the original Act along with the year and chapter number of the more recent amending legislation. The numbers of sections repealed and amended in the original Act are then listed.

> **TIPS** • *Use the "Table of Legislative Effects" in the Statute Law Database to trace how an Act has amended earlier legislation.*

### How to use the Westlaw UK Legislation search

**4.18** ▶ To check commencement dates, amendments and relevant case law using the Westlaw UK Legislation search, first search for the Act which interests you as noted in para.4.14, using the full title and year. When a particular section of an Act is displayed, a "Legislation Analysis" section alongside the legislation text provides links to commencement information and a list of any amending legislation, along with a list of cases citing the particular section displayed.

If you search for information on the Dangerous Dogs Act 1991 (the example used in para.4.12) and select the entry for s.4 (s.4), the "Legislation Analysis" notes first the date at which the version now in force came into effect. This was April 1, 2005, following a minor change made by the Courts Act 2003. The commencement date for the section as it first came in to force is then given (August 12, 1991), along with a link to the statutory instrument which brought it into force. The "Modifications" section gives the amended text with notes of the changes in wording which were introduced by the Dangerous Dogs (Amendment) Act 1997. The "Historic Law" section, in turn, makes it possible to view the section as it was before the 1997 amendments. Finally, ten cases which have cited the section are listed, the most recent being *R v Flack* [2008] EWCA Crim 204; [2008] 2 Cr. App. R. (S.) 70. There are no journal citations at this level, but the "General Materials" link displayed alongside all sections of the Act lists 13 journal articles citing the Act.

### How to use the Current Law Legislation Citator

**4.19** ▶ The *Current Law Legislation Citator* enables you to track changes to legislation in print, using a series of bound volumes listing references to amending legislation. Commencement orders can also be traced. The first volume details changes to Acts (of whatever age) that took place between 1947 and 1971. A number of other volumes cover the changes made in following years (again irrespective of the date of the statute changed), concluding with the most recent full year. More current developments can be checked in the Statute Citator section of the *Current Law Monthly Digest*. The *Current Law Legislation Citator* volumes feature both a "Statute Citator" section and a "Statutory Instrument Citator" section. The exception is the first volume in the series, which was published as the *Current Law Statute Citator*.

Acts are listed by year and in chronological (i.e. chapter number) order in each of the volumes. A helpful alphabetical list of statutes at the start of each bound volume can be used to check the chapter number if this is not already known. If changes have occurred to an Act, these are listed section by section in the volume covering the years in which the changes were

## Dangerous Dogs Act 1991 c. 65

### Legislation Analysis

#### Current Law in Force

| | |
|---|---|
| April 1, 2005 | s. 4(9)(d) - words substituted by 2003 c. 39, Sch. 8 para. 353(b) |

#### Commencement

| | |
|---|---|
| s. 4(1)-(9)(d) | August 12, 1991 SI 1991/1742 art. 3; 1991 c. 65 s. 10(4) |

#### Extent

| | |
|---|---|
| s. 4(1)-(9)(d) | England, Wales, Scotland |

#### Modifications

| | |
|---|---|
| s. 4(2) | Dangerous Dogs Act 1991 c. 65, s. 4(9)(a) |
| s. 4(3)(a) | Dangerous Dogs Act 1991 c. 65, s. 4(9)(b) |
| s. 4(5) | Dangerous Dogs Act 1991 c. 65, s. 4(9)(c) |
| s. 4(6) | Dangerous Dogs Act 1991 c. 65, s. 4(9)(d) |

#### Historic Law

**Version in force**

| | |
|---|---|
| April 1, 2005 | s. 4(6) - words substituted by 2003 c. 39, Sch. 8 para. 353(a) |
| June 8, 1997 | s. 4(3)(a) - words repealed by 1997 c. 53, s. 1(4) |
| June 8, 1997 | s. 4(2) - words repealed by 1997 c. 53, s. 1(3) |
| June 8, 1997 | s. 4(1A) - added by 1997 c. 53, s. 1(2) |
| June 8, 1997 | s. 4(1)(a) - words inserted by 1997 c. 53, s. 1(1) |
| April 1, 1996 | s. 4(9) - words substituted by 1995 c. 40, Sch. 4 para. 81(b) |
| April 1, 1996 | s. 4(9) - words substituted by 1995 c. 40, Sch. 4 para. 81(a) |
| August 12, 1991 | initial commencement |

#### Cases Citing s. 4

1. **Gordon v Reith** 1997 S.L.T. 62; [1998] E.H.L.R. Dig. 137 (HCJ Appeal)
2. **Normand v Freeman** 1992 S.L.T. 598; 1992 S.C.C.R. 417 (HCJ Appeal)
3. **R. v Bogdal (Michael Edward) (aka Tadeusz (Marjan))** [2008] EWCA Crim 1; (2008) 172 J.P. 178; Times, January 17, 2008; (2008) 172 J.P.N. 403; (2008) 105(4) L.S.G. 23; (2008) 152(4) S.J.L.B. 30 (CA (Crim Div))
4. **R. v Donnelly (Ian)** [2007] EWCA Crim 2548 (CA (Crim Div))
5. **R. v Flack (Michael James)** [2008] EWCA Crim 204; [2008] 2 Cr. App. R. (S.) 70 (CA (Crim Div))
6. **R. v Haynes (Rodney)** [2003] EWCA Crim 3247; [2004] 2 Cr. App. R. (S.) 9 (CA (Crim Div))
7. **R. v Holland (Elizabeth)** [2002] EWCA Crim 1585; [2003] 1 Cr. App. R. (S.) 60 (CA (Crim Div))
8. **R. v Knightsbridge Crown Court Ex p. Cataldi** [1994] 1 W.L.R. 296; [1999] Env. L.R. 62; [1999] E.H.L.R. 426; [1999] E.H.L.R. Dig. 105 (QBD)
9. **R. v Liverpool Stipendiary Magistrate Ex p. Slade** [1998] 1 W.L.R. 531; [1998] 1 All E.R. 60; [1998] 1 Cr. App. R. 147; [1998] E.H.L.R. 103; Independent, June 13, 1997; [1997] C.O.D. 414 (DC)
10. **Stewart (Patricia Geraldine) v Donnelly (Sentencing)** 1994 S.C.C.R. 545 (HCJ Appeal)

© 2008 Sweet & Maxwell Ltd

**Fig 4.5**
Example Legislation Analysis page from Westlaw UK

made. The year and chapter numbers are given of amending Acts, and commencement orders are referred to by statutory instrument number. As a result, the information contained in each volume can take time to decode, as the relevant Act or statutory instrument needs to be found in order to check the details of an amendment, or the date legislation came into force. Citations are also given for Cases which have interpreted a particular section of an Act.

It is important to remember that it may be necessary to use more than one volume of the Citator to gain a complete picture of legislative change or relevant case law. Details of the changes made to the Dangerous Dogs Act 1991, for example, need to be traced in the *Current Law Legislation Citator* volumes covering 1989 to 1995 and 1996 to the present. The changes made by the Dangerous Dogs (Amendment) Act 1997 can only be found in the volume covering 1996 to 1999. For the most recent case law interpreting the Act, and details of the change made by the Courts Act 2003, you need to use the volume covering 2002 to 2004.

### Chronological Table of the Statutes

**4.20** ◗ The *Chronological Table of the Statutes* is an official publication which lists every statute which has been passed since 1235, and shows, for each one, whether it is still law. This is done by the use of different type faces—an entry in italic type indicates that the statute in question is no longer law, whilst entries in bold type represent Acts which are still wholly or partly in force.

Entries for Acts are arranged in date order in two print volumes. Part 1 currently covers 1235–1974; Part 2 covers 1974–2006. If a complete section of an Act, or an entire Act, has been repealed, the abbreviation "r" is used, followed by a note of the repealing legislation. Other abbreviations used are explained at the front of Part 1.

Unfortunately, the *Chronological Table* is usually two or three years out of date. It is updated by the annual publication entitled The *Public General Acts and General Synod Measures: 20 . . .: Tables and Index*, under the heading "Effect of legislation". This shows whether the Acts passed during that year have amended or repealed any previous legislation. As in the *Chronological Table*, the entries in this index are arranged by the date of the original Act, so that it is possible to tell at a glance if there has been any change to a particular statute. The *Public General Acts: Table and Index* is published separately by TSO and it is also printed at the end of the annual volumes of the *Public General Acts and Measures*. Recent amendments to statutes can also be checked using the "Table of legislative effects" in the Statute Law Database (at *www.statutelaw.gov.uk*), as noted in para.4.17.

## OLDER STATUTES

**4.21** ◗ Acts, or sections or Acts, which are in force, whatever their date, can be found in the online and print sources introduced in para.4.12. However, it will sometimes be necessary to look at an Act of Parliament which is no longer in force and dates back beyond 1831 when the Public General Acts series (para.4.6) was first published. These can be found in the collections described below and in the Justis UK Statutes database (para.4.9).

The earliest statute which is still part of the law of the land was passed in 1267. The first parliamentary statute dates from 1235 (the Statute of Merton), although some collections of the statutes commence in 1225. Collections of the legislation prior to 1225 do exist (e.g. A. J.

Robertson, *The Laws of the Kings of England from Edmund to Henry I*) but they are not regarded as forming part of the statutes of the realm.

## Statutes of the Realm

Produced by the Record Commission, *Statutes of the Realm* is generally regarded as the most authoritative collection of the early statutes. It covers statutes from 1235 to 1713, including those no longer in force, and prints the text of all Private Acts before 1539. There are alphabetical and chronological indexes to all the Acts and there is a subject index to each volume, as well as an index to the complete work. An online version of the *Statutes of the Realm* volumes covering the period from 1628 onwards can be found on the British History Online website (at *www.british-history.ac.uk*). This is a non-subscription website and the volumes form part of the "Parliamentary" pages. If your University subscribes to the *English Reports* from HeinOnline, all 11 volumes of the Statutes are available as part of the English Reports Library.

▶ **4.22**

## Statutes at Large

The title of *Statutes at Large* was given to various editions of the statutes, most of which were published during the eighteenth century. They normally cover statutes published between the thirteenth and the eighteenth or nineteenth centuries. The text used in the Justis UK Statutes database (para.4.9) is taken from Ruffhead's editions of *Statutes at Large* for the period predating the *Public General Acts* series. Scanned online versions of Ruffhead's editions can be found in Eighteenth Century Collections Online (ECCO), available to all UK universities, though the screen images of the original volumes can be difficult to use.

▶ **4.23**

## Acts and Ordinances of the Interregnum

Acts passed during the Commonwealth are excluded from the collections of the statutes mentioned above. They can be found in C.H. Firth and R.S. Rait, *Acts and Ordinances of the Interregnum 1642–1660*. The Firth and Rait edition of the *Acts and Ordinances* can be found online from the British History Online website (at *www.british-history.ac.uk*) in the "Parliamentary" section, along with the Statutes of the Realm.

▶ **4.24**

## Local and Personal Acts

In addition to *Public General Acts*, which apply to the whole population or a substantial part of it, there are also passed each year a few Local and Personal Acts. These Acts affect only a particular area of the country or a particular individual or body, e.g. Transport for London Act 2008; St. Austell Market Act 2008.

▶ **4.25**

The chapter number of a Local Act is printed in roman numerals, to distinguish it from the Public General Act of the same number. Thus the Transport for London Act may be cited as 2008, c. i (i.e. the first Local Act passed in 2008), whilst 2008, c. 1 is the citation for a Public General Act, the European Communities (Finance) Act 2008.

Personal Acts are cited in the same way as Public General Acts, but with the chapter number printed in italics, e.g. *c. 3*. The citation of Local and Personal Acts was amended in 1963. Prior to that date, they are cited by regnal years, in the same way as Public General Acts, e.g. 12 & 13 Geo. 5, c. xiv relates to a Local Act, whilst 12 & 13 Geo. 5, c. 14 is a Public General Act (para.4.3).

Local and Personal Acts are listed in alphabetical order in the annual *Local and Personal Acts 20 . . .: Tables and Index*, which can also be found in the bound volumes of the *Public General Acts and Measures*. From 1991 onwards, Local Acts are available on the OPSI legislation web pages (at *www.opsi.gov.uk/legislation*). In addition, HMSO published two cumulative indexes: the *Index to Local and Personal acts 1801–1947* and the *Supplementary Index to the Local and Personal Acts 1948–1966*.

Although most libraries will possess copies of the Public General Acts in some form, printed copies of the Local and Personal Acts are not so widely available. Those which are published are listed in the TSO Daily Lists, which are cumulated in the TSO Catalogues. Local Acts since 1992 are printed in the final volume of *Current Law Statutes Annotated* each year. To obtain a copy of the text of an older Local Act or a Personal Act, you may need to contact the local library or the organisation affected by the legislation.

## STATUTORY INSTRUMENTS

**4.26** ▶ In order to reduce the length and complexity of statutes and increase flexibility in the light of changing circumstances Parliament may include in an Act an "enabling" section, which grants to some other authority (usually a Minister of the Crown) power to make detailed rules and regulations on a principle laid down in general terms by the Act. The various Road Traffic Acts, for example, give the Secretary of State for Transport power, amongst other things, to impose speed limits on particular stretches of road, to vary these limits at any time, to create experimental traffic schemes, to introduce new road signs, to control the construction and use of vehicles and to impose regulations concerning parking, pedestrian crossings, vehicle licences, insurance and numerous other aspects of the law relating to motor vehicles. An advantage of this power is that the rules can be readily changed, without the necessity for Parliamentary debate and approval of every amendment.

Statutory instruments, together with statutory codes of practice and byelaws, form what is called *secondary* or *subordinate* legislation, often also called *delegated* legislation, since Parliament has delegated the power to make this legislation to another authority.

The term *statutory instruments* is a generic one, and includes rules, regulations and orders. Commencement orders are a particularly important type of statutory instrument, since they set the date for the commencement of an Act or bring certain provisions of an Act into force (see point 7 of para.4.2). Like statutes, statutory instruments may be of general or of purely local interest. Local instruments are not always printed and published in the normal way. An Order of Council, made by the Queen and her Privy Council, is also a form of statutory instrument. These are printed as an appendix to the annual volumes of statutory instruments, together with Royal Proclamations and Letters Patent.

### Citation of statutory instruments

**4.27** ▶ Each statutory instrument published during the year is given its own number. The official citation is: SI year/number. For example, the Fluorinated Greenhouse Gases Regulations 2008 was the 41st statutory instrument to be passed in 2008 and its citation is therefore SI 2008/41.

Statutory instruments typically have a title which includes the word "Rules", "Regulations" or "Order", e.g. Rules of the Supreme Court, the Safety of Sports Grounds

(Designation) Order, the Registration of Births and Deaths Regulations. If you are undecided whether the document you are seeking is a statutory instrument, check in the Alphabetical List of Statutory Instruments in *Halsbury's Statutory Instruments* .

## Tracing statutory instruments

Statutory instruments are listed by year and number on the legislation page of the OPSI website (at *www.opsi.gov.uk/legislation*). The full text is available and coverage begins in 1987. Paper copies of single statutory instruments can also be purchased from TSO and your library may hold these for the current year. Details of new statutory instruments are published in the TSO Daily Lists (para.6.15). Bound volumes are available for previous years. The instruments have been printed in numerical order since 1962; before that date, they were arranged by subject. The last volume of each yearly set contains a subject index to all the instruments published during the year. ▶ 4.28

All the statutory instruments that were still in force at the end of 1948 were reprinted in a series of volumes entitled *Statutory Rules and Orders and Statutory Instruments Revised*. This was arranged in subject order, showing all the instruments which were then in force.

The full, unrevised, text of statutory instruments from 1987 onwards is also available online from the BAILII website (para.2.15) and the Justis UK Statutory Instruments database (para.2.6). The Justis UK Statutory Instruments Archive provides online access to the full, unrevised, text of all statutory instruments published between 1671 and 1986. Both Justis databases are subscription databases, so you will need to check if your library can provide access.

The databases of law in force noted in para.4.12 contain both statutes and statutory instruments in their legislation searches. Use the full title (including year and statutory instrument number if known) when searching these databases. Database results are presented as described in para.4.12. The print volumes of *Halsbury's Statutory Instruments* (para.4.29) provide an alternative approach to tracing statutory instruments in force.

## Halsbury's Statutory Instruments

*Halsbury's Statutory Instruments* provides up-to-date information on every statutory instrument of general application in force in England and Wales. It does not reproduce the text of all statutory instruments in force. Instead it reproduces the text of a selected number and provides summaries of others. The work consists of 22 volumes, in which the statutory instruments are arranged in broad subject categories. The service is kept up to date by a *Service* binder containing notes of changes in the law and the text of selected new instruments. ▶ 4.29

If you know the year and number of a statutory instrument, the easiest way to locate it in *Halsbury's Statutory Instruments* is through the Chronological List of Instruments in the *Service* binder. Alternatively, if you know the name of the statutory instrument, look in the Alphabetical List in the back of the annual paperback volume of the *Consolidated Index*. You may, for example, be looking for information on the Part-Time Workers (Prevention of less Favourable Treatment) Regulations 2000. The relevant page from the Alphabetical List is shown on page 78. The list tells us that the number of the statutory instrument is 1551 and that it has been allocated the subject title "Employment" in *Halsbury's Statutory Instruments*. (Entries in the Chronological List in the *Service* binder are displayed in the same way.)

On the inside front cover of each of the main volumes, there is a list of subject titles,

**Fig 4.6**
'Example page from the Consolidated Index of Halsbury's Statutory Instruments'

| Serial No | Description | Title |
|---|---|---|
| 3470 | Parliamentary Commissioner Order 2007.............................................. | Constit Law (Pt 2) |
| 494 | Parliamentary Commissioner's Pension (Amendment) Regulations 1972 ........ | Pensions |
| 846 | Parliamentary Commissioner's Pension Regulations 1967........................... | Pensions |
| 1041 | Parliamentary Constituencies and Assembly Electoral Regions (Wales) Order 2006....................................................................................... | Elections |
| 1116 | Parliamentary Copyright (National Assembly for Wales) Order 2007 ............. | Copyright |
| 3146 | Parliamentary Copyright (Northern Ireland Assembly) Order 1999 .............. | Copyright |
| 676 | Parliamentary Copyright (Scottish Parliament) Order 1999 ....................... | Copyright |
| 1457 | Parliamentary Corporate Bodies (Crown Immunities etc) (Amendment) Order 2006....................................................................................... | Parliament |
| 1732 | Parliamentary Corporate Bodies (Crown Immunities etc) Order 1992............ | Parliament |
| 780 | Parliamentary Elections (Returning Officers' Charges) Order 2005 .............. | Elections |
| 3470 | Parliamentary Elections (Welsh Forms) (Amendment) Order 2005 ............... | Elections |
| 1105 | Parliamentary Elections (Welsh Forms) Order 2005 ................................ | Elections |
| 1014 | Parliamentary Elections (Welsh Forms) Order 2007 ................................ | Elections |
| 780 | Parliamentary Pension Scheme (Additional Voluntary Contributions) (Amendment) Regulations 1999 ....................................................... | Parliament |
| 3252 | Parliamentary Pensions (Additional Voluntary Contributions) Regulations 1993 ..................................................................... | Parliament |
| 2417 | Parliamentary Pensions (Additional Voluntary Contributions Scheme) (Amendment) Regulations 2004 ....................................................... | Parliament |
| 1887 | Parliamentary Pensions (Amendment) (No 2) Regulations 2002 .................. | Parliament |
| 1965 | Parliamentary Pensions (Amendment) (No 2) Regulations 2006 .................. | Parliament |
| 2649 | Parliamentary Pensions (Amendment) (Pension Sharing) Regulations 2001 ..... | Parliament |
| 599 | Parliamentary Pensions (Amendment) Regulations 1992............................ | Parliament |
| 2867 | Parliamentary Pensions (Amendment) Regulations 1995............................ | Parliament |
| 2406 | Parliamentary Pensions (Amendment) Regulations 1996............................ | Parliament |
| 2100 | Parliamentary Pensions (Amendment) Regulations 1999............................ | Parliament |
| 835 | Parliamentary Pensions (Amendment) Regulations 2001............................ | Parliament |
| 1807 | Parliamentary Pensions (Amendment) Regulations 2002............................ | Parliament |
| 2416 | Parliamentary Pensions (Amendment) Regulations 2004............................ | Parliament |
| 887 | Parliamentary Pensions (Amendment) Regulations 2005............................ | Parliament |
| 920 | Parliamentary Pensions (Amendment) Regulations 2006............................ | Parliament |
| 270 | Parliamentary Pensions (Amendment) Regulations 2007............................ | Parliament |
| 3253 | Parliamentary Pensions (Consolidation and Amendment) Regulations 1993 .... | Parliament |
| 605 | Parliamentary Writs Order 1983............................................................ | Elections |
| 2850 | Parochial Fees Order 2007 ................................................................. | Ecclesiastical |
| 862 | Parsonages Measures (Amendment) Rules 2007 ...................................... | Ecclesiastical |
| 3171 | Parsonages Measure Rules 2000 .......................................................... | Ecclesiastical |
| 926 | Part 7 of the Anti-terrorism, Crime and Security Act 2001 (Extension to Animal Pathogens) Order 2007.......................................................... | Criminal |
| 425 | Particle Physics and Astronomy Research Council Order 1994.................... | Education |
| 569 | Partnerships (Accounts) Regulations 2008 ............................................ | Partnership |
| 1987 | Partnerships and Unlimited Companies (Accounts) (Amendment) Regulations 2005 ......................................................................... | Companies Partnership |
| 1820 | Partnerships and Unlimited Companies (Accounts) Regulations 1993 ........... | Companies Partnership |
| 2017 | Partnerships (Restrictions on Contributions to a Trade) Regulations 2005...... | Taxation |
| 1639 | Partnerships (Restrictions on Contributions to a Trade) Regulations 2006....... | Taxation |
| 1551 | Part-time Workers (Prevention of Less Favourable Treatment) Regulations 2000 ............................................................................. | Employment |
| 2240 | Part-time Workers (Prevention of Less Favourable Treatment) Regulations 2000 (Amendment) Order 2005...................................... | Employment |
| 2035 | Part-time Workers (Prevention of Less Favourable Treatment) Regulations 2000 (Amendment) Regulations 2002............................. | Employment |
| 1107 | Part-time Workers (Prevention of Less Favourable Treatment) Regulations 2001 ............................................................................. | Employment |
| 670 | Party Wall etc Act 1996 (Commencement) Order 1997 ........................... | Building |
| 671 | Party Wall etc Act 1996 (Repeal of Local Enactments) Order 1997 .............. | Building |
| 3276 | Passenger and Goods Vehicles (Community Recording Equipment Regulation) Regulations 2006 ....................................................... | Transport |

indicating in which volume they are printed. "Employment" is located in Vol.7. Turn to the Chronological List of Instruments at the beginning of the section headed "Employment" in Vol.7. A page reference is given for the entry in the volume for the statutory instrument itself. The text of the Part-Time Workers (Prevention of Less Favourable Treatment) Regulations 2000 is printed in full in the 2003 issue of Vol.7 with a note stating that the Regulations are printed as amended by SI 2002/2035.

Subsequent changes are recorded in the Monthly Survey Section of the Service binder. The Monthly Survey is arranged by subject titles as in the main volumes. Look for the number of the instrument in the "Amendments and Revocations" section.

### Checking whether a statutory instrument is in force or has been amended

If you have searched for and found a statutory instrument using one of the online sources of legislation in force (para.4.12), you do not need any further confirmation that it remains in force. The same applies if you are using the print volumes of *Halsbury's Statutory Instruments* (para.4.29). However, for some important statutory instruments, you may wish to track whether the statutory instrument has been amended, and if so, the dates at which different provisions came into force. This might be the case, for example, if you were tracking the way EU directives have been implemented in the UK, since implementation generally makes use of statutory instruments rather than statutes. The Westlaw UK "Legislation" search provides the best way of tracking such changes. Suppose you wish to track changes to the Working Time Regulations which implement EU legislation on working time. You might begin by searching for the Working Time Regulations 1998/1833 using the Legislation title search. Commencement information and amending legislation can then be checked for the separate parts of the Regulations using the entries under "Legislation analysis", just as it can for the sections of an Act (para.4.18). The Working Time Regulations 1998/1833 have been amended a number of times, for example, by the Working Time (Amendment) Regulations 2003/1684 and the Working Time (Amendment) Regulations 2007/2079 as changes concerning different categories of workers have been made to the original regulations. Case law citing the different parts of the 1998 Regulations can also be found.

The Statutory Instrument Citator section of the *Current Law Legislation Citator* provides a print alternative to the Westlaw UK "Legislation" search. Search for statutory instruments by year and number.

▶ **4.30**

### Tracing statutory instruments made under a particular Act

The Westlaw UK "Legislation" search (para.4.18) provides an effective way of searching for statutory instruments made under a particular Act. Search for an Act by title and check the entries for individual sections to find a list of statutory instruments made under powers granted in that section. Links are available to the full text of the relevant statutory instrument. In the entry for section 1 of the Dangerous Dogs Act 1991, for example, an entry can be found for the Dangerous Dogs (Designated Types) Order 1991/1743. A similar can be used with the LexisNexis Butterworths legislation search (para.4.13)

Lawtel (para.2.5) provides an alternative online approach to tracing statutory instruments made under an Act. For statutes passed since 1984, Lawtel provides links to all statutory instruments which are enabled by the Act. Again, search by the title of the Act. The "Statutory

▶ **4.31**

Status Table" provides a links to the relevant statutory instruments. *Halsbury's Statutes* (para.4.16) provides a print alternative for tracing statutory instruments made under an Act.

### Wales legislation

**4.32** Under the Government of Wales Act 1998, the National Assembly for Wales has taken over powers formerly exercised by the Secretary of State for Wales. This means in practice that the Assembly is able to debate and approve secondary or delegated legislation for Wales. Its legislation takes the form of statutory instruments which are cited in the same way as other statutory instruments, e.g. Children's Homes Amendment (Wales) Regulations 2001. This particular statutory instrument is numbered as no.140 (W. 6), the "W. 6" denoting the sixth regulation made by the Assembly for 2001.

The Government of Wales Act 1998 does not lay out broad areas of legislative competence; instead the powers of the Assembly are defined in relation to some 300 Acts of Parliament. The Acts themselves are listed in the National Assembly for Wales (Transfer of Functions) Orders made in 1999 and 2000. Broadly speaking, the Assembly can make regulations in the areas of industrial and economic development, education and training, health, agriculture, local government, housing, social services, transport and the environment and arts and cultural heritage.

Statutory instruments made by the National Assembly can be found on the Wales Legislation page of the OPSI website (at *www.opsi.gov.uk/legislation*). Draft statutory orders can be found on the National Assembly of Wales website (at *www.wales.gov.uk*), along with links to Assembly business and other information about the Assembly. Proceedings of the Assembly are not available in print form. The Wales Legislation Online website (at *www.wales-legislation.org.uk*), managed by Cardiff Law School, contains a Digest of National Assembly Functions & Subordinate Legislation which lists the powers of the National Assembly for Wales and its subordinate legislation by subject area. Using the site it is possible to take a given Act, e.g. the Environment Act 1995, and find out which sections list functions that are exercised solely by the Assembly, which list functions that are shared between the Assembly and a Minister of the Crown, and which list functions which have not been devolved to the Assembly. Legislation made by the Assembly is to be added to the entries for each Act where relevant.

# ▶ 5
# Journals

## TYPES OF JOURNALS

Journals (or periodicals) are important to lawyers: they keep you up to date with the latest ▶ **5.1**
developments in the law, and provide comments and criticisms of the law. In your preparations
for seminars, essays and moots, it is essential to show that you are aware of what has been
written in journals. You cannot rely exclusively on textbooks which are always, to some degree,
out of date, and which may provide inadequate information on some topics. Journals help to
keep you up to date with recent cases, statutes, official publications, comments and scholarly
articles.

For convenience, we can divide journals into four different types, although there is some
overlap between them. However, they are treated similarly in libraries. There are a number of
weekly publications, such as the *New Law Journal*, *Justice of the Peace*, the *Solicitors Journal* and
the *Law Society Gazette*, which aim to keep practitioners and students up to date. They provide
reports and comments on recent cases, statutes, statutory instruments and the latest trends
and developments in the law, together with some longer articles, usually on topical or practical subjects. In contrast are the academic journals, which are published less frequently. They
contain lengthy articles on a variety of topics, comments on recent cases, statutes and government publications, and book reviews. Some examples are the *Law Quarterly Review*, the *Modern
Law Review* (six issues a year) and the *Journal of Law and Society* (four issues a year). The third
category is the specialist journal dealing with particular aspects of the law. Some specialist
journals combine notes of recent developments with longer articles on aspects of that area of
the law. Examples of these journals include the *Criminal Law Review* (monthly), *Legal Action*
(monthly) and *Family Law* (ten issues a year). Other specialist journals are more like newslet-
ters and are designed as current awareness bulletins for practitioners. These journals (e.g.
the *Property Law Bulletin*, *Simon's Tax Intelligence*) are only a few pages in length and summarise and briefly comment on the latest developments. The final category is foreign journals.
English-language publications, particularly from common law jurisdictions, are of assistance
in providing a comparative view of similar UK issues. Examples of this group are the *Yale Law
Journal* (eight issues a year), the *Harvard Law Review* (eight issues a year), the *Canadian Bar
Review* (four issues a year) and the *Australian Law Journal* (monthly).

## Online Access to Journals

Since the late 1990s, most legal journal publishers have allowed access to online versions ▶ **5.2**
of journal articles, either from their own website, or from an intermediary site. Some law

journals can be accessed using web-based services such as SwetsWise or ScienceDirect, which act as agents for publishers, many more can be found in the full text journal databases available from LexisNexis Butterworths (para.2.3) and Westlaw UK (para.2.4). This means there is no single route to online versions of journal articles, making access unnecessarily complicated.

Your library website is the best place to start if you wish to access a journal online. It is here that you can discover the appropriate online source for a particular journal. A—Z lists of journals by title are often linked to the appropriate website for accessing the full text of articles online. Entries made for a journal in the library catalogue may also feature links to websites providing full-text access. In many cases you will have to find the library link to the online source of a journal in order to gain access to the full text. As noted in para.2.8, you need to use the library (or other institutional) link to a journal website in order to confirm that you have access rights. A subscription must be paid for online access to journals; often the same subscription covers both online access and the print copies of journals on the law library shelves. The appropriate access route is one which confirms that your university has subscribed to a journal or database service. The relatively small number of law journal articles that can be found on public internet sites (perhaps placed there in "pre-print" versions by the author) can be found using Google Scholar (at *www.scholar.google.com*). This is worth trying if subscription routes have failed. If you are using Google Scholar on a university network, full text articles may also be available from publisher websites. This is because publishers' sites are set to automatically allow full text access to anyone using the university network. However, once again, access to the full text of an article published in a particular journal is only possible if the library has first paid a subscription.

As many of the law journals available online can be found on either LexisNexis Butterworths or Westlaw UK, it is worth familiarising yourself with the journal titles available from the two database services if both are available. This can be done by selecting the "Browse" option from the "Journals" search page present in both LexisNexis Butterworths and Westlaw UK. LexisNexis Butterworths, as might be expected, holds the full text of LexisNexis Butterworths journal titles, along with journals from some other publishers (over 60 titles in all). Westlaw UK provides access to approximately 80 titles, including those from Sweet & Maxwell. There is no overlap in the journal coverage provided by the two services. However, some of the journals available from LexisNexis Butterworths and Westlaw UK are also available from the websites of the relevant journal publishers. This is true of the *Oxford Journal of Legal Studies*, for example, which can be found on LexisNexis Butterworths and also accessed from the Oxford University Press website, using the appropriate subscription access route.

Online access to journals published before the mid 1990s has also increased greatly in recent years as universities have added online access to journal archives to their current subscriptions. Almost all universities have a subscription to the JSTOR journals archive, for example, which contains a significant number of politics and social science journals of potential value for legal research. Most university libraries also subscribe to HeinOnline, an American archive of online journal articles which has been adding increasing numbers of UK and European journals. Non-US titles include the *Modern Law Review* and the *European Journal of International Law*. Some journal publishers have also created digital archives of all past issues of particular journals and made these available as separate archive subscriptions. Check library

*Oxford Journal of Legal Studies*, Vol. 28, No. 3 (2008), pp. 409–441
doi:10.1093/ojls/gqn020

Fig 5.1
'Example page from an article in the Oxford Journal of Legal Studies'

# Institutional Approaches to Judicial Restraint

JEFF A. KING*

**Abstract**—This article addresses the pressing issue of what process courts should use to identify those questions whose resolution lies beyond their appropriate capacity and legitimacy. The search for such a process is a basic constitutional problem that has defied a clear answer for well over a hundred years. The chequered history of earlier attempts illustrates why commentators have once again begun to gravitate towards institutional approaches. The general features of institutional approaches include emphasis on uncertainty, judicial fallibility, systemic impact, collaboration between branches of government and incrementalism in judging. These features, however, are relied upon in support of two conflicting views of the role of judges in public law adjudication. One is restrictive, and advocates sharp limitations to the ambit of judicial review. The other is contextual, and, in stark contrast, it proposes to expand the ambit of review in reliance on the idea of using principles of restraint to structure the exercise of judicial discretion. While this article does not take sides between them, it nonetheless seeks to refine the contextual institutional approach by outlining a general framework for reasoning with principles of restraint, and by addressing some of the key difficulties such a reasoning process would face.

Judges often adjudicate disputes that raise the question of how strictly they should scrutinize government or legislative action. The question arises in a number of contexts: statutory interpretation, judicial review of administrative discretion, review of tribunal findings, adjudication of human rights claims and in the interpretation of international law to mention a few. In all of these contexts, judges have identified certain questions as being inappropriate for judicial resolution, or have refused on competency grounds to substitute their judgment for that of another person on a particular matter. I will use the expression 'judicial restraint' to describe this type of judicial conduct, and intend it to be neutral among competing conceptions of judicial restraint. How judges should exercise judicial restraint is a fundamental matter of constitutional principle that concerns

* Research Fellow and Tutor in Law, Keble College, Oxford. Email: jeff.king@law.ox.ac.uk. The author thanks Paul Craig, Catherine Donnelly, Graham Gee, Jeffrey Jowell, Aileen Kavanagh, Dimitris Kyritsis, Kai Möller, Roger Shiner, Jan van Zyl Smit, Gréggoire Webber, Alison Young, and the participants of the 2008 Annual Meeting of the Society of Legal Scholars (Ireland) for helpful feedback on earlier drafts.

database and journal lists for access. Online journal archives always provide access from the first published issue of a journal onwards, but the most recent issues are only available if they form part of a single publisher archive. One peculiarity of the JSTOR and HeinOnline archives is that they contain scanned page images of the original journal articles, rather than re-keyed text. As a result, the text of the articles cannot be copied into word-processed text. Printing may also be slow and email attachments relatively large.

## FINDING A JOURNAL ARTICLE ONLINE IF YOU ALREADY HAVE A REFERENCE

**5.3 ▶** Journal references, or citations, found in the bibliographies of books, or on course reading lists, need to be deciphered before you can find the article online. A journal citation, like those for law reports, uses standard abbreviations for the journal name, whereas library catalogues and databases use the full spelled-out version. The Cardiff Index to Legal Abbreviations (at *www. legalabbrevs.cardiff.ac.uk*) provides the best online source for interpreting abbreviations and additional print sources are noted in para.3.5.

Once you have the full title of the journal, check library A–Z journal lists or the library catalogue for access. If access is provided from the publishers website or an intermediary database (such as SwetsWise), library links may simply provide access to the source website. You then have to search the publisher's site or the intermediary database in order to find the relevant year and issue of a journal, before selecting the full text of an article. Most sites provide access using web versions of the contents page of individual journal issues. You will almost certainly be asked to provide your university authentication (id and password) if you are accessing the journal off-campus. Many universities have now simplified this process through the use of software which provides an additional search menu when you select a link to a journal. The menu prompts for the year, volume, issue number and first page of the journal article and then provides a direct link to the full text of the article on the appropriate website. The search menu page often also links to additional services—the ability to search other catalogues for a reference for example, or perhaps request an inter-library loan if your library does not have a subscription to a journal.

If the journal article you wish to find is available on either LexisNexis Butterworths (para.2.3) or Westlaw UK (para.2.4), you need to use an entirely different approach. If the journal is available from LexisNexis Butterworths, select the "Journals" page from the LexisNexis Butterworths home page. Title, author and citation searches are available, but be sure to enter the details you have accurately. A small error in title or citation, for example, means that an article will be missed.

The process is much the same for the "Journals" search on Westlaw UK. Select the search from the home page, then enter the title of the journal article in the "Article Title" search box. As the journals search in Westlaw UK includes article details drawn from the wide-ranging entries of the *Legal Journals Index* (para.5.5), you may also find it necessary to add an author surname in the "Author" search box, in order to narrow down the number of potential title matches.

Both LexisNexis Butterworths and Westlaw UK also include a browse facility on their "Journals" pages. Selecting "Full Text Articles" in the browse section of the Westlaw UK journals page, for example, displays an alphabetical list of the journals available in full text versions on Westlaw UK. Particular publication years can then be selected and the contents list for individual issues displayed with full text links to the articles themselves.

## FINDING A JOURNAL ARTICLE IN THE LIBRARY

If you have a reference to a journal article, the relevant abbreviations will need to be deciphered as noted in para.5.3 before you can find the article in print. The Library catalogue can then be searched using the full title of the journal in order to confirm that the library holds the journal. You may find this is not the case. Even the largest law libraries lack print copies of some journals. If a journal is not listed in the catalogue, check online access, as print and online access are not always identical. Then consider requesting an inter-library loan (para.5.23).

⟩ **5.4**

If a journal is held by your library, there should be some indication of its location. Often the last copy received is noted if there is a current subscription to the journal. Law journals are usually arranged alphabetically by title in a single sequence. Remember though, that the most recent issues may well be shelved in a separate current journals or periodicals area.

## TRACING ARTICLES IN LEGAL JOURNALS

You could rely on footnotes in recent books or journal articles to provide references to articles on a particular topic. If an article is well researched, it may give numerous citations to journal articles worth reading. You are likely, however, only to get coverage of those articles which support the view of the author. Using footnotes from textbooks and citations from key articles is a good way to widen your search for documents on a subject, but for the most comprehensive and recent coverage, you must also make use of indexes to journal articles.

⟩ **5.5**

There are several indexes you can use to find journal articles on a subject or on a particular case, statute or other document. All of them are available online. The most relevant indexes are described below. Although you would not need or wish to consult every index every time you require articles on a topic, you should remember that the information given, and the journals covered, varies. If you use only one index, you may miss helpful material.

### Legal Journals Index

The *Legal Journals Index* began publication in 1986 and is the most useful source for tracing law articles in journals published in the UK. It is available online as part of the Westlaw UK service (para.2.4) and since 2007 has been fully integrated into the Westlaw UK "Journals" search. It formally constituted a separate search area. All *Legal Journals Index* coverage is included in Westlaw UK from 1986 onwards, along with entries from the print *European Legal Index*, which has carried references to articles on EU law since 1993. The index covers articles from approximately 260 legal journals and provides the most comprehensive coverage of articles on UK law. Some libraries may continue to keep the print volumes of both the *Legal Journals Index* and the *European Legal Index*, though online access has made them largely redundant.

⟩ **5.6**

Each entry in the *Legal Journals Index* database includes details of the title and the author (or authors) of the journal article, along with details of the journal in which the article is published. The volume, issue and page numbers of the article are also included. An abstract, or summary, of the content of each journal article is also provided, though some of the earlier summaries contained in the database may only consist of a single sentence. In addition to the summary, subject terms and keywords are added, to aid searching. The subject entries correspond to the subject headings used in the subject index of the printed volumes and use a standard vocabulary. The keywords are additional identifying subject words taken from the each journal article.

To use the *Legal Journals Index*, first select the "Advanced Search" within the Westlaw UK "Journals" search. The "Subject/Keyword" search box found on the "Advanced Search" page provides the entry point for *Index* searches. Any words you enter in the "Subject/Keyword" search box must match the subject terms and keywords added to a *Legal Journals Index* entry for a result to be displayed. This might seem an extremely restrictive way of searching for journal articles which match a subject which interests you. You will soon discover though, that an enormous number of legal journal articles are published in the UK during the course of a single year, with the result that the problem facing the researcher is usually that of sifting out only those which are directly relevant to the research being undertaken. An index provides an aid to selection.

Using the "Subject/Keyword" search requires that you first to think of keywords which might be added to the articles which you would like to find. These keywords can then be combined using "and" to focus and refine your search (see para.2.11). The "List of Terms" link below the "Subject/Keyword" search box displays the subject terms used by the *Index* arranged in a subject hierarchy. However, it is usually sufficient to try searching using the first keywords which seem likely and then noting the subject terms and keywords used in any index entries you find. These can then be used in further searches.

Suppose that you are interested in finding articles which discuss privacy issues in the context of the Human Rights Act. You might start by searching for index entries that contain both "privacy" and "human rights". To do this, enter "privacy and human rights" in the "Subject/Keyword" search. Your search then retrieves all index entries for articles that contain both "privacy" and "human rights" in either the subject or keyword entries. This initial search will find well over 2,000 index entries—far too many to begin looking at the index entries and deciding which articles might be useful. Further search words will need to be added to reduce the number of matching index entries. At this point it becomes important to think more precisely about your research topic. Perhaps media intrusion is the focus of your interest, in which case simply add "media" and search for "privacy and human rights and media".

Once you have begun to narrow the range of articles found in this way, take a look at the index entries made for some of the most relevant articles found and pay particular attention to the subject keywords which have been used in the index entries. There are still around 500 matching index entries. Search again using the keywords which now seem to offer the closest match to your interests, or use the "Search within results" feature to achieve the same end. You might note that "celebrities" has been used as a keyword, or that articles discussing the various *Douglas v Hello!* cases have been found, and that these are indexed under "breach of confidence". If your interest in privacy issues had been sparked by the *Douglas v Hello!* cases, you could narrow your search using "breach of confidence and privacy and human rights". As noted in para.2.11, there are no right answers, and it is advisable to try out different searches,

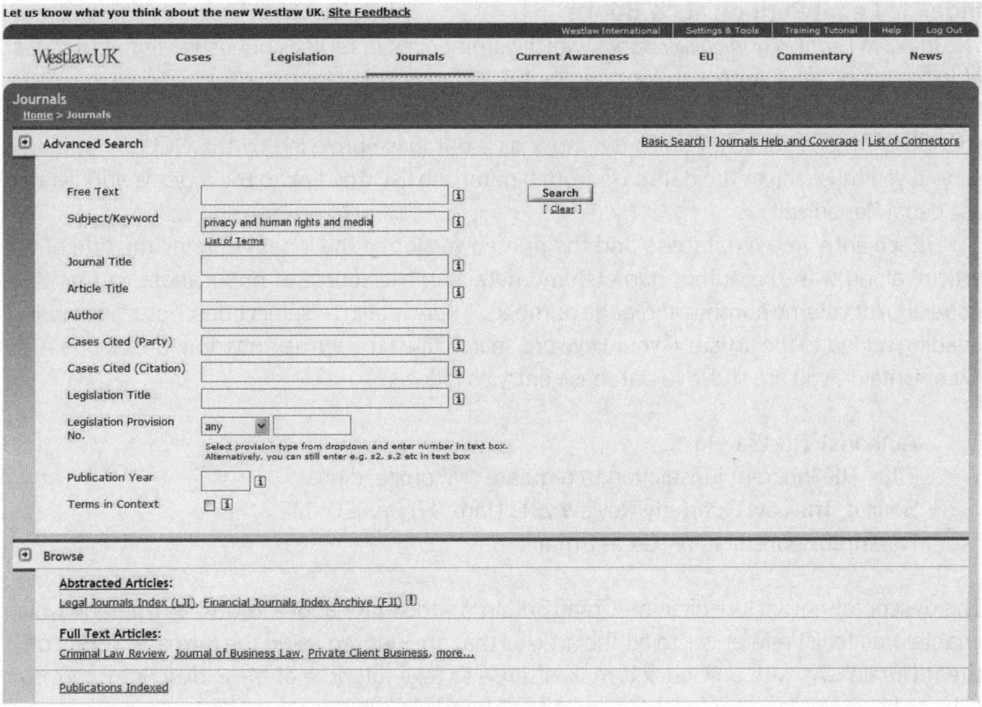

**Fig 5.2**
"Advanced Search" page in the Westlaw UK "Journals" section'

saving references of particular interest as you examine the results of each search. Individual entries can be marked (ticked) on the results screen and details of those articles later emailed or saved to a file. There is no need to write down the references you find to useful articles.

Select the "Legal Journals Abstract" link against any of the article details displayed to read the summary provided by the *Legal Journals Index*. A "Full Text Article" link is also displayed if the article text is available directly from Westlaw UK. Bear in mind though, that Westlaw UK contains only some of the journal articles available online. Once references to articles have been found using the "Subject/Keyword" search, all of the potential online and print sources of the articles need to be pursued as described in para.5.3 and para.5.4. It would be unduly restrictive to narrow your interest to articles available in full text on Westlaw UK (effectively to articles published by Sweet and Maxwell).

Note also that the results achieved using this index-based approach to searching differ greatly from those achieved using a "Free Text" search. The "Free Text" search on the Westlaw UK "Journals" page includes not just the full text of the *Legal Journals Index* summaries, but also the entire text of all journals held in full text versions in the Westlaw UK journals database. One consequence is that many articles are found in which your subject terms are only mentioned in passing. More importantly, articles available in full text are displayed first in the results screens. An important article which happens not to be available in Westlaw UK may be easily missed. Other articles which may only have a tangential relation to your research will be displayed first.

> **TIPS** • *Make an initial search for articles using the "Journals" "Advanced Search" in Westlaw UK. Then look at the keywords added to the entries for the articles found. They can give you ideas for new searches.*

### Index to Legal Periodicals & Books

**5.7** ▶ The *Index to Legal Periodicals & Books*, which commenced in 1908, is published in the US. Most of its coverage is of American journals, but it includes some journals from the UK, Canada, Ireland, Australia and New Zealand. The *Index* is available online from a number of sources. If your library has a subscription to the *Index* as a database provided by the OCLC FirstSearch service you must select the database from a database list. The link to the *Index* is abbreviated as "Legal Periodical".

Each entry in the database and the printed version of the Index contains the title of the article, along with the author name(s) and details of the source of publication: journal title, issue and/or volume number and page numbers. There is also a "subject descriptor", or subject heading added to the article. If your keyword search used the terms "inherent jurisdiction AND Great Britain", you are shown a database entry as follows:

> Author(s): Dockray, M. S.
> Title: The inherent jurisdiction to regulate civil proceedings.
> Source: The Law Quarterly Review v 113 (Jan. '97) pp. 120–132
> Descriptor: Jurisdiction—Great Britain.

The descriptor entry "Jurisdiction—Great Britain" in the entry above, is also a hyperlink which enables you to list references to all the articles that are indexed using the terms "Jurisdiction—Great Britain". As with any index it makes sense to take full note of these descriptor terms or subject headings, as they provide a means of improving the accuracy and relevance of your search results. The headings use American terminology and spelling which may occasionally cause difficulties.

If you wish to search for articles indexed before 1981, you must use the print volumes of the *Index*. Check if these are available in your library.

### Lawtel

**5.8** ▶ The Lawtel service includes an articles index which contains references to the contents of 57 UK publications. The emphasis is on publications that are likely to be of interest to legal practitioners. *Corporate Briefing, Counsel and Pensions World* are included, for example, along with academic law journals such as the *New Law Journal* and *Modern Law Review*. References to the legal sections of *The Times, The Guardian* and *The Independent* are included. Most of the publications are indexed from 1998 onwards, a few from 1995.

Each entry for the article index has a paragraph summarising the contents of the article along with references to any case law or legislation cited in the article. As with other indexes it is possible to search for articles using a case name or the name and section of a statute. You can also search using subject headings.

### Index to Foreign Legal Periodicals

**5.9** ▶ The *Index to Foreign Legal Periodicals* commenced in 1960. It indexes articles on international and comparative law and the municipal law of countries other than the US, the UK and the common law of Commonwealth countries. Close to 500 legal journals are indexed. The *Index* is available online from 1985 onwards.

## Legal Resource Index (LegalTrac)

The *Legal Resource Index* indexes over 800 legal publications, most of which are American, although a few UK journals are included. The index is made available online as the LegalTrac database.

▶ 5.10

## Halsbury's Laws

*Halsbury's Laws of England* is available from LexisNexis Butterworths and references to journal articles are included. Only a small range of journals is covered. The print version of *Halsbury's Laws* includes a Table of Articles in Binder 2. References to articles are arranged alphabetically by title within broad subject areas. As a result, this is not the easiest way to locate specific articles.

▶ 5.11

The Table of Articles in Binder 2 is updated by the latest copy of the *Monthly Review* in Binder 1. The *Monthly Review* summarises changes in the law by broad subject area and new articles are listed at the beginning of each section.

The Annual Abridgement to *Halsbury's Laws* includes a Table of Articles. This gives a selection of the journal articles written on a subject during that year. The Annual Abridgement replaces the information in the Table of Articles in Binder 2. *Halsbury's Laws* is described in more detail in para.7.3.

# TRACING LAW-RELATED JOURNAL ARTICLES

The effective study of law will of necessity take you into other disciplines. Articles on law-related aspects of housing, delinquency, sentencing, families and education are found in a wide range of journals, many of which are not solely concerned with law and which as a consequence are not usually found in a law collection. You may wish to consult journals which carry articles by sociologists, economists, criminologists, social administrators or historians. To trace social science and humanities material, you need to use a different selection of databases. The coverage of some of these databases is noted in the following paragraphs.

▶ 5.12

If your library has a "search portal" for database searching on its website, the contents of these indexes can be searched using a single search page which forms part of the library website. This means that you do not have to learn how to use a new set of search pages when you turn to an unfamiliar index. It is usually also possible to search more than one index at a time. To do this, select the indexes you wish to use from subject lists on the portal web pages. Search results are amalgamated into a single web page with links provided to the full-text source of journal articles if available. Unfortunately, search portals cannot currently be used to search law indexes (with the exception of the *Index to Legal Periodicals*).

The indexes listed below are by no means the only subject indexes to the contents of journals. Indexes exist covering many different subjects. The library staff will help you find out which indexing or abstracting services are available to cover the subjects that interest you.

## Index to Periodical Articles Related to Law

This index commenced in 1958. It contains a selective coverage of English-language articles not included in the *Legal Journals Index*, or the *Index to Legal Periodicals & Books*. It is available online from HeinOnline having ceased print publication at the end of 2005. There is an index

▶ 5.13

to articles by subject, a list of journals indexed and an author index. All the entries from 1958 to 1988 have been published in one cumulative volume. Annual indexes appeared thereafter.

### Applied Social Sciences Index and Abstracts (ASSIA)

**5.14** ▶ ASSIA is aimed at those in practice in social services, prison services, employment, race relations, etc., and includes articles on many aspects of the law. Articles from approximately 650 journals are indexed. Although produced in Britain, the index covers English-language journals from 16 countries.

### British Humanities Index

**5.15** ▶ This covers a broad range of subjects and includes articles from British newspapers and popular weekly journals, as well as more scholarly periodicals. Online coverage is from 1985 onwards.

### Social Sciences Index

**5.16** ▶ This index, which took over from the *Social Sciences and Humanities Index*, includes articles on law, criminology, sociology, political science, sociological aspects of medicine and other socio-legal topics. Online coverage is from 1983 onwards.

### Psychological Abstracts (PsycINFO)

**5.17** ▶ The scope of this is far wider than the title suggests, covering abortion, drug use, alcoholism, etc. Over 1,300 journals are indexed and dissertations, books and book chapters are included. Online coverage begins as early as 1887.

### International Bibliography of the Social Sciences (IBSS)

**5.18** ▶ Produced in the London School of Economics, the *International Bibliography of Social Sciences* has the most wide-ranging coverage of the social science indexes. It is particular strong in its coverage of European journals. Coverage goes back to 1961.

### The Philosopher's Index

**5.19** ▶ This index contains references (with abstracts) to articles found in almost 500 philosophy journals from a wide range of countries. Records of books and contributions to anthologies are included. Online coverage is from 1940 onwards.

### Sociological Abstracts

**5.20** ▶ *Sociological Abstracts* includes coverage of law, penology and the police and is available from a variety on online sources. Online coverage is from 1963 and abstracts are added to records from 1974 onwards.

### Social Sciences Citation Index

**5.21** ▶ The *Citation Index* is so called because, in addition to the usual bibliographic details, every entry in the index database carries a list of the articles referred to (or "cited") by the article in question. It is possible, using the index, to begin with a particular article, found perhaps after a subject search, and then trace details of the articles which have in turn discussed or used the article you started with. This is particularly useful if you already know of a key article and wish to find the latest articles in a long-running debate in the literature. In addition to the Social Sciences Citation Index, there is also an *Arts and Humanities Citation Index* and a *Sciences Citation Index*, all of which are available online as part of the Web of Science service (itself part of "Web of Knowledge").

## NEWSPAPER ARTICLES

In addition to factual reporting, newspapers often contain commentary, analysis and background information on recent legal developments and controversial topics. If your law library has a subscription to Nexis UK, the full text of UK national (and many regional) newspapers is available from the mid 1980s onwards. ▶ **5.22**

A menu choice on the Nexis UK "News" page allows news sources to be chosen from the wide range of English language sources available. Once a particular source is chosen, "UK Broadsheets" for example, a list is displayed of the constituent elements of the source. In this case *The Guardian*, *Times*, *Independent* etc. Any of these sources can be chosen individually at this point.

The news coverage of even a single newspaper over a number of years is, however, considerable, so it is advisable to make full use of the options which restrict the way in which your search is carried out. To continue with the example used in para.5.6, you might wish to find newspaper articles which discuss privacy as a human rights issue, so the keywords "privacy" and "human rights" would need to be included in the search boxes at the top of the "News" page. It would not be especially helpful, though, to find all articles which happen to include these words. Once you have entered your search terms, menu choices can be used to specify, for example, that only a "major mention" of a term retrieves an article, or that the search term must occur in the headline or the first paragraph. As a search for articles including "privacy" and "human rights" combines two search terms, the proximity of the two terms can also be specified using an additional drop-down menu. Instead of both terms simply appearing somewhere in the article, it can be specified that the terms must occur within five words of each other, or in the same sentence. Finally, date limits can be set, to restrict the search to a particular period of time. Limiting searches in this way can mean that a search for "privacy" and "human rights" can be restricted to produce a long but manageable results list of perhaps a hundred or so articles over a number of years, some of which will provide useful leads to important legal issues. These might be pursued using the academic coverage provided by legal journals.

The current awareness features of both LexisNexis Butterworths and Westlaw UK can also be used to find newspaper articles on recent legal developments. The LexisNexis Butterworths "Current Awareness" search includes brief summaries of articles of legal interest drawn from UK national newspapers. Legal news can also be found using the Westlaw UK "Current Awareness" search.

## LOCATING JOURNALS FROM OTHER LIBRARIES

If the journal is not available in your library, you may wish to obtain it from elsewhere. One approach would be to use the online catalogues of other libraries, which contain details of the journal titles held by the library (see para.7.29). Most online catalogues allow you to limit your title search to a "journals only" section of the catalogue. If you are searching for older journal titles, the *Union List of Legal Periodicals*, published by the Institute of Advanced Legal Studies, may be of use. It lists the locations of journals throughout the UK, though it is now extremely dated. The second edition was published in 1978 (although take comfort from the knowledge that libraries are unlikely, for the most part, to discard journal collections).

If you wish to consult a large number of journals or reports, it may be more convenient to go to another library and use the material there. If only a few articles are required, it may be easier to obtain them through the inter-library loan service. Details of this service are available from your librarian. If you wish to use this service, plan ahead and allow time for your request to be processed and for the material to arrive. The process can take several weeks, but usually around one to two weeks.

> **TIPS** • *Use the options available in the Nexis news databases to limit your search words e.g. to "major mentions". If using multiple search words ensure that they must be found close to each other in the text of newspaper articles.*

Copies of journal articles can be obtained directly from a wide range of organisations offering a document supply service. Even if you have to pay for copies from your own library, copies supplied by these services are likely to be more expensive, as a copyright fee is usually charged by publishers. This fee is added to the cost of supply. A university or other educational or public library does not charge this copyright fee. The British Library has a British Library Direct service (at *www.direct.bl.uk*), for example, which caters for individual one-off orders, but the copyright fee for a single article might be £6 (it can vary). Service charges will be added to this.

# ▶ 6
# UK official publications

## INTRODUCTION

A great deal of official publishing now takes place on the internet. This includes parliamentary ▶ 6.1 publications and the publications of government departments and other official bodies. As a result, official publications have become much more accessible than they once were. However, tracing official publications is not always straightforward. This is a field in which you should not hesitate to seek the advice of library staff whenever you have a difficulty. Most libraries which have a collection of official publications have at least one person who is responsible for helping readers find this material, whether online or in print.

The Stationery Office (TSO) publishes a high proportion of UK official publications. As a result, TSO web pages, and the TSO bookshop catalogue, are significant sources for tracing official publications (para.6.15). TSO is not, however, the only source of UK official publications. Some of the publications you may wish to consult will have been published elsewhere, often on the websites of government departments and other official bodies. Databases are available to help trace these publications (para.6.16).

Before privatisation in 1996, UK official publishing was undertaken by Her Majesty's Stationery Office (HMSO), which acted as the government printer. HMSO still exists as a residual body, responsible for Crown copyright. Since 2005, it has been part of the Office of Public Sector Information (OPSI). For this reason, legislation is found on OPSI web pages.

Parliamentary publications are the most important category of UK official publications for the law student. These include papers brought before Parliament (Command Papers), Bills, House of Commons Papers and *Hansard* reports of parliamentary debates. Most of this chapter is concerned with these sources. Acts of Parliament, which are also official publications, are covered in Ch.4. Parliamentary papers are published by TSO.

Documents other than parliamentary publications published by, or on behalf of, government departments or other official bodies, are often referred to as non-parliamentary publications. These items vary considerably and include, for example, public information pamphlets such as the *Highway Code* and directories such as the *Civil Service Yearbook*, which lists Civil Service departments, provides contact details, and gives the names of senior civil servants. TSO publishes only some of these non-parliamentary publications.

## PARLIAMENTARY PUBLICATIONS

**6.2**▶ Recent parliamentary papers are available online either from TSO (at *www.official-publications. gov.uk*) or the Parliament website (at *www.parliament.uk*). There are four main categories:

> House of Commons Papers;
> House of Commons Bills;
> House of Lords Papers and Bills;
> Command Papers.

All Command Papers and House of Commons Papers from the 2005/2006 parliamentary session onwards are available online from TSO. Selected papers are also available for the period 1994–2005. Command Papers are covered in more detail in para.6.3. Access to the text of Bills before Parliament is explained para.6.9 and *Hansard* debates (both online and in print) in para.6.11. If print versions of recent parliamentary papers are available, they are usually gathered into boxes corresponding to some or all of the categories noted above. Every parliamentary paper has its own number and the papers are usually arranged in number order.

If your library has a complete collection of printed parliamentary publications, they may be bound together in volumes containing all the material produced during a particular session of Parliament. These volumes are known as *sessional papers* or *sessional sets*. A Sessional Index provides a subject approach to the material. Other index approaches are covered in para.6.16.

Libraries with large collections of official publications do not usually enter parliamentary publications in the library catalogues, relying instead on the indexes produced by TSO and others (para.6.14—para.6.16) to trace relevant material. You will probably also find that all the parliamentary publications have been housed in an official publications collection in a separate area of the library (which may not form part of the law library). Therefore, you should ask the librarians whether there is a collection of official publications available and get them to show you where they are located and how they are arranged. If, however, your library has only a small collection of parliamentary publications, they may be catalogued and shelved individually.

Older parliamentary papers are available from the House of Commons Parliamentary Papers database from Proquest, which can be accessed from any UK university library. The database contains scanned versions of papers available in sessional sets and includes papers from 1688 to 2003/2004. Even large libraries are relatively unlikely to have original print volumes pre-dating 1801. Parliamentary papers may also be available on microfiche or microfilm, or in the form of reprints published by bodies such as the Irish University Press. (These reprints are arranged in subject order.)

Material which is still in print may be purchased from any branch of TSO or through any bookseller. Photocopies of out-of-print publications can be purchased from TSO. Publications may also be available on loan through the inter-library loan service.

### Command Papers

**6.3**▶ This is a very important category of parliamentary papers and one to which you may frequently be referred. It includes many major government papers, e.g. The *Governance of Britain* (2007).

Some, though not all, of the reports of the Law Commission are also included, along with the reports of all Royal Commissions. A Command Paper is, as it states on the front cover, presented to Parliament "By Command of Her Majesty." In practice, this means that it is presented to Parliament by a Minister of the Crown on his or her own initiative; its preparation has not been requested by Parliament. Command Papers are often statements of government policy, which are likely to be the subject of future legislation, or they are presented for the information of the Members of Parliament. Command Papers include:

statements of government policy (often referred to as *White Papers*);
some annual statistics and annual reports (many more are issued as non-parliamentary publications);
reports of Royal Commissions;
reports of some committees (other committee reports may be issued as non-parliamentary publications);
reports of tribunals of inquiry;
state papers (including the Treaty Series).

## Citation and location of Command Papers

Command Papers are each given an individual number, prefaced by an abbreviation for the word "command". This abbreviation and the number are printed at the bottom left-hand corner of the cover of the report. The numbers run on continuously from one session of Parliament to another. The present abbreviation "Cm." has been used for publications issued since 1986. Prior to 1986, different abbreviations of the word "command" were used. They are:

▶ **6.4**

| | |
|---|---|
| 1st series 1833–1869 | [1]–[4222] (the abbreviation for "Command" was omitted in the first series) |
| 2nd series 1870–1899 | [C. 1]–[C. 9550] |
| 3rd series 1900–1918 | [Cd. 1]–[Cd. 9239] |
| 4th series 1919–1956 | [Cmd. 1]–Cmd. 9889 |
| 5th series 1956–1986 | Cmnd. 1–Cmnd. 9927 |
| 6th series 1986– | Cm. 1– |

(The use of square brackets was abandoned in 1922.) It is important to note exactly the form of the abbreviation so that you have some idea of the date of the report. For instance, Cmd. 6404, which relates to social insurance and allied services (the Beveridge Report), is a different item from Cmnd. 6404, which is an international agreement relating to pensions. One was published in 1942 and the other in 1976.

The "Browse" section of the TSO Official Documents website (at *www.official-publications. gov.uk*) displays links to Command Papers for 2004 onwards, organised by year and Command Paper number. A listing by subject is also provided. The "Advanced Search" enables keyword searches to be limited to Command Papers only. The browse facility within the Proquest House of Commons Parliamentary Papers database can be used to display Command Papers predating 2004/2005 by year. Keyword searches can be limited to Command Papers from the main search page.

If your library keeps print versions of Command Papers in boxes arranged by command number, you will have no difficulty in tracing the report you want (assuming your reference is correct). However, if the publications are arranged by sessions or are bound into sessional sets (see para.6.2), it will be necessary to have some idea of the date of the Command Paper. An online approach using the sources noted above would be the easiest way to proceed. However there are print sources which can help. You might, for example, find the Concordance of Command Papers 1833–1972, which is in J.E. Pemberton, *British Official Publications* (2nd edn.), pp. 66–66, useful for older papers.

Occasionally, a report is published later than the Command Papers with adjoining numbers, with the result that it appears in a different session of Parliament (and is therefore in a different sessional set (para.6.2)). If you know the Command Paper number of a publica-tion issued before 1979–80 and wish to locate it in the bound sessional sets, first ascertain the correct session by consulting Pemberton's list or the *HMSO Annual Catalogues* (see para.6.14). Until the 1979–80 session, Command Papers were not arranged in number order in the sessional sets. They were arranged alphabetically by subject in a sequence with all reports, accounts and papers. To find a Command Paper in the sessional sets before 1979–80 there-fore, you need to consult the Sessional Index at the back of the last volume of the session. There you will find a list of Command Paper numbers indicating, for each one, the volume and page within the sessional set where it can be found. Command Papers bound in the sessional sets since 1979–80 can be readily traced under the Command Paper number.

Some Command Papers also form part of another series. For instance, some of the reports of the Law Commission (but not all) are Command Papers: but each Law Commission report also bears its own running number. For convenience, law libraries may keep all law Commission reports together, regardless of whether they are issued as Command Papers, House of Commons Papers, or non-parliamentary papers (and some of the series have been issued in all these categories). Another major series within the Command Papers are the state papers known as the Treaty Series. These are Command Papers and each has a number, but, in addition, each has its own Treaty Series number. If they are not bound into the sessional sets, the library may keep all the Treaty Series together. There are separate annual and three– or four–yearly consoli-dated indexes to the series; in addition, they also appeared in annual *HMSO* or *TSO Catalogues*. Both the Treaty Series number and the Command Paper numbers are given. In 1970, HMSO published an *Index of British Treaties 1101–1968* (compiled by Clive Parry and Charity Hopkins). There are entries under subjects (Vol.1) and by the date of the treaties (Vols 2 and 3).

## Papers of the House of Lords and House of Commons

**6.5** ▶ Until 1988, the House of Lords Papers and Bills were issued in a common numerical sequence, so the Papers and Bills were integrated. Since then, they have been issued in separate numer-ical sequences in the same way as the House of Commons Papers.

The number of each House of Lords Paper is printed in round brackets at the foot of the front cover. The citation is: H.L. session (paper number), e.g. H.L. 1993–94 (7) 1st Report [Session 1993–94]: Enforcement of Community Competition Rules: Report with Evidence— Select Committee on the European Communities.

The Papers of the House of Commons include reports of some committees, together with accounts, statistics and some annual reports which are required by Parliament for its work. The citation of a House of Commons Paper contains the initials H.C., the session and the paper number. e.g. H.C. 2006–07 716 is the *Annual Report* 2006/07 of the Legal Services Commission.

House of Commons Papers, like Command Papers, can be found online using the TSO website and Proquest database of House of Commons Parliamentary Papers. The approach is much the same. Papers are listed by session in both sources and keyword searches can be limited to House of Commons Papers. House of Lords Papers, however, are not currently available online.

As House of Commons and House of Lords Papers are numbered by session, they are usually straightforward to find in print if you have the correct session and number. Note though, that though complete collections of House of Commons Papers are not unusual, fewer libraries have collections of House of Lords Papers.

## BILLS

Bills are the draft versions of Acts, laid before Parliament for its consideration and approval. If your library has a complete collection of parliamentary papers, the Bills will be shelved with this collection; if not, they may be available in the law library. If the library's parliamentary papers are bound up into sessional sets, the Bills will form the first volumes of each set. The most recent Bills are likely to be shelved separately in boxes.

▶ **6.6**

A Bill may be introduced into Parliament by a Member of Parliament (or by a peer) as an independent action (called a Private Member's Bill), or it may be introduced by a Minister as a Government Bill. Ultimately, however, if it is passed, it becomes a Public General Act whoever introduces it. Private Members' Bills are not always published by TSO: if not otherwise available, they can usually be obtained by writing directly to the Member of Parliament concerned.

### Stages in the passage of a Bill

Before a Bill can become law, it passes through a number of stages. The exact stage which any Bill has reached on its passage through Parliament can be discovered by consulting the "Bills before Parliament" page of the Parliament website (at *http://www.parliament.uk*), or the *House of Commons Weekly Information Bulletin* (para.6.8). A Bill may be introduced into the House of Lords or the Commons. If they commence in the House of Commons, Bills progress through the following stages. Bills fail if they do not pass through all these stages before the end of the parliamentary session.

▶ **6.7**

(i) First Reading—a purely formal reading of the Bill's title by the Clerk of the House; after this, the Bill is printed, a day is fixed for its Second Reading and it becomes available to the public.

(ii) Second Reading—the principles of the Bill are debated. If the Bill fails to gain the approval of the House at this stage, it cannot proceed. The debate is reported in *Hansard* (see para.6.11).

(iii) Committee stage—the whole House may sit in committee to examine the clauses of a Bill. More usually, the Bill is discussed in a Public Bill Committee (previously a "Standing Committee") consisting of approximately 20 Members of Parliament. The Public Bill Committee debates are found on the Parliament website (at *www.parliament.uk*), on the "Hansard" pages. The link to the debates is under the main *Hansard* heading, where they are arranged by session (chronologically), and then alphabetically by the name of the Bill under discussion. TSO also prints the text of the debate on the particular Bill as an individual item. Bound volumes are issued as *Parliamentary Debates. House of Commons Official Report. Standing Committees* (Public Bill Committees from 2006/2007 onwards). A number of volumes are published for each session and their publication lags two to three years behind the debates themselves.

If you are using the print copies of the debates you will need to find out which committee discussed the Bill you are interested in. This can be done by looking in the *House of Commons Information Bulletin* (para.6.8). Standing Committees can also be traced using the TSO website (para.6.15) or the UKOP catalogue (para.6.16). If you are searching using UKOP you will find that the name of the committee appears in the title area of the records used. Particular debates can be found by combining the Bill's title with "standing committee" or "grand committee" or "Public Bill Committee", as appropriate.

(iv) Report stage—if the Bill has been amended by the Public Bill Committee, this stage gives the House an opportunity to consider the changes. If necessary, the Bill may be referred back to the committee. (If the Bill was debated and approved without amendment in a Committee of the Whole House, then this stage is a formality.)

(v) Third Reading—a general discussion of the Bill as amended, after which it is passed to the House of Lords for its approval.

(vi) Lords' stages—The Bill is reprinted when it is passed to the Lords for their consideration and approval. If the Lords make any amendments, these are referred back to the Commons for their approval. Normally, both Houses must be in agreement on the text before the Bill can receive the Royal Assent. The Parliament Acts 1911 and 1949 provide for certain exceptions to this rule. Finance Bills are the standard exception.

## Changes to the text of a Bill

6.8 ▶ Bills before Parliament are found on the Parliament website (at *www.parliament.uk*). Public Bills are arranged in an alphabetical sequence on the "Bills before Parliament" page. This can be found from the Parliament home page under "Business" and "Bills and Legislation". Bills which originated in the House of Lords have [H.L.] after the title. The Bills most recently debated are displayed in a "What's new" list. Selecting any of the Bills listed for the current session displays first a table noting a Bill's current progress through Parliament. A particularly useful feature of the table is the ability to link directly to the *Hansard* debates for the various readings and committee stages the Bill has already passed through. Dates for future debates are also present. Further down the page, a list is displayed of the various versions of the Bill. Against each one is a note of its status at that point, e.g. "as introduced", as amended in "Public Bill Committee".

Perhaps confusingly, the number of a Bill changes with each new version (there is a running sequence for the session). The Climate Change Bill debated in the 2007–08 session was introduced in the House of Lords, for example, as HL Bill 9, and would be fully cited as

Climate Change Bill [H.L.] [2007–08] 9. It was brought forward from the House of Lords to the House of Commons as Bill 97, and renumbered again as Bill 129 following amendments at the Public Bill Committee stage (becoming the Climate Change Bill [H.C.] [2007–08] 129).

The different versions of the Bill can be viewed as PDF files, and these correspond to the printed versions of the Bill published by TSO. If you wish to refer to a Bill, and significant amendments have been made, it is clearly important to state which version of a Bill you are using. If a significant number of amendments have been moved, e.g at the committee stage of a Bill, marshalled lists of amendments are also published by TSO. These bear the same number as the original Bill, but add a roman number, e.g. 123 II.

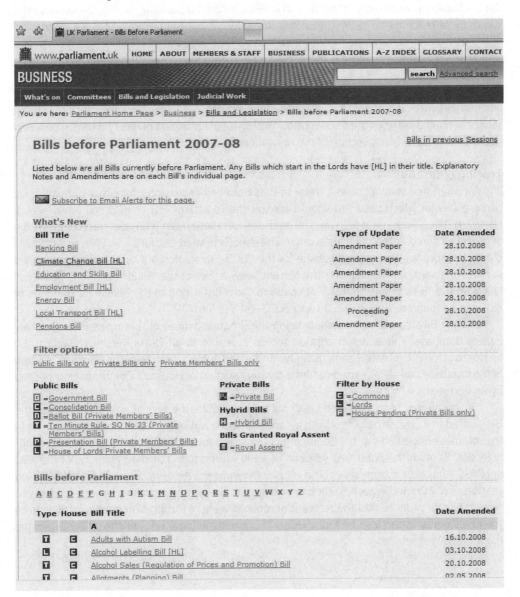

**Fig 6.1**
'"Bills before Parliament" web page on the Parliament website'

### Tracing recent Bills

**6.9** ▶ Finding the full text of a Bill as currently before Parliament is relatively straightforward using the "Bills before Parliament" page of the Parliament website (at *www.parliament.uk*). Earlier versions are also easy to find online, as noted in the previous section.

If you wish to trace the development of legislation using printed versions, however, you need first to confirm the numbers of the various versions of a Bill. Only then can the Bills which interest you be found in a number sequence. The "Bills before Parliament" web page is the most obvious source. The *House of Commons Weekly Information Bulletin* provides another approach. It is available in print and also online from the Parliament website under the "Publications and Records" section. The "Bills before Parliament" section provides a brief summary of readings for a Bill and notes the different printed versions of a Bill. These are noted as bracketed numbers in bold text. The various versions of a Bill can also be traced using the TSO catalogue (para.6.15), or the UKOP catalogue (para.6.16). Both catalogues list individual printings.

If your library holds a set of the printed copies of Bills, these should be shelved in session and number order. If not, printed Bills can be requested through your libraries inter-library loan service or purchased from the TSO website. The House of Lords text of recent Bills can be found under the House of Lords section of the *Hansard* web pages.

### Tracing older Bills

**6.10** ▶ It is not often that you will need to refer to Bills from earlier sessions, for either they will have become law (in which case you should consult the resultant Act) or they will have lapsed. However, Bills from relatively recent sessions of Parliament can be traced using the approaches noted in the previous section. The various printed versions of a Bill are all available online from the Parliament website for the 2005–06 session onwards and are organised in much the same way as Bills for the current session. Select the "Bills in previous Sessions" link from the "Bills before Parliament" page to see a full listing of the Bills. First printings of Bills can be found for the 2002–03 and 2003–04 sessions.

Earlier Bills can be found online using the Proquest House of Commons Parliamentary Papers database. This is a subscription service available to all UK universities. Bills can be found from the main search page using both title and subject searches. The "Browse" section of the database can also be used to find a complete listing of House of Commons Bills printed by session year.

If your library has the bound sessional sets available, the text of all the versions of the Bill printed in a session, together with all amendments, will be found in alphabetical order in the volumes entitled *Bills* at the beginning of the sessional set. If the bound sets are not available, details of all the published versions of a Bill will be found at the beginning of the *TSO* or *HMSO Annual Catalogue* and in the *House of Commons Weekly Information Bulletins* during that session. As noted in para.6.9, it becomes important to consider which version of a Bill you wish to find, in order to find the relevant numbered version. Publication details for Bills from the 1970s onwards can also be found using TSO's website (para.6.15) or the UKOP catalogue (para.6.16).

# PARLIAMENTARY DEBATES (HANSARD)

The first semi-official reports of Parliament's debates were published in 1803 by William **▶6.11** Cobbett. The man whose name is so closely linked with the publication, Hansard, was a subsequent printer of the reports. There have been six series of *Parliamentary Debates*. The first series covered 1803–20, with subsequent series for 1820–30, 1830–91, 1892–1908 and 1909–1981. The sixth series covers 1981 to the present. Since 1909, the *Official Reports of Parliamentary Debates* have been published by the House of Commons itself. The House of Lords Debates have been published separately since 1909; previously, Lords and Commons Debates were published together.

House of Commons debates are available online from the 1988/89 sessions onwards on the Parliament website (at *www.parliament.uk*). House of Lords debates can be found in full text on the same site from 1994/95. A project to digitize the volumes of *Hansard* covering the entire period from 1803 to 2005 is also now well underway, and a link to the Historical Hansard site is displayed on the Parliament "Hansard" page.

Current debates can be viewed online as *Hansard Daily Debates* for either the House of Commons or House of Lords. Ministerial statements and oral and written answers are also included, along with an index. Comparatively recent debates are then listed online by month. Daily and weekly printed editions of *Hansard* provide the same up-to-date coverage. After a few months, the debates are organised, both online and in print, into numbered volumes. It is these volumes which constitute the "record copy". Each volume covers debates taking place over a two or three week period. One peculiarity of these volumes worth noting is that both print and online versions use column rather than page numbering. All *Hansard* references to the record copy are to column numbers.

Indexes to the *Hansard* volumes appear, both online and in print, some months after the volume itself. These can help trace a debate if you do not have an exact date. The indexes are bound with the volumes in print, and appear online alongside the volume entry in the *Hansard* listing for the session. The indexes contain an alphabetical listing of debates by subject matter and by name of speaker. The subject of written questions and the names of those asking them are also included. References are to the column number of the printed *Hansard*, rather than page numbers. Index references ending in 'w' indicate written questions. Online index entries all link to the relevant *Hansard* text.

The search engine for the Parliament website provides an alternative approach to tracing debates. To make the best use of its abilities, select the "Advanced Search" link from any of the Parliament web pages. The advanced search menu allows your search to be restricted, so that only *Hansard* debates (or indexes) are searched. Searches can also specify that an exact phrase must be matched, to ensure, for example, that the phrase "greenhouse gas emissions" must be matched in the results page. As *Hansard* pages are extensive, it usually makes sense to add date limits wherever possible.

> **TIPS** • *Use the "Advanced Search" on the Parliament website to search Hansard using keywords. Searches can be limited to Hansard indexes (rather than debates) increasing the potential relevance of your results..*

## Electronic conveyancing

Pilot schemes 1428w

## Electronic government

Local government 111-2w, 1024w, 1034-5w

## Electronic surveillance

Members (04.02.2008) 660-70, 948-9, 954
Ministerial statements (06.02.2008) 959-71

## Electronic tagging

1187-8w

## Ellman, Mrs Louise

*Westminster Hall Debates*

Driving, Young people (07.02.2008) 310-3wh

*Questions*

Asylum 1209w
Muslim Brotherhood, Entry clearances 1389w
Offender Management Act 2007 133-4w
Palestinians, Overseas aid 302-3
World War II, Education 646-7

## Ellwood, Tobias

*Chamber Debates*

National Insurance Contributions Bill, Rep and 3R (31.01.2008) 542-4

*Westminster Hall Debates*

### Using online sources to trace debates on a Bill

**6.12** ▶ For the period from 2005/06 onwards, the most effective way to find debates on a particular Bill is to use the "Bills before Parliament" web page on the Parliament site, described in para.6.8. The table displaying the progress of a particular Bill can be used to find the *Hansard* debates relating to each stage the Bill has passed through.

The POLIS database maintained by the House of Commons Library can be used to trace debates on Bills from earlier sessions of Parliament. It indexes proceedings of both Houses of Parliament from 2001 onwards. Access is free from the Parliamentary Data website (at *www.polis.parliament.uk*). To search the database enter the title of a Bill (not the subsequent

**4 Feb 2008 : Column 660**

# HMP Woodhill (Inquiry)

**3.34 pm**

**The Secretary of State for Justice and Lord Chancellor (Mr. Jack Straw):** With permission, Mr. Speaker, I should like to make a statement. As the House will be aware, there appeared in *The Sunday Times* yesterday allegations that conversations between my hon. Friend the Member for Tooting (Mr. Khan) and a constituent of his, Mr. Babar Ahmad, detained in prison on an extradition warrant, had been subject to covert recording when my hon. Friend visited Mr. Ahmad on two occasions in 2005 and 2006 at Her Majesty's prison Woodhill.

I was made aware of the burden of these allegations on Saturday afternoon. My right hon. Friend the Home Secretary and I discussed the matter and we agreed that an immediate inquiry should be established. In a statement to *The Sunday Times* issued on my behalf early on Saturday evening I announced this, and expressed my concerns about the allegations, if true.

It may assist the House if I now give some detail of the differing ways in which the statutory authorisation regimes for intercept, and for intrusive surveillance, operate. But just before I do so, let me underline the fact, drawn from my experience as a Minister directly involved in these matters over many years, that no authorisations are granted unless by law they are necessary for the detection or prevention of crime or the protection of national security or for related matters, and are proportionate, and unless the information concerned cannot be obtained by other means. Any authorisation for the interception of telephone calls and other public telecommunications requires a warrant personally signed by the relevant Secretary of State— usually the Home Secretary in respect of the police, Security Service and other domestic law enforcement agencies, and the Foreign Secretary in respect of the Secret Intelligence Service and GCHQ. Such a Secretary of State warrant is also required for surveillance operations— including eavesdropping—where sought by the three intelligence agencies. The telecommunications regime is overseen by the interception of communications commissioner—normally a retired member of the senior judiciary, currently Sir Paul Kennedy. This is laid down in the Regulation of Investigatory Powers Act 2000—known as RIPA. Surveillance under this regime is overseen by the intelligence services commissioner under the Intelligence Services Act 1994.

Under the 2000 Act, the regime in respect of intrusive surveillance operations by the police and other domestic law enforcement agencies is different. Under these provisions, which originated with the Police Act 1997, passed in the closing months of the previous Administration, with our support, there is a hierarchy of approvals depending on the nature of the surveillance concerned. In the case of eavesdropping operations, authorisation by a chief officer of police or officer of equivalent rank in the Metropolitan Police Service is required. This regime is supervised by the chief surveillance commissioner—currently Sir Christopher Rose, formerly a senior judge of the Court of Appeal. Ministers play no part in these authorisations.

**Fig 6.3**
'Example Page from the House of Commons Parliamentary Debates (Hansard)'

Act) in the "Legislation" search box, i.e. "Prevention of Terrorism Bill", rather than "Prevention of Terrorism Act". Results are displayed in chronological order and notes of debates are provided along with references to oral and written questions. Though the database itself provides only index entries for debates, noting *Hansard* references, links are provided to the full text of *Hansard* debates available from the Parliament website. It is possible to find, for example, the oral statement that introduced a Bill to one of the Houses of Parliament, and follow the link to the *Hansard* full text. Some libraries may also provide access to the Justis Parlianet. This is a subscription service, based on the POLIS database, that provides index entries for proceedings from 1979 onwards.

## NON-PARLIAMENTARY PUBLICATIONS

**6.13** ▶ These are publications which are not presented to Parliament. The term covers a vast range of government publications, including statutory instruments (para.4.26). In most libraries, these publications (other than statutory instruments) are entered in the library catalogue, so you should start your search for them in the catalogue. Checking the catalogue is particularly important in those libraries where non-parliamentary publications are scattered among the book collections according to the subject matter of their content, rather than being kept in a single central location. If a central collection exists, additional copies may also be kept in subject collections.

Non-parliamentary publications are increasingly available on the internet, usually on the website of the body responsible for their publication. As there are many official bodies, a useful starting point is the UK online website (at *www.direct.gov.uk*), as this features an alphabetical list of government, or government funded or controlled bodies under the "A–Z of central government" link. This allows you to trace relevant or potentially relevant home pages. Home pages of public bodies as diverse as the Child Support Agency, the Employment Tribunals Service and the Equality and Human Rights Commission, can be found using the site. Your next step is to explore the site, looking for a publications link, a site map, or a search engine.

Previously, a great deal of non-parliamentary publishing was undertaken by HMSO, but this is no longer the case, so TSO catalogues and the TSO website (para.6.15) are only of limited use. If you wish to trace non-parliamentary papers, the UKOP catalogue is of more use as it includes official publications not published by TSO (see para.6.16). The UKOP database also includes links to non-parliamentary publications found on departmental sites, along with archived copies of some publications from 2000 onwards.

## TRACING OFFICIAL PUBLICATIONS

**6.14** ▶ A number of sources are available for tracing both parliamentary and non-parliamentary papers. These include TSO Daily Lists and catalogues (para.6.15), along with the UKOP catalogue and the BOPCRIS database (all covered in para.6.16). It often may not be clear whether a document—an annual report perhaps—is a parliamentary, or a non-parliamentary paper, so the ability to search for all kinds of official publications is helpful.

> **TIPS** • *Use the "Boolean Search" (under "Advanced Search") when searching the UKOP database. Combine search keywords using "AND".*

## Stationery Office catalogues, indexes and website

The *TSO Daily Lists* are useful for tracing very recent legislation and other recent government publications. The lists appear both in print and on the TSO websites. The
current list is on the TSO website (at *www.tsoshop.co.uk/parliament*). The site also features links to previous lists by month and year. Using the *Daily List* parliamentary
section, you can find publication details of House of Lords and Commons Papers and
Bills, Command Papers, Acts, and Debates. Non-parliamentary publications appear in
the official publications section. Other sections are devoted to Scottish Parliament publications, Northern Ireland Assembly publications and Northern Ireland official publications. The final section is devoted to agency publications. These are publications, by
bodies such as the Council of Europe, the UN and the WHO, that are sold, but not
published, by TSO.

▶ **6.15**

If your required publication is more than a few days old, it is easier to search using
TSO's online bookshop (at www.tsoshop.co.uk)—other sources for keyword searching are
covered in para.6.16. The TSO bookshop site includes details of all publications sold by TSO
and it is possible to keyword search for any TSO publication, along with HMSO publications, including some "print on demand" titles from as early as 1930. Click the link for the
"Advanced Search" to limit your search to Bills, Acts, House of Commons Papers, etc. The
author search allows searches by the names of chairmen of committees and date limits can
also be set. The TSO bookshop site is designed to act for the Stationery Office as an internet
bookshop, so along with pricing information, the site provides the ability to order online.
If the item you are interested in is out of print, a price is given for TSO's print on demand
facility.

Should you want to trace relatively recent publications using print sources, you will find
that many libraries hold the printed TSO Weekly List. As the name suggests, this is a cumula-
tion of the week's Daily Lists.

If you are looking for earlier material, which may not appear on the TSO website,
you should use the annual catalogues which appeared as either the *HMSO Annual Catalogue
19 . . .*, or before that, *Government Publications 19 . . .* As you go back through the catalogues
you see that where the name of the Ministry began with the word "Ministry" or "Department",
the entry was inverted, as, for example, Environment, Department of. Otherwise the structure and layout of the catalogues is much like the structure of the current daily and weekly
lists.

Every five years a *Consolidated Index* was produced for the older catalogues, e.g. for
1961–65, 1966–70, 1971–75, 1976–80 and in many libraries, the catalogues for these years are
bound together. To allow for this, the pagination of the catalogues was continuous over the
five year period.

## Other sources for tracing official publications

The UKOP (UK Official Publications) database combines details of official publications published by TSO with details of official publications published by other sources. This means that
almost all publications by government departments are included—whether published by TSO
or not—along with the full range of TSO published parliamentary papers. Coverage begins in
1970 and since 2000 links have been added to the full text source of many publications. Some

▶ **6.16**

**Fig 6.4**
'TSO "Parliamentary and Legal" web page'

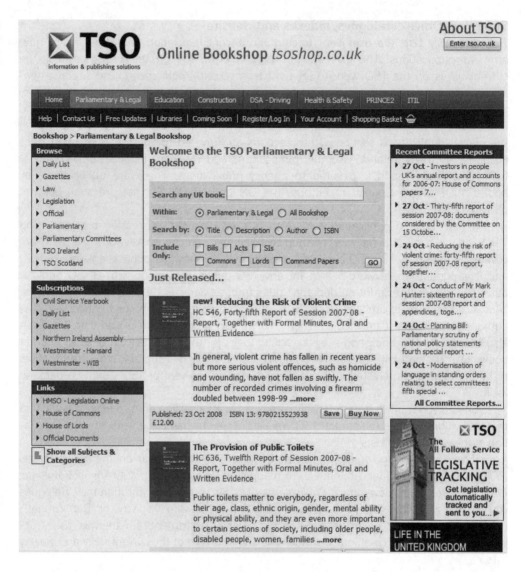

of these are archived digital copies only available from UKOP. UKOP is a subscription database, so you need to check if your library can provide access.

UKOP can be searched for publications by title, in much the same way as the TSO bookshop catalogue, in order to trace Command Paper or other parliamentary reference numbers, or information on which branch of government was responsible for the publication. But be warned, the use of automatic keyword searching, and the relevance ranking of results, means that some documents can be almost impossible to find. A search for the government white paper *Justice for All* (Cm. 5563), retrieves a list of 1,000 possible matches featuring "Justice". Further details, preferably including a date, are needed to find the document with its Command Paper number.

UKOP is better designed for subject searching, allowing a trawl through often long results lists for potentially useful or relevant documents on a subject. Its "Advanced Search" facilitates subject searching using either a "Flexible Search" or a "Boolean Search" (see para.2.11 for more on Boolean searching). The "Flexible Search" option automatically adds additional search words to the ones you have entered using the UKOP thesaurus of subject terms, so that if you search for publications relating to "asylum seekers", publications with titles featuring the words "immigration" and "refugees" are also found. However, this kind of searching can be all too inclusive. A "Flexible Search" for "asylum seekers" finds over 1,000 references, so additional, more specific, search terms need to be added to create a meaningful search. A "Boolean Search" for "asylum AND seekers" finds well under 200 references.

The Justis Parlianet service provides another subscription route for tracing recent official publications. Like the previous databases, it includes both parliamentary and non-parliamentary papers. A "search wizard" can be used to specify "Publications", excluding the details of parliamentary debates and other material held on the database. Subject keywords can then be used to search for official publications. Title and author searches are also possible.

If you wish to trace older official publications, the BOPCRIS database (at *http://www. bopcris.ac.uk*) provides selective coverage of the entire period from 1688 to 1995. The database provides abstracts for 23,000 key documents, most of which are parliamentary papers, though some non-parliamentary papers are included. Selection is based on the Ford lists and breviates, a series of print publications which have provided the standard selection of important official publications for most of the period covered by the database. Many of the abstracts are extensive, making keyword subject searching particularly effective. The database was funded by UK universities enabling database access to be free of charge.

If you already know that the publication which interests you is a parliamentary paper, the Proquest database of House of Commons Parliamentary Papers can be used both to trace and access papers prior to the 2004/05 parliamentary session. Keyword searches can be restricted to document titles, which can be preferable to searching the full text of the entire database, as large papers of documents are often found using full text searching, even if date limits are set. A more structured approach to searching the papers by subject is possible using the subject search box. Subject terms can be chosen from a searchable list, and range from the relatively general ("asylum"), to the very specific ("asylum and immigration bill 1995/96"). The "hierarchical 19th century subject list" is derived from the *Subject Catalogue of the House of Commons Parliamentary Papers, 1901–1900*, by Peter Cockton. Using the subject list, detailed subject entries can be found within broad categories.

A comprehensive approach to finding older material requires the use of printed indexes. Along with the indexes published by HMSO (para.6.15), the general indexes printed for the House of Commons covering the nineteenth Century should be examined. These provide a detailed alphabetical approach to finding parliamentary papers and were published as the *General Index to the Accounts and papers . . . Printed by Order of the House of Commons or Presented by Command for 1801–1852, 1852/53 to 1868/69 and 1879–1878/79*. The Ford lists and breviates, already mentioned, were published as *Select list of British parliamentary papers for 1833–99*; *A Breviate of Parliamentary Papers*, with volumes covering the period from 1900 to 1954; *Select List of British Parliamentary Papers, 1955–1964*; and *Ford List of British*

*Parliamentary Papers*, with volumes covering 1965–83. Your library may also retain the Index to the House of Commons Parliamentary Papers on CD-ROM, which contains references to Bills, Command Papers and House of Commons Papers. Coverage begins in 1801.

### Tracing Law Commission reports and working papers

**6.17** ▶ Some of the Law Commission reports are published as Command Papers and others are House of Commons Papers, whilst many more are non-parliamentary papers. As a result you may find that in your library they are not all shelved as one collection. Every report and working paper has its own individual number. A complete list of all the reports and working papers which have been published is given in the latest copy of the Law Commission's Annual Report (issued as a House of Commons Paper). The list gives the Command Paper number or Paper numbers, where relevant, and indicates, for each report, whether the Commission's proposals for reform have been implemented. Law Commission papers can also be traced using TSO's website for recent publications and the HMSO catalogues for older reports and publications.

### Tracing press releases

**6.18** ▶ The press releases of government departments are relatively easy to trace thanks to the UK online website (at *www.direct.gov.uk*). This provides a means of tracing the departmental websites and the press releases they carry.

Updates on press releases with brief summaries can also be found in the "Current Awareness" section of Westlaw UK. Press releases can be browsed "by document type" or searched as part of the current awareness database. Press releases of legal interest are included from UK government departments, the Commission of the European Communities and the European Court of Human Rights.

### Tracing statistics

**6.19** ▶ The UK Statistics Authority website (at *www.statistics.gov.uk*) provides a particularly useful starting point for official statistics. The site includes a link to the web pages of the Office for National Statistics (ONS), which provides access to official data sources, products and services. In most cases statistical data are provided directly, and in others you are given details of a print source or a relevant government department. It is possible to browse the ONS website by theme (e.g. crime and justice), and then select a more detailed subject area (e.g. justice). Specific data can then be found, e.g on sentencing.

The Home Office Research Development Statistics website (at *www.homeoffice.gov.uk/ rds*) is a particularly good departmental site for legal research.

# ▶ 7
# How to find information on a subject

## INTRODUCTION

It is probable that you will frequently be asked to discover the law relating to a particular topic. Your essays, tutorial and seminar preparation will often require you to know not simply the present state of the law but also its development and such criticisms and suggestions for reform as have been made.

▶ 7.1

To find information on a subject you will need to consult some or all of the following sources:

Acts of Parliament;
Delegated legislation;
EU law, and International Treaties and Conventions;
Cases;
Textbooks;
Journal articles;
Relevant government publications, including Law Commission Reports (especially those which have made suggestions for reform of the law);
Reports and comments in newspapers;
Bills and Parliamentary Debates.

In order to tackle a legal problem, you may need to ask yourself the following questions:

QUESTION: Where can I find a general statement of the law on this subject?
ANSWER: In encyclopedias, such as *Halsbury's Laws* (para.7.3) and in textbooks (para.7.29).

QUESTION: What books are there on this subject?
ANSWER: Consult library catalogues (para.7.29) and bibliographies (para.7.30).

QUESTION: What journal articles have been written on this subject?
ANSWER: Consult indexes to journals (para.5.5).

QUESTION: What cases have there been on this topic?
ANSWER: Use either online databases or print indexes (para.7.8).

QUESTION: What judicial interpretation has been placed on particular words?

ANSWER: Look in *Words and Phrases Legally Defined* and similar works (para.7.19).

QUESTION: Which Acts of Parliament deal with this subject and are in force?
ANSWER: Use online databases (para.7.21) and (para.7.22) or *Halsbury's Statutes* (para.7.24).

QUESTION: Are there any relevant statutory instruments?
ANSWER: Use online databases (para.7.26) or *Halsbury's Statutory Instruments* (para.7.27).

QUESTION: Have there been any government reports or Law Commission reports on this topic?
ANSWER: Use the TSO or UKOP databases (para.6.15 and para.6.16) and the *Annual Reports* of the Law Commission (para.6.17).

QUESTION: Are there any Bills before Parliament which would change the law on this subject? Has the issue been discussed in Parliament?
ANSWER: Consult the "Bills before Parliament" web page (para.6.8) and *Parliamentary Debates* (para.6.11 and para.6.12).

Having mapped out the ground, you can now proceed to tackle these questions. If you encounter any difficulties in carrying out a search on a legal subject, never be afraid to ask the library staff or your lecturer for help. Remember that other students may also be working on the same subject—start work well within the time limits set, otherwise you may discover that the material is unavailable because of high demand.

## LEGAL ENCYCLOPEDIAS

**7.2 ▶** These contain detailed up-to-date statements of the law on a particular subject. The major general legal encyclopedia is *Halsbury's Laws of England*, which is now in its fifth edition. It is a most useful source of information on a wide variety of topics. In addition, there are a number of more specialised encyclopedias, many of them available online, or issued in looseleaf form so that the information can be kept up to date.

### Halsbury's Laws of England
**7.3 ▶** *Halsbury's Laws* covers all areas of English law and is a useful starting point for research on any legal topic. Because it is kept up to date, it has the advantage over textbooks of including recent information.

The encylopedia is available either online from LexisNexis Butterworths (para.2.3), or as 60 print volumes. The fourth edition was completed in 1987 and its volumes periodically updated and re-issued until 2008, which marked the start of the fifth edition. The volume arrangement of the printed encyclopedia also forms the basis of the online version, which features separate on screen updating sections. Recent updates to the printed encyclopeda are handled by a *Cumulative Supplement* and a *"Noter-Up"* binder. The print volumes selected for re-issue are those which have been most affected by changes in the law.

Whether online or in print, *Halsbury's Laws* provides an effective statement of the whole of the law of England and Wales. The print volumes are arranged alphabetically by subject, from "Administrative Law" to "Wills" and these divisions are also present in *Halsbury's Laws* online. Each print volume covers between one and seven subjects. The subjects are in turn divided into numbered paragraphs and each paragraph gives a description of the law relating to a particular topic, together with copious footnote references to relevant statutes and cases. Remember that *Halsbury's Laws* gives a useful summary of the law: you will need to go to other works to find the actual text of an Act of Parliament or law report.

## How to use Halsbury's Laws online

Select the "Commentary" page from the LexisNexis Butterworths home page (para.2.3), to check if your library has a subscription to *Halsbury's Laws of England*. *Halsbury's Laws* can be found using the "Sources" drop-down menu. If your library has subscriptions to other LexisNexis Butterworths works providing commentary on the law, their titles are displayed on the same menu. These might include *Clarke Hall and Morison on Children*, for example, or *Tolley's Employment Law Service*.

▶ 7.4

If you are sure of the area of law you wish to research, one approach is to use the "Browse" link available under the commentary heading. The subject headings found in the print volumes of Halsbury's Laws are then displayed alphabetically. Within each heading, contents listings can be used to work through the hierarchy of sub-headings used in the encyclopedia, until the full text of a particular section is reached. The "British Nationality, Immigration and Asylum" heading might be selected, for example, followed by "Immigration", then further subheadings, in order to reach sections on the law relating to deportation.

However, the subject heading to choose may not be obvious. In this case, a more effective way of using *Halsbury's Laws* is to search the full text of the entire encyclopedia using the "Search Terms" section displayed on the commentary search page. As this is a full text source it is important to consider the different ways in which the subject you are interested in might be described, in order to be sure that you have adequately explored the database (see para.2.11 for more on database searching). Suppose, for example, you wish to discover the current law on bomb hoaxes. How should you phrase your search? Fortunately, the LexisNexis Butterworths commentary sources can be searched using the same proximity limiters that operate in LexisNexis Butterworths generally. This means that you can specify how close you wish terms to be found in the text of the encyclopedia in order to ensure that all potentially relevant results are found. Searching for "bomb w/6 hoax", for example, specifies that the two words should be between six words of each other. This means that text including the phrase "bomb hoax" is found, but also text including the phrase "hoax bomb call", or "hoax call suggesting that a bomb", etc. A further refinement of the search would be to use "hoax!", where the exclamation mark ensures that all words beginning "hoax" are found, e.g. "hoax" and "hoaxes". Using proximity searches in this way ensures that you are not defeated by the variety of natural language.

In this particular case, searching *Halsbury's Laws* for matches to "bomb w/6 hoax!" finds two relevant sections in the encyclopedia. One can be found under the "Criminal Law" heading, on "Improper use of a public electronic communications network", the other, on "Criminal liability for public nuisance", can be found under the "Nuisance" heading. The print index (see para.6.9) only lists the first section.

Once you have found the encyclopedia's description of the law on a subject, it is

**Fig 7.1**
'Example results
page from Halsbury's
Laws online'

Halsbury's Laws of England/NUISANCE (VOLUME 34 (REISSUE))/1. SCOPE OF NUISANCE/
(1) DESCRIPTION AND CLASSIFICATION/(i) Public, Private and Statutory Nuisances/6.
Criminal liability for public nuisance.

## 6. Criminal liability for public nuisance.

There are statutory provisions[1] which impose penalties for nuisances affecting public
health and comfort. However, the common law liability remains, and any person who by
any act unwarranted by law or by any omission to carry out a legal duty endangers the
life, health, property, morals or comfort of the public commits an offence known as public
nuisance[2]. A landowner may be criminally liable for public nuisance if he should have
known of the likely consequences of activities taking place on his land, even if he had no
actual knowledge[3].

[1] See the Environmental Protection Act 1990 ss 79-82 (as amended); and paras 15, 85-87 post. See
also PROTECTION OF ENVIRONMENT AND PUBLIC HEALTH vol 38 (2006 Reissue) para 413 et seq.

[2] Examples are the keeping of a corpse unburied (*R v Vann* (1851) 2 Den 325 at 331, CCR), provided the
person charged has the means for paying for its burial (see CREMATION AND BURIAL vol 10 (Reissue) para
904); the exposure in a public place of a person infected with smallpox (*R v Vantandillo* (1815) 4 M &
S 73), although it would be a defence to an indictment if it could be shown that there was lawful and
sufficient excuse for so doing (*R v Burnett* (1815) 4 M & S 272; and see *Metropolitan Asylum District
Managers v Hill* (1881) 6 App Cas 193 at 204, HL, per Lord Blackburn; *A-G v Nottingham Corpn* [1904]
1 Ch 673); the keeping of explosives or highly inflammable matter in a manner calculated to terrify
the neighbourhood or to do damage to neighbouring property (*R v Lister and Biggs* (1857) Dears & B
209, CCR; *R v Taylor* (1742) 2 Stra 1167; *R v Bennett* (1858) Bell CC 1; and see EXPLOSIVES; for statutes
now regulating the keeping of explosives see EXPLOSIVES); going about a public street armed so as to
terrify the public (*R v Meade* (1903) 19 TLR 540); making obscene telephone calls on many occasions
to numerous women (*R v Johnson* [1997] 1 WLR 367, CA; cf *R v Ireland* [1997] QB 114, [1997] 1 All ER 112,
CA, where there was a series of telephone calls to three women, and when the calls were answered
there was silence, and this was held to constitute assault). The actual, not potential, danger to the
public must be considered, so that a **hoax telephone call about the planting of a bomb was held
not to be a public nuisance**: *R v Madden* [1975] 3 All ER 155, [1975] 1 WLR 1379, CA; cf *R v Soul*
(1980) 70 Cr App Rep 295, CA. As to criminal liability for bomb hoaxes see CRIMINAL LAW, EVIDENCE AND
PROCEDURE vol 11(2) (2006 Reissue) para 853. As to the common law and statutory liability for selling
unwholesome food see FOOD.

[3] *R v Shorrock* [1994] QB 279, [1993] 3 All ER 917, CA. As to where an injunction restraining public or
private nuisance may exceptionally be granted in aid of the criminal law see *City of London Corpn v
Bovis Construction Ltd* [1992] 3 All ER 697, 49 BLR 1, CA; and paras 62 note 2, 92 note 3 post. See also
INJUNCTIONS.

## UPDATE

## 6 Criminal liability for public nuisance

TEXT AND NOTE 2--The common law offence is compatible with the legal certainty requirements
of the common law and the European Convention on Human Rights, but the circumstances in
which there should be resort to the common law offence are now rare in view of the existing
statutory provisions: *R v Goldstein; R v Rimmington* [2005] UKHL 63, [2006] 1 AC 459.

important to check if there is an update section at the end of the main text. The section on criminal liability for public nuisance, for example, includes the statement that the "common law offence is compatible with the legal certainty requirements of the common law and the European Convention on Human Rights". A 2005 case is then cited, *R. v Rimmington* [2005] U.K.H.L., [2006] 1 AC 459.

> **TIPS** • *Be as specific as you can when searching Halsbury's Laws using keywords. Use single words and short phrases and combine them with "AND".*

### How to use Halsbury's Laws in print

▶ 7.5

To use *Halsbury's Laws* in print, start by looking up the subject that interests you in the *Consolidated Index* (Vols 55 and 56). The entry refers you to the appropriate volume number (in bold type) and paragraph number (not page number). The presence of "n" followed by a small number indicates that you are being referred to one of the footnotes at the end of the appropriate paragraph number. For information on the law related to bomb hoaxes, you would turn to Vol.11(1), para.484. Paragraph 484 gives a statement of the law relating to bomb hoaxes, together with footnotes which refer you to relevant statutes. *Halsbury's Laws* also refers you to cases and other sources of information, as appropriate.

Remember that it is possible that the information in the volumes is out of date. New legislation, or other changes in the law, could have made the information incomplete or inaccurate. To find out if there have been any changes in the law since the volumes were published, make a note of the relevant volume and paragraph numbers, and turn to the *Cumulative Supplement*. For example, the information on bomb hoaxes was contained in Vol.11(1), para.484. If you turn to the latest *Cumulative Supplement* (only the latest Supplement should be used) and look up the entry for Vol.11(1), para.484, you can check to see if there have been changes in the law since Vol.11(1) was written. It is therefore important to read the information in the Cumulative Supplement in conjunction with that found in the main volume.

These two volumes bring the information up to date to the end of last year. But have there been changes in the law since then? To find out, turn to the looseleaf *Noter-Up* in Binder 2. The *Noter-Up* is arranged in the same way as the *Cumulative Supplement*, in volume and paragraph number.

## SUMMARY: HOW TO USE HALSBURY'S LAWS IN PRINT

1. Look up the subject in the *Consolidated Index*. This tells you the number of the volume and paragraph which contains the information.
2. Find the relevant volume and paragraph number in the main work.
3. To make sure the information is up to date, consult:
   (a) the *Cumulative Supplement*, and
   (b) the *Noter-Up* in Binder 2, under the relevant volume and paragraph number.

Remember there are four steps in using Halsbury's Laws:

Consolidated Index;
Main Work;

Cumulative Supplement;

Noter-Up.

At the back of each volume of the main work, there are separate indexes to each of the subject areas dealt with in the volume.

The *Monthly Reviews* (published as booklets and filed in Binder 1) can be used as a general means of keeping up with new developments in subjects you are studying since they give, under subject headings, recent changes in the law with summaries of cases, statutes, statutory instruments and other materials. The *Monthly Reviews* are not arranged in the same volume and paragraph order as the main volumes, so in order to find relevant information you will need to look up the subject again in the *Cumulative Index* to the *Reviews* at the back of the Binder. The *Monthly Reviews* are replaced by an *Annual Abridgment*, which summarises all the changes in the law during a particular year. At the beginning of the volume, a section headed "In brief" summarises the major development in the law of each subject during the year. At the beginning of each subject, there is a reference to the main volume of *Halsbury's Laws* which deals with that subject and there is a highly selective list of journal articles written on the subject during the year.

### Specialised encyclopedias

**7.6** ▶ There are a number of specialised encyclopedias which can provide you with an up-to-date statement of the law in particular subject areas. They are particularly useful in subjects such as taxation, where the law changes very rapidly. Many are issued in looseleaf format, so that the information can be updated by the insertion of replacement pages whenever there is a change in the law. Many are also available online or on CD-ROM. *Woodfall: Landlord and Tenant*, for example, can be searched or browsed from the "Commentary" section of Westlaw UK. Other specialised encyclopedias available from Westlaw UK cover topics such as copyright, tort, and sale of goods. The titles you will be able to use will depend on library subscriptions. Specialised encyclopedias from LexisNexis Butterworths cover, among other subject areas, education law, family law and landlord and tenant. As with Westlaw UK, the titles available online from LexisNexis Butterworths will depend on library subscriptions. Check the "Commentary" section of the service to discover the titles available.

When using the looseleaf version of a specialised encyclopedia, you should check the pages near the beginning of the volume which tell you how recent the information is. This will enable you to be certain that the latest supplementary pages have all been inserted. Specialised encyclopedias usually contain an explanation of the law, together with the up-to-date versions of the relevant statutes, statutory instruments and government circulars, and notes of relevant cases. Publishers are now issuing some books for practitioners, such as *Ruoff & Roper: Registered Conveyancing*, in looseleaf format, so that the text can be kept up to date. This is a development of the long-established practice of issuing cumulative supplements in between editions, to update the last edition.

### Precedent books and rule books

**7.7** ▶ These are principally intended for the practitioner. The basic object of precedent books is to provide specimens of wills, conveyances, tenancy agreements or other forms of legal documents which solicitors are called upon to draw up. In addition, there are some precedent books which provide specimens of the types of forms that will be required whenever a case is taken to court. Rule books contain the rules that govern procedure in court, and specimen copies of the various orders and forms used by the courts and by the parties to litigation.

The multi-volume *Encyclopaedia of Forms and Precedents* aims to provide a form for every transaction likely to be encountered by practitioners, except for court forms. The *Encyclopaedia* is also available from LexisNexis Butterworths (para.2.3). The entries are arranged by subject, e.g. "Animals", "Mortgages". Some idea of the wide scope of the work can be obtained by glancing through the subject headings. For instance, the section on animals covers such diverse topics as the sale and leasing of animals, applications for a licence to keep mink or to keep an animals' boarding establishment; a veterinary surgeon's certificate for the destruction of an animal, and the relevant documents prohibiting movement of animals during an outbreak of disease. If you are using the print version, the looseleaf service volume keeps the information up to date. The *Cumulative Index* refers you to the volume (in bold type) and paragraph number that you require. Each individual volume also has its own index. References in the index to paragraph numbers in square brackets refer to precedents: paragraph numbers not enclosed in brackets refer to the preliminary notes. Checklists of procedures to be followed are provided under some subject headings.

*Atkins Court Forms* is a complementary publication, covering the procedure in civil courts and tribunals. Again, the volume is available from LexisNexis Butterworths. The print volume on divorce, for instance, contains all the necessary documents needed during the court action, together with a detailed list of the steps to be taken and the forms required at each stage. The volumes are reissued from time to time to incorporate new material. An annual supplement keeps the information up to date. The *Consolidated Index* is also published yearly.

There are many precedent books dealing with specific areas of the law, e.g. the looseleaf *Jackson & Powell: Professional Liability Precedents*. In addition, some textbooks designed for practitioners will include precedents.

The rules and procedures governing various courts are set out in a number of places. Sweet & Maxwell's *White Book* service and *Bullen & Leek & Jacob's Precedents of Pleading* are available online from Westlaw UK (para.2.4) and can be searched or browsed from the "Commentary" page. *Archbold: Criminal Pleading, Evidence and Practice* is used by those engaged in criminal work. It is also available from the Westlaw UK "Commentary" page.

The coloured pages in each issue of the *Law Society Gazette* are of particular interest to practitioners. These often include specimen forms and precedents, and details of Home Office circulars and practice directions. Practice directions are also published in the major series of law reports, e.g. the *All England Law Reports* and the *Weekly Law Reports*.

## TRACING CASES ON A SUBJECT

Cases on a particular subject can be traced by consulting the following sources.     ▶ **7.8**

The Westlaw UK Subject/Keyword search (para.7.9);
Full-text case law databases (para.7.10);
Databases of recent judgments (para.7.11);

*Current Law* (para.7.12 and para.7.13);
*The Digest* (para.7.14 and para.7.15);
*Halsbury's Laws of England* (para.7.4);
Indexes to individual series of law reports (para.7.16);
Updates on recent cases (para.7.17);
Indexes to articles in legal journals (para.5–5);
Relevant textbooks (para.7.29).

### How to use the Westlaw UK Subject/Keyword search

**7.9** ▶ To find cases on a subject using the Westlaw UK "Cases" search, it can help greatly to restrict your search, so that only keywords or subject terms are searched. The database used in the cases search contains abstracts of almost all England and Wales cases reported since 1947, whether present in full text or not. These are the abstracts which appear in print in the *Current Law Year Books* (para.7.13). Standard subject terms and keywords are added to the abstracts, and your search can be restricted to search only those terms. Abstracts are available for an extremely wide range of cases and it is highly likely that the cases found using abstract keywords will be highly relevant to your subject search. Suppose, for example, that you wish to find cases that might concern privacy and human rights (you might already have found some relevant journal articles using Westlaw UK "Journals" search as suggested in para.5.6). If you were to use keyword search terms such as "privacy" and "human rights" in a standard "Free Text" search, your results list would contain numerous minor and incidental mentions of the search words, making it difficult to find relevant cases. The inclusion of both "human rights" and "privacy" in the added keywords for a case, on the other hand, means that the case is much more likely to be of interest.

To restrict the cases search to keywords, select the "Advanced Search" from the "Cases" search page. Then enter your search words using the "Subject/Keyword" search box. To continue with the privacy and human rights example, a "Subject/Keyword" search finds 60 cases. Just over 1,000 cases are found using a "Free text" search. However, the cases found are still quite wide ranging, and you might then decide to narrow the search using another standard keyword phrase, such as "right to respect for private and family life". If you are unsure which keywords to use, try a "Free text" keyword search first and note the keywords and keyword phrases which appear in "Case Analysis" entries of some of the cases that seem relevant. If you were interested in cases related to the *Douglas v Hello* cases mentioned in para.3.15, for example, keywords such as "breach of confidence", "celebrities" or "media" will prove relevant, along with "privacy".

**TIPS** • *Only search using the Westlaw UK "Subject/Keyword" search when you have already identified standard subject and keyword terms for a subject.*

Using the Cases search in this way allows you to explore subject areas and find relevant cases, many of which can then be found in full text.

### How to use full-text databases to find case law by subject

**7.10** ▶ The full text databases of case law found in LexisNexis Butterworths (para.2.3) and Westlaw UK (para.2.4) provide the largest archives of law reports and judgments available for subject searching. Your library may also have particular series of law reports available from Justis Publishing (para.2.6) in particular, constituting additional potential sources of case law. If you wish to include the widest possible range of relatively recent judgments, the judgments on the BAILII website (para.2.13) should also not be ignored. The nature of law reporting means that a particular judgment is likely to appear in more than one of these databases. However, there remain specialist law reports whose judgments only appear online in one of these sources. As a result, a comprehensive approach to subject searching using full text sources of case law, requires that you repeat your search on all of the databases to which you have access.

For all of these databases, the process of searching is straightforward. They all have some form of free text search box in which you can enter your search words and they accept the search syntax described in para.2.11, in particular the use of "AND", "OR" etc. to combine search words. Some form of proximity searching will also be available, ensuring that your search words must occur close together in the text being searched.

If you are using a full text database of case law, the most important thing to remember is that you must be as specific as possible in your choice of search words. As noted in para.2.11, if you enter general terms such as "copyright" or even "copyright AND software", you will obtain as a search result, either a list of the many thousands of cases in which the word "copyright" appears on its own, or the many hundreds of cases in which both the word "copyright" and the word "software" appear, but not necessarily in any proximity to each other. Most databases halt a search which would retrieve a very large number of cases. A corollary is that you need a good understanding of what it is you are researching in order to be able to home in on the important keywords. It makes sense to use full text databases as the last stage in your subject searching. Try looking at likely textbooks before you make your search, in order to select key terms to use. *Halsbury's Laws of England* (para.7.3), either online or in print, can also help you in the initial stages of a subject search, clarifying terminology and listing key cases.

You should think of different ways your topic is likely to be discussed in a judgment. For the most part you are only searching the text of the words used in the judgment and you will need to think about the different ways the same basic issue can be expressed. Ensure also that you use the symbol or "search operator" for the database that specifies that your keywords must be found close to each other in the long text of a judgment. Many databases allow "NEAR" to specify a standard proximity, LexisNexis Butterworths uses "w/" so that "w/6" specifies within six words. The "w/" proximity operator can also be used in Westlaw UK. Once you have considered various possibilities and tried different searches, the time will come to read the law reports you have found and see which cases they have cited.

> **TIPS** • *Use textbooks or Halsbury's Laws to clarify the keywords you should use when searching full text databases of case law.*

### How to use databases of recent judgments

The sources of recent judgments described in para.3.20 provide a means of searching for judgments from a range of UK courts. BAILII, Casetrack and Lawtel all allow the full text of judgments to be searched using keywords. The need to decide your key search words and think of alternative ways in which the same idea can be expressed applies to these databases just as much as it does to the databases noted in para.7.10. Keywords and phrases can be combined and "proximity" searches are possible. Check the search and help screens of the databases you are using for further information on how to combine search words.

▶ 7.11

### How to use the Current Law Monthly Digest

**7.12** ▶ *Current Law* is published monthly under the title *Current Law Monthly Digest*. The main part is arranged by subject and under each subject heading is given a summary of recent cases on the subject, new statutes and statutory instruments, government reports and recent books and journal articles on that subject. Full details are given to enable you to trace the cases and other materials mentioned in your own library. A page from the Monthly Digest is shown on p.119. On this page alone, articles are mentioned (item 388), a case is summarised (item 389) and a statutory instrument is outlined (item 387).

At the back of each issue is a Table of Cases which contains a list of all the cases which have been reported during the current year. It is therefore only necessary to look at the Table of Cases in the latest issue of the *Current Law Monthly Digest* to trace a case reported at any time during the year. (This list of cases brings the information in the *Current Law Case Citators* up to date (para.3.16)).

The *Current Law Monthly Digest* also contains a subject index. Again it is cumulative, so it is only necessary to consult the index in the latest month's issue. This enables you to trace any development in the law during the current year. The reference given, e.g. Feb 80, is to the appropriate monthly issue (in this example, the February issue) and the item number in the issue, i.e. item 80. If the reference is followed by an S (e.g. Jan 821S), the item contains Scottish material.

The Table of Cases provides a list of reports of cases. Suppose, however, that you know that there has been a recent case on the subject, but you do not know the name of the parties. In this instance, you can trace the cases on the subject during the current year by looking in the cumulative Subject Index in the latest issue of the *Current Law Monthly Digest*. The Subject Index can also help when you have spelt the name of the parties incorrectly or have an incomplete reference.

### How to use the Current Law Year Books

**7.13** ▶ The issues of the *Current Law Monthly Digest* are replaced by an annual volume, the *Current Law Year Book*.

The *Year Book* is arranged by subject, in the same way as the *Monthly Digest*, and contains a summary of all the cases, legislation and other developments in that subject during the year. Lists of journal articles and books written on a subject during the year are printed at the back of the volume. (The 1956 *Year Book* contains a list of journal articles published between 1947 and 1956.)

Since 1991, the *Current Law Year Book* contains Scottish material as well as that from England. Before then, there was a separate Scottish version, called the *Scottish Current Law Year Book*. Despite the name, this included all the English material, plus a separate section at the back of the volume containing Scottish developments during the year. The Scottish section remains separate from the English material in the *Current Law Year Book* and there are separate indexes to the two sections.

At the back of the 1976 *Year Book*, there is a Subject Index to all the entries in all the *Year Books* from 1947 to 1976. Entries give the last two digits of the year, and a reference to the individual item number within that year's volume, e.g. 69/3260 is a reference to item 3260 in the 1969 *Year Book*. Entries which have no year in front of them will be found in the *Current Law Consolidation 1947–1951*. Cumulative indexes were also published in the 1986 and 1989 *Year*

# SPORT

**387. Football–Football grounds–Seating**

FOOTBALL SPECTATORS (SEATING) ORDER 2008, SI 2008/1749; made under the Football Spectators Act 1989 s.11. In force: July 25, 2008; £3.00.

This Order directs the Football Licensing Authority to include in any licence to admit spectators to the Liberty Stadium, Swansea; the Keepmoat Stadium, Doncaster; and the Don Valley Stadium, Sheffield, a condition imposing the requirements that only seated accommodation is to be provided for spectators at a designated football match and that spectators shall only be admitted to watch such a match from seated accommodation. In order to admit spectators to a designated football match, which would include any association football match played at those grounds, a licence is required under the Football Spectators Act 1989.

**388. Articles**

Ability matters *(Lyons, Christina; Carr, Craig)*: N.L.J. 2008, 158(7331), 1064. Explains the events which led to the restrictions on athletes with intellectual disabilities from competing in the Paralympic Games after the games held in Sydney in 2000 and questions whether such athletes should be allowed to compete in the 2012 Paralympics to be held in London. Highlights Government initiatives to encourage schoolchildren to become involved in Olympic sports in preparation for the 2012 Olympics and whether the exclusion of intellectually disabled children from the School Games is discriminatory. Calls for agreement on eligibility criteria and compliance provisions.

The White Paper on Sport as an exercise in "Better Regulation" *(Weatherill, Stephen)*: I.S.L.J. 2008, 1/2, 3-8. Comments on the European Commission White Paper on Sport in light of the EC initiative to simplify rules, reduce compliance burdens and base regulation on impact assessment. Discusses to what extent sporting organisations' autonomy in sporting matters should be balanced with EC intervention, and sport should be treated as a special case.

Will the new WADA Code plug all the gaps? Will there be by-catch? *(Marshall, John; Hale, Amy Catherine)*: I.S.L.J. 2008, 1/2, 37-42. Discusses the revised World Anti-Doping Agency (WADA) Code against drug abuse by athletes in force January 1, 2009. Considers the elements of flexibility introduced to the Code, athletes' duty to report their whereabouts for out-of-competition testing, athletes' privacy, atypical findings in drug tests, breach of a sanction, sanctions on teams, rights of appeal, and recreational drugs. Examines whether the revised Code will prevent drug cheats from avoiding sanctions and increase the risk of sanctions for innocent athletes.

# SUCCESSION

**389. Administration of estates–Burials and cremation–Dispute about form or place of funeral or interment–Reasonable wishes and requirements of family and friends**

'The court was required to determine whether the body of the deceased (D) should be released to his father (F) or to his mother (M). D had died intestate in a road traffic accident. M and F were divorced. F lived in Worcester but wanted D to be buried in Kington whilst M wanted D to be cremated in Worcester where she lived. D had been brought up in Worcester but for some eight years before his death he had made his home, his work and his personal life with his former wife and then with his fiancee and his brother and friends in the Kington area. M maintained that she still had a relationship with D whilst F disputed the existence of that relationship. M maintained that the journey to Kington to visit D's grave would be problematic as she did not drive whereas F lived in Worcester and could visit D's grave without difficulty.

*Held*: Judgment accordingly. In the instant case, the factors that were relevant in determining the form or place of the funeral or interment were the deceased's own wishes and the reasonable wishes and requirements of family and friends who were left, *Grandison (Deceased), Re, The Times*, July 10, 1989 considered. The place with

**Fig 7.2**
'Example page from the Current Law Monthly Digest'

*Books*. These indexes, together with the *Year Books* since 1989 and the latest *Current Law Monthly Digest*, provide complete coverage of any developments in the law of that subject since 1947.

*Master Volumes* were published in the 1956, 1961, 1966 and 1971 *Year Books*. These volumes contain, under the usual subject headings, detailed entries for all developments during the year in which they were published, together with a summary of the developments during the previous four years. References are given to enable you to trace the full details in the appropriate *Current Law Year Book*. Thus it is possible, by using the *Master Volumes* and the *Current Law Consolidation 1947–1951*, to see at a glance a summary of every entry that has appeared in *Current Law* on a particular subject over a five-year period.

## SUMMARY: HOW TO USE CURRENT LAW IN PRINT

(1) If you know the name of a case and want to find out where it has been reported and whether the case has subsequently been judicially considered, consult:
the *Current Law Case Citator* volumes (see para.3.16); and
the Table of Cases in the latest *Current Law Monthly Digest*.

(2) To trace any developments (cases, statutes, etc.) on a particular subject, consult:
The Cumulative Index covering 1947–1976 at the back of the 1976 *Current Law Year Book*;
the Cumulative Index at the back of the 1986 *Year Book* covering the years 1972–1986;
the Cumulative Index at the back of the 1989 *Year Book* covering the years 1987–1989;
the Indexes in the back of the *Year Books* since 1989; and
the Subject Index in the latest issue of the *Current Law Monthly Digest*.

(3) To obtain a general view of developments in a topic over a number of years, consult:
the *Current Law Consolidation 1947–1951*;
the *Master Volumes* (1956, 1961, 1966, 1971 *Year Books*);
all the *Year Books* published since the last *Master Volume* was issued; and
all the issues of the *Current Law Monthly Digest* for this year.

(4) To trace books and journal articles on a subject, look in the back of the 1956 *Year Book* and each subsequent Year Book and in the *Current Law Monthly Digests* under the appropriate subject heading. There are, however, quicker and more comprehensive sources for tracing journals (para.5.5) and books (para.7.29 et seq.).

Remember that *Current Law* only contains information on cases reported or mentioned in court since 1947 and other developments in the law since 1947. To trace earlier cases, use *The Digest*.

### The Digest

**7.14** ▶ *The Digest* (formerly known as the *English and Empire Digest*) contains summaries of cases that have appeared in law reports from the thirteenth century to the present day, arranged in subject order. It enables you to trace cases of any date that deal with your particular subject. In addition to English cases, reports of Irish, Scottish and many Commonwealth cases are included, together with cases on EU law. These are printed in smaller type to enable them to be easily distinguishable from English cases.

For each case, a summary of the decision is given, followed by the name of the case, and a list of places where the case is reported. The subsequent judicial history of the case is also shown, in the annotations section. A list of the abbreviations used for law reports will be found in the front of Vol.1 and also in the front of the *Cumulative Supplement*.

### How to use The Digest to trace cases on a subject

To find cases on a particular subject using *The Digest*, start by looking at the multi-volume ▶ **7.15** *Index*. This is re-issued every year. The *Index* includes both broad subject categories and highly specific entries for particular subjects. These can take you directly to a summary of the judgment in a particular case. Suppose you are interested in finding human rights cases related to the European Convention right to manifest religion or belief. You will first need to try likely subject entries in the *Index*. A number of relevant cases will be found, for example, under the main "Freedom of Conscience" heading, grouped under a European Convention on Human Rights sub-heading (see the illustration on p.122). Of these, you might be particularly interested in the case noted under "religious and philosophical convictions". The reference for "religious and philosophical convictions" gives a volume number, and notes the relevant subject heading within the volume:

26(3) H Rghts [i.e. Human Rights] 560.

In the main volumes, cases are listed in number order for the volume under appropriate subject headings. Turn to case number 560 to see a summary of *R (on the application of K) v Newham LBC* (2002) Times, February 28 (see the illustration on p.123). Scots, Irish and Commonwealth cases are grouped together at the end of each section within the volume.

After finding the relevant case in the main volumes, you should now check to see if there have been more recent cases on the subject since the volume was written. To do this, consult the *Cumulative Supplement*. Make a note of the volume number, subject heading and case number(s) in the main volumes which contain relevant information. Now turn to the *Cumulative Supplement* and look to see if there is an entry for that volume, subject heading and case number. If there is an entry, this will provide information on any later cases relevant to the subject area. A number of cases are, in fact, noted against Vol 26(3) 560 and these are noted as 560a, 560b etc. (see the illustration on p.124). All these cases are more significant than the case summarised in the main volume. 560b, for example, is the case, *R (on the application of Begum) v Head Teacher and Governors of Denbigh High School* [2006] U.K.H.L. 15; [2006] 2 W.L.R. 719 on the right to wear particular clothing (a jilbab) in a school for religious reasons. A further line notes a case which applied the ruling in the Begum case:

**Apld** *Miss Behavin' Ltd v Belfast City Council* [2007] 3 All ER 1007.

The *Cumulative Supplement* is revised annually; the front cover tells you how recent the information is. If you are looking for new cases on a particular subject, within the last few months, then *The Digest* is not sufficiently up to date and you should use online sources (para.7.8) or print publications, such as *Current Law*, the latest *Pink Index* to the *Law Reports* or the *Monthly Reviews* in *Halsbury's Laws of England*.

**Fig 7.3**
'Example page from
The Digest Index'

*R (on the appln of Ullah) v Special Adjudicator* (2002) Times, 5 September

**559 Recognition of religious bodies — Refusal by state to recognise church divided from recognised church — State's duty to remain impartial**

Under Moldovan law, religions practised in Moldovan territory had to be recognised by the government and, accordingly, the applicant church sought official recognition. Recognition was refused on the basis that the church was a schismatic part of a recognised Moldovan church rather than a distinct religious body, and that the state authorities should not intervene in the dispute. The applicant church complained that this refusal violated its members' freedom of religion guaranteed by the European Convention on Human Rights art 9. *Held*, the freedom of religion implied the freedom to manifest one's religion, but it did not protect every act motivated or inspired by a religion. Where several religions co-existed in a population, it may be necessary to impose restrictions on this freedom in order to reconcile the different interests of different groups. However, the state had a duty to remain neutral and impartial in the exercise of its regulatory power, and should not seek to remove tensions in a divided society by doing away with pluralism. The Moldovan government had failed in this duty by considering that the applicant church was not a new religious body and making its recognition dependent on the will of a recognised ecclesiastical authority. In a democratic society, the state did not need to take steps to ensure that religious communities were subject to a single governing body. Similarly, where the exercise of the right to freedom of religion was made subject to a system of prior approval, intervention by a recognised ecclesiastical authority in the approval procedure could not be reconciled with art 9. Judgment would be given accordingly.

*Metropolitan Church of Bessarabia v Moldova (Application 45701/99)* (2002) 35 EHRR 306, European Court of Human Rights

**560 Religious and philosophical convictions — Right to education — Allocation of places in schools — Parental preference**

The respondent local education authority provided a pamphlet to parents setting out its admissions policy. One criteria for selection was the preference of parents for a single-sex school. The applicant, a devout Muslim, indicated that he wished to send his daughter to a local single-sex school, but his application was rejected on the basis that it would be against the efficient use of resources. The applicant sought judicial review of that decision on the ground that the respondent ought to have taken into account

his religious convictions. *Held*, it was accepted that the applicant's religious convictions were genuine and fell within the European Convention on Human Rights First Protocol art 2, which provided that member states had to respect the right of parents to ensure education in conformity with their own religious convictions. Since the coming into force of the Human Rights Act 1998, religious convictions were to be taken into account and there was no doubt that the applicant's religious convictions were an important consideration in the instant case. Further, it had to be borne in mind that under the School Standards and Framework Act 1998 s 86(1)(*b*), parents had to be enabled to supply reasons for their preferences. In order to comply with the Convention First Protocol art 2, the state was obliged to take some positive action. First, the respondent had to recognise religious convictions and take them into account in formulating its admissions policy. It followed that there ought to be a means of recognising religious convictions. In that respect, all that was needed was space to include reasons on the relevant application form. In the instant case, the respondent had failed to fulfil the requirements of the Convention First Protocol art 2. Accordingly, the decision would be quashed and remitted for reconsideration.

*R (on the appln of K) v Newham London Borough Council* (2002) Times, 28 February

**561 Right to freedom of thought, conscience and religion — Application to company**

A profit-making corporation can neither enjoy nor rely on the right to freedom of thought, conscience and religion guaranteed by the European Convention on Human Rights art 9(1).

*Company X v Switzerland (Application 7865/17)* (1981) 16 DR 85; (1981) 16 Decisions and Reports 85, European Commission of Human Rights

**562 Right to freedom of conscience — Pacifism — Objection to payment of taxes directed towards military purposes**

The applicant, a pacifist, did not wish any part of her income tax to be used for military purposes. She alleged that the fact that this was not allowed in the UK amounted to a violation of the European Convention on Human Rights art 9 (right to freedom of conscience): *Held* in declaring the complaint inadmissible, art 9 primarily protected the sphere of personal beliefs and religious creeds together with acts which were intimately linked to these attitudes such as acts of worship or devotion which were aspects of the practise of a religion or a belief in a generally recognisable form. However, in protecting this personal sphere art 9 did not necessarily guarantee the right to behave in the public sphere in a way which was dictated by such a belief, as, for

**Fig 7.4**

'Example page from The Digest Vol 26(3)'

**Fig 7.5**
'Example page
from the Digest
Cumulative
Supplement

**560b Freedom to manifest religion or belief — Pupil believing wearing of particular clothing required for religious reasons — Particular clothing not within school uniform code — Pupil refusing to attend school without particular clothing — School refusing to allow pupil to attend without adhering to uniform code — Whether unlawful denial of pupil's freedom to manifest religion or belief**

The defendant school was a maintained secondary school for children of both sexes. The school's uniform requirements for girls included a shalwar kameeze which was seen as satisfying the religious requirements that Muslim girls should wear modest dress, and girls from other faith groups, such as Hindus and Sikhs, also wore it. The school went to some lengths to explain its dress code to prospective parents and pupils. The claimant, who was a pupil at the school, adhered to the dress code for some two years. She later came to believe that the shalwar kameeze was not an appropriate form of dress for herself as a Muslim girl who had reached puberty. She, therefore, attended the school dressed in a jilbab, a form of dress which concealed the shape of her arms and legs. She was told to change into proper school uniform. She refused to attend school unless she was wearing a jilbab and the school refused to allow her to attend unless she complied with the uniform code. She was told of other schools where she could wear a jilbab, but her application to one of those was rejected, and she did not seek a place at the others. She applied for judicial review of the decision of the head teacher and the governors not to admit her to the school while wearing a jilbab. She argued that she had been unlawfully excluded and unlawfully denied her right, inter alia, to manifest her religion or beliefs guaranteed by art 9(1) of the European Convention for the Protection of Human Rights and Fundamental Freedoms 1950 (as set out in Sch 1 to the Human Rights Act 1998) and which was, by art 9(2) of the convention, subject only to such limitations as were prescribed by law and were necessary in a democratic society for, inter alia, the protection of the rights and freedoms of others. The judge dismissed her application, but the Court of Appeal made a declaration that her rights under art 9 had been infringed. The school appealed. The main question for consideration was whether the claimant's freedom to manifest her belief by her dress was subject to interference within the meaning of art 9(2) and, if so, whether such interference was justified under that provision. *Held*, the appeal would be allowed for the following reasons.

(1) Per *Lord Bingham of Cornhill*, *Lord Hoffmann* and *Lord Scott of Foscote*. Article 9 of the Convention did not require that one should be allowed to manifest one's religion at any time and place of one's own choosing. It was settled law that the right to manifest belief was qualified and that what constituted interference would depend on all the circumstances of the case, including the extent to which in the circumstances an individual could reasonably expect to be at liberty to manifest her beliefs in practice. Strasbourg jurisprudence made it clear that in the circumstances of the instant case there had been no infringement of art 9. The claimant's family had chosen the school for her with knowledge of its uniform requirements. She could have sought the help of the school and the local education authority in solving the problem. They would no doubt have advised her that if she was firm in her belief, she should change schools. Indeed, there was nothing to stop her from going to a school where she was allowed to wear a jilbab. It followed that there had been no interference with the claimant's right to manifest her belief in practice or observance.

(2) Per *Lord Nicholls of Birkenhead* and *Baroness Hale of Richmond*. The school's refusal to allow the claimant to wear a jilbab at school did interfere with her art 9 right to manifest her religion, but the school's decision was objectively justified. It had the legitimate aim of protecting the rights and freedoms of others.

*R (on the appln of Begum) v Head Teacher and Governors of Denbigh High School* [2006] UKHL 15; [2006] 2 All ER 487; [2006] 2 WLR 719; [2006] 1 FCR 613; [2006] NLJR 552; 150 Sol Jo LB 399; [2006] 4 LRC 543; [2006] All ER (D) 320 (Mar); (2006) Times, 23 March, HL

**Apld** Miss Behavin' Ltd v Belfast City Council [2007] 3 All ER 1007

**560c Freedom to manifest religion or belief — Ban on wearing Islamic headscarf in university — Author excluded from university for refusing to remove headscarf worn in accordance with her beliefs — Whether author's right to freedom of thought, conscience and religion violated**

The author was a student at the Tashkent State Institute. As a practising Muslim, she dressed appropriately, in accordance with the tenets of her religion, and in her second year of studies started to wear a headscarf. The institute adopted new regulations, under which students had no right to wear religious dress. The author was requested to sign the new regulations, which she did although she refused to remove her headscarf. Subsequently the deputy dean called her to his office during a lecture and showed her the new regulations again and asked her to take off her headscarf. She refused to do so and was excluded from the institute because of her

One consequence of putting the cases in number order is that case numbers change when a volume is re-issued. This is because additional cases have been inserted into the sequence. In the back of each volume of *The Digest* is a Reference Adaptor. Wherever you find a cross-reference to a volume which has been reissued very recently, you need to look in the volume's Reference Adaptor to convert the reference. The Reference Adaptor consists of a long list of all the case numbers in the old volume, alongside the number which replaces it in the reissued volume.

## SUMMARY: TRACING CASES ON A SUBJECT IN THE DIGEST

1. Look up the subject in the *Index*. This will refer you to the volume, subject heading and case numbers where cases on that subject can be found.
2. To see if there have been any more recent cases on the same subject, look in the *Cumulative Supplement* under the relevant volume, subject heading and case number. This will provide you with up-to-date information.

### How to use individual indexes to series of Law Reports to trace cases on a subject

If the facilities in your library are limited, you may need to use the indexes to individual series ▶ 7.16
of law reports to trace relevant cases on a subject. The most useful is the *Law Reports Index* (para.3.18) because it covers a number of other important series in addition to the *Law Reports*. Indexes are available covering each 10-year period since 1951 and supplementary indexes (an annual *Red Index* and the latest *Pink Index*: para.3.18) bring the information up to date to within a few weeks. The *Law Reports Index* is easier to use than *The Digest*, but remember that it covers fewer series of English law reports and no foreign cases.

In addition to the *Law Reports Index* (and the series of *Digests*, which preceded it, going back to 1865) there are indexes to other series, such as the *All England Law Reports*, which have a *Consolidated Tables and Index* in three volumes, covering 1937–2007. This is kept up to date by supplements (para.3.18). In addition, there is an Index volume to the *All England Law Reports Reprint*, which includes a subject index to selected cases from 1558–1935.

### Finding updates on recent cases by subject

The "Current Awareness" section of LexisNexis Butterworths provides summaries of a wide ▶ 7.17
range of recent judgments. These can be found by entering keywords in the "Search terms" box on the current awareness search page, or by clicking the "Add topics to search" link. The Add topics option allows subject headings to be selected from a hierarchy, e.g. first "Banking", and then more specifically, "International Banking", within the Banking heading. Selected search terms are then entered into a "Topics You Added" search box. Searches can also be limited by period, to find results for the previous month, six months, etc. The resulting search returns results from case digests, along with summaries of legislation and journal articles. To view case summaries only, click the "Cases" link on the left margin of the search page.

A similar approach can be used with the Westlaw UK "Current Awareness" search. Keywords can be entered in the "Free text" search box, or selected from a subject hierarchy using the "List of terms" link. The standard search is for current awareness items added in the last 90 days; alternative date ranges can be selected using "Advanced Search". To limit searches so that only case summaries are found, click the "By Document Type" entry under

"Browse" and select "Cases". Searches using the "Free Text" and "Subject/Keyword" boxes are then restricted to cases only.

The summaries of journal and newspaper articles available from the current awareness sections of both LexisNexis Butterworths and Westlaw UK should not themselves be over-looked as a route to the identification of recent cases. To read the text of the articles, you need to turn to a source such as the Nexis service for newspapers (para.5.22), or the various online and print sources of journal articles (para.5.3 and para.5.4). However the citation for the case included in the summary of the journal or newspaper articles may be all you need. The case itself can then be located directly.

### Tracing the Subsequent Judicial History of a Case

**7.18** Judges often rely on earlier cases to support the reasons they have given for a decision, and from time to time a judge will review the case law in an attempt to explain the principles stated in earlier cases, or to use them as a springboard to create a new application of the principles. Occasionally a case will be "distinguished" in order that the judge will not feel obliged to follow it. Less frequently, a superior court will state that an earlier case was wrongly decided, and will overrule it, so that the principles laid down in the case will not be followed thereafter.

The treatment a case receives when it is subsequently judicially considered has a direct bearing on its importance and reliability. For example, if in an essay you cited as an authority the common law rules laid down in a particular case, you would be embarrassed to discover that the rules were later abolished by statute. Similarly, you should check that a particular case you have referred to, e.g. *Gillick v West Norfolk and Wisbech AHA* [1984] 1 All E.R. 365, was not later reversed on appeal to the House of Lords, as happened in *Gillick v West Norfolk and Wisbech AHA* [1985] 1 All E.R. 533. Consequently, you must be alert to the need to trace the full judicial history of a particular case.

The simplest way to do this is to use the "Case Analysis" information available from the Westlaw UK "Cases" search (para.3.15). The well-known old case *Carlill v Carbolic Smoke Ball Co.*, for example, can be found using the "Party Names" search because it has been considered several times since 1947 (the case itself dates from 1893). The "Cases citing this Case" section of the case analysis page for *Carlill v Carbolic Smoke Ball Co.* shows that the decision in the case has been most recently applied by *Bowerman v Association of British Travel Agents Ltd* [1996] C.L.C. 451. It was also distinguished in *Pharmaceutical Society of Great Britain v Boots Cash Chemist (Southern) Ltd* [1952] 2 Q.B. 795. The most recent case to consider *Carlill* was *Bardissy v D'Souza* [2003] W.T.L.R. 929. The case analysis suggests, in other words, that the case is still of relevance. The case analysis page also gives a citation for a 2008 journal article in the "Journal Articles" section, which discusses the case in the context of contracts of indemnity, gambling and insurance contracts, J.B.L., 2008, 5, 432–447.

If you were using the print volumes of the *Current Law Case Citator* the same informa-tion could be traced by checking first the volume covering 1947 to 1976. This gives page and volume numbers to entries in the *Current Law Year Book* after the case citations. These enable you to check the *Year Book* summaries for cases which have applied, approved, distinguished or considered the *Carlill* case between 1947 and 1976. Subsequent volumes of the *Current Law Case Citator* then need to be checked in order to discover *Year Book* summaries of the 1996 and 2003 cases mentioned earlier.

### How to Find Words and Phrases Judicially Considered

The meaning of words is of great importance to lawyers. The interpretation of statutes and documents may hinge upon the meaning of a single word. For example, does "day" in banking terms mean 24 hours, or does it end at the close of working hours? How should the words "on a road" be interpreted in the Road Traffic Act 1988?

▶ **7.19**

Two specialised dictionaries record the courts' decisions on problems such as these. *Stroud's Judicial Dictionary* provides the meaning of words as defined in the case law and in statutes. *Words and Phrases Legally Defined* is a similar publication; both are kept up to date by supplements.

The *Law Reports Index* includes a heading "Words and Phrases", in which full details of cases defining a particular word or phrase are given (see the figure on p.128).

The *Current Law Monthly Digests* and *Year Books* also include an entry "Words and Phrases" and the Index to the *All England Law Reports* and the Consolidated Index to *Halsbury's Laws* have a similar heading.

### How to Trace Statutes on a Subject

Full-text databases (para.7–21);
Other online sources (para.7–22);
*Halsbury's Statutes of England* (para.7–23);
*Current Law* (para.7–24).

▶ **7.20**

### How to use full-text databases of legislation

The LexisNexis Butterworths "Legislation" search (para.4.13) and the Westlaw UK "Legislation" search (para.4.14) can both be used to trace statutes in force by subject. The Justis UK Statutes database (para.4.9) adds the ability to search for statutes no longer in force.

▶ **7.21**

Subject searching these databases works best, however, when you already know the wording of a section of an Act, or of a phrase unique to a piece of legislation; there are no added keywords or subject links that might help guide you to a piece of legislation. As a result the advice given in section para.7.10, on keyword searching full text case law databases, remains valid when searching the legislation databases. It makes sense to turn to textbooks and other secondary searches first if you are taking a subject approach to legislation, in order to have a firm grasp of the key terms before you make use of legislation databases.

Suppose, for example, you are reviewing the legislation in force on an aspect of the law of civil partnerships. Even though legislation in this area is straightforward, simply typing "civil partnerships" finds 397 results. Remember that these databases list their results section by section, so all the sections of Acts that feature the word "civil partnership" will be displayed (though there is only one Act in this case).

However, you may have clarified in advance that it is the recognition of overseas relationships that interests you. In this case, if you are using the LexisNexis Butterworths "Legislation" search for example, put "civil partnerships" in the title search box to search for legislation with "civil partnership" in the title and combine this with the words "overseas relationship" in the

WORDS AND PHRASES—*continued*

*"Balanced"*—Education Act 1996, s 407(1)
R (Dimmock) v Secretary of State for Education and Skills, Burton J [2008] 1 All ER 367
*"Bankruptcy debt"*—Insolvency Act 1986, s 382(1)
R (Balding) v Secretary of State for Work and Pensions, CA [2008] 1 WLR 564
*"Beneficiary"*—Judicial Trustees Act 1896, s 1 (as amended)
Thomas and Agnes Carvel Foundation v Carvel, Lewison J [2008] 2 WLR 1234
*"Beneficiary"*—Council Regulation (EC) No 44/2001/, art 5(6) Gomez v Gomez-Monche Vives,
Morgan J [2008] 3 WLR 309
*"Breach of duty"*—Limitation Act 1980, s 32(2) (as amended) Giles v Rhind (No 2),
CA [2008] Bus LR 1103
*"Cannot be found"*—Criminal Justice Act 2003, s 116(2)(d) R v Adams,
CA [2008] 1 Cr App R 430
*"Circles specialised in the sector concerned"*—Council Regulation (EC) No 6/2002, art 7(1)
Green Lane Products Ltd v PMS International Group Ltd, Lewison J [2008] Bus LR 338
*"Civil . . . matter"*—Council Regulation (EC) No 44/2001, art 1(1)
Grovit v De Nederlandsche Bank NV, CA [2008] 1 WLR 51
*"Civil matter"*—Council Regulation (EC) No 2201/2003, art 1
Proceedings brought by C (Case C-435/06), ECJ [2008] 3 WLR 419
*"Civil matters relating to . . . parental responsibility"*—Council Regulation (EC) No 2201/2003, art 1
Proceedings brought by C (Case C-435/06), ECJ [2008] 3 WLR 419
*"Claims made against a member firm . . . insured"*—Insurance policy
Brit Syndicates Ltd v Italaudit SpA,
HL(E) [2008] 2 All ER 1140; [2008] 2 All ER (Comm) 1
*"Clerical error"*—Administration of Justice Act 1982, s 20(1) Pengelly v Pengelly,
Judge Hodge QC [2008] 3 WLR 66
*"Collection"*—Powers of Criminal Courts (Sentencing) Act 2000, s 140(1)
Director of Public Prosecutions v Greenacre, DC [2008] 1 WLR 438
*"Compensation"*—Civil Liability (Contribution) Act 1978, s 6(1)
Charter plc v City Index Ltd (Gawler, Part 20 defendants),
CA [2008] Ch 313; [2008] 2 WLR 950
*"Concerning compensation"*—Arbitration agreement Czech Republic v European Media Ventures SA,
Simon J [2008] 1 All ER (Comm) 531; [2008] 1 Lloyd's Rep 186
*"Connected"*—Council Regulation (EC) No 44/2001, art 6(1) Freeport plc v Arnoldsson
(Case C-98/06), ECJ [2008] QB 634; [2008] 2 WLR 853
*"Consumer hire agreement"*—Consumer Credit Act 1974, s 15 (as amended)
TRM Copy Centres (UK) Ltd v Lanwall Services Ltd, CA [2008] Bus LR 1231
*"Control"*—Sexual Offences Act 2003, s 53(1) R v Massey, CA [2008] 1 WLR 937
*"Criminal proceedings to which the strict rules of evidence apply"*—Criminal Justice Act 2003, s 134
R v Chal, CA [2008] 1 Cr App R 247
*"Custody"*—Prison Rules 1999, r 9 R v Montgomery, CA [2008] 1 WLR 636
*"Dangerousness"*—Criminal Justice Act 2003, s 229 R v Considine, CA [2008] 1 WLR 414
*"Deprived of . . . liberty"*—Human Rights Act 1998, Sch 1, Pt I, art 5(1)
Austin v Comr of Police of the Metropolis,
CA [2008] QB 660; [2008] 2 WLR 415
*"Designed or adapted for living in"*—Leasehold Reform Act 1967, s 2
Boss Holdings Ltd v Grosvenor West End Properties Ltd, HL(E) [2008] 1 WLR 289
*"Disposal of material as waste"*—Finance Act 1996, s 40(2)(a)
Waste Recycling Group Ltd v Revenue and Customs Comrs, Barling J [2008] STC 1037
*"Dues"*—Convention on International Civil Aviation, art 15
R (Federation of Tour Operators) v HM Treasury,
Stanley Burnton J [2008] STC 547
*"Employee"*—Employment Rights Act 1996, s 230(1) New Testament Church of God v Stewart,
CA [2008] ICR 282
*"Employer"*—Council Regulation (EC) No 44/2001, art 20(1)
Samengo-Turner v J & H Marsh & McLennan (Services) Ltd, CA [2008] ICR 18
*"Employment conditions"*—Council Directive 99/70/EC, Annex, cl 4(1)
Del Cerro Alonso v Osakidetza (Servicio Vasco de Salud) (Case C-307/05),
ECJ [2008] ICR 145
*"Enforcement"*—Powers of Criminal Courts (Sentencing) Act 2000, s 140(1)
Director of Public Prosecutions v Greenacre, DC [2008] 1 WLR 438
*"Engagements"*—Trade Union and Labour Relations (Consolidation) Act 1992, s 97(2)
Unison v Allen, EAT [2008] ICR 114
*"Engine"*—Offences against the Person Act 1861, s 31 R v Cockburn, CA [2008] 2 WLR 1274
*"Engine calculated to . . . inflict grievous bodily harm"*—Offences against the Person Act 1861, s 31
R v Cockburn, CA [2008] 2 WLR 1274
*"Equipment . . . used by an employee . . . at work"*—Provision and Use of Work Equipment
Regulations 1998, reg 3(2) Smith v Northamptonshire County Council, CA [2008] ICR 826
*"Fair and accurate"*—Defamation Act 1996, Sch 1, Pt I, para 1 Curistan v Times Newspapers Ltd,
Gray J [2008] 1 WLR 126
*"Fees and expenses"*—Conditional Fee Agreement Regulations 2000, reg 3A (as inserted)
Jones (A Child) v Wrexham Borough Council, CA [2008] 1 WLR 1590

"Search term" box. A box can also be ticked to ensure that only statutes are searched and not both statutes and statutory instruments. Your search then finds 22 separate sections of the relevant Act which contain the words "overseas relationship". These include s.54, for example "Validity of civil partnerships registered outside England and Wales". A later section, 212, "Meaning of overseas relationship", suggests that in fact, Part 5 of the Act needs to be studied as a whole, "Civil Partnership Formed or Dissolved Abroad etc".

The "Legislation" search in Westlaw UK is not so precise and searches must be made in two stages. First enter "civil partnership" in either the "Free Text" or "Act/SI Title" search box. A large number of references will be found. Then enter "overseas relationship" in the "Search within Results" box at the top of the results screen. Just over 100 results remain, though relevant sections of the Act are near the top of the list. Enclosing the two phrases in quotes reduces the results list slightly. Westlaw UK does not automatically treat "civil partnership" and "overseas relationship" as phrases. It is not possible to restrict the search to statutes only.

If you do not have access to a subscription database of legislation, the Statute Law Database (para.4.15) and the OPSI website (para.4.6) provide alternative sources of legislation for subject keyword searching.

The "Advanced Search" within the Statute Law Database allows much the same approach to searching as that possible in LexisNexis Butterworths. "Civil Partnership" can be entered in the "Title" search box, and "overseas relationship" entered in a "Text Search" box. Matching legislation is then displayed by title. If the Civil Partnership Act 2004 is then selected, all sections of the Act or displayed, but those containing the words "overseas relationship" are usefully highlighted with a red star. However, the delayed updating of the database noted in para.4.15 means that the legislation displayed cannot be relied upon as a statement of law in force.

The OPSI website, importantly, only includes Acts in their original, unamended form. Also, legislation is only included from 1988 onwards. This makes is a less suitable source for subject searching. However, keyword searching is possible using the "Advanced Search" available on the OPSI legislation pages. Your search can be restricted to Acts and the relevant keywords entered. The relevance ranking used by the OPSI advanced search places legislation in which the keywords are close together at the top of the results list.

The BAILII database (para.4.8) allows more conventional database searching from its "Legislation" search. Search terms are highlighted within the text of a whole Act or statutory instrument. BAILII contains legislation drawn from both the OPSI website and the Statute Law Database.

> **TIPS** • *Place phrases in quotation marks when searching Westlaw UK, otherwise your search will find sections of Acts in which the search words appear, but not necessarily next to each other. LexisNexis Butterworths treats consecutive words as phrases.*

## Other online sources for tracing legislation by subject

Catalogues of official publications offer an alternative to full text databases of legislation for tracing legislation by subject. The TSO bookshop catalogue (para.6.15) enables statutes to be searched by title keyword and the "Advanced Search" allows searches to be restricted to Acts. Using the UKOP database (para.6.16) "Flexible Search" widens the range of subject searching,

▶ **7.22**

as the UKOP thesaurus enables results to be found using both the search words you have entered and alternative, closely related, terms.

### Halsbury's Statutes of England

**7.23** ▶ *Halsbury's Statutes* provides the amended text of legislation which is still in force, along with annotations detailing, for example, statutory instruments made under the Act, case law, judicial interpretation of words and phrases and references to relevant sections of *Halsbury's Laws*.

The 50 volumes of the main work are arranged alphabetically by broad subject areas. Acts dealing with agriculture, for example, are found in Vol.1, whereas statutes on the subject of wills are found in Vol.50.

The annual *Table of Statutes and General Index* provides a comprehensive subject index to the volumes to enable you to find statutes on a particular topic. The index will refer you to the appropriate volume and page number. In the *Table of Statutes and General Index* volume there is a separate subject index to the *Current Statutes Service*, which contains those Acts that were passed after the main volumes were issued. If you are looking for the latest Acts on a particular subject, look also in the subject index at the front of the looseleaf Volume 1 of the *Current Statutes Service*. This indexes the material that has been added to the Service since the annual *Table of Statutes and General Index* was published.

Once you have identified those Acts which are of relevance to you, it is essential to consult both the *Cumulative Supplement* and the *Noter-Up* to see if there have been any changes in the law. An explanation of how to do this, along with further details of *Halsbury's Statutes*, can be found at para.4.17.

### Other print sources for tracing legislation on a subject

**7.24** ▶ *Halsbury's Laws* (para.7.3) contains references to relevant statutes, although the text of the Acts is not printed. The *Current Law Monthly Digests* and *Year Books* (para.7–12 and para.7–13) are arranged by subject and include entries for new statutes and statutory instruments as well as for cases on a subject. A brief summary appears under the appropriate subject heading.

## HOW TO TRACE STATUTORY INSTRUMENTS ON A SUBJECT

**7.25** ▶ Statutory instruments on a particular subject can be traced by consulting:

> Online sources (para.7.26);
> *Halsbury's Statutory Instruments* (para.7.27).

For an explanation of the nature and purpose of statutory instruments, refer back to para.4.26.

### Online sources for tracing statutory instruments

**7.26** ▶ The full-text databases of legislation noted in para.7.21 all provide access to statutory instruments. The considerations relevant to searching for statutory instruments are consequently much the same. The LexisNexis Butterworths "Legislation" search is a particularly useful starting point for searching for statutory instruments, as the database source can be limited so that only statutory instruments are searched. In Westlaw UK, the legislation search includes both statutes and statutory instruments. Both LexisNexis Butterworths and Westlaw UK contain statutory instruments in force. The Justis UK Statutory Instruments database contains the full text of all statutory instruments from 1987 onwards, and a further archive database contains statutory instruments published between 1671 and 1986. However, only a few libraries are likely to subscribe to the archive.

The "Advanced Search" of both the Statute Law Database and the OPSI website provide an alternative approach to searching for statutory instruments and key search considerations are as noted in para.7.21. The Statute Law Database currently contains statutory instruments from 1991 onwards. OPSI coverage begins in 1987.

### Halsbury's Statutory Instruments

*Halsbury's Statutory Instruments* is a series which covers every statutory instrument of general application in force in England and Wales. It reproduces the text of a selected number and provides summaries of others. The series is arranged alphabetically by subject and is kept up to date by a Service binder containing notes of changes in the law and the text of selected new instruments. A full description of the work can be found in para.4.29.     ▶ **7.27**

If you are looking for statutory instruments dealing with a particular subject, you should start by looking up your subject in the *Consolidated Index*. This paperback volume is issued annually and indexes the contents of all the main volumes. The entries give you the volume number (in bold type) and page number in the main work and the number of the statutory instrument (in brackets).

Occasionally you will find that the volume to which you are referred has been re-issued since the latest *Consolidated Index* was published. The references from the *Consolidated Index* will no longer be correct and in this case you will need to refer to the subject index at the back of the new volume.

Once you have traced the relevant statutory instruments on your subject in the main volumes, it is important to turn to the *Service* binder to find out if the information you have traced is still up to date. To do this, turn to the *Monthly Survey* section of the *Service* binder and look up the relevant subject title. This shows new statutory instruments which have appeared since the main volume was compiled. It tells you which statutory instruments printed in the main volumes are no longer law and provides you with a page-by-page guide to changes made since the main volume was published.

## SUMMARY: HOW TO USE HALSBURY'S STATUTORY INSTRUMENTS TO FIND INFORMATION ON A SUBJECT

1.  Consult the *Consolidated Index*. This tells you the volume, page number and statutory instrument numbers you require.
2.  To check if there have been any changes in the law, look in the *Monthly Survey* pages of the *Service* binder.

### Tracing recent statutory instruments

The OPSI legislation site (at *www.opsi.gov.uk/legislation*) lists statutory instruments in number order making it possible to check for the most recent statutory instruments added to the site.     ▶ **7.28**

If you suspect that a statutory instrument is very recent, it might also be convenient to check entries in the TSO *Daily List* (para.6.15), available both online and in print. The print *Current Law Monthly Digest* has the advantage of listing relatively recent statutory instruments under subject headings.

All draft statutory instruments awaiting approval are also published in full text on the OPSI legislation website and they remain on the site until they are superseded by a statutory instrument, or, in some cases, until they are withdrawn.

### Finding Books on a Subject

**7.29** ▶ Your first task is to find out what suitable books are available in your own library. Start with your library catalogue. All catalogues allow you to search for keywords in the titles of books. This means you can search for title words that match your subject. A keyword search on "negligence", for example, picks up the titles "Introduction to negligence", "The law of negligence" and so on. If you do not find books on your subject, try some alternative headings or look under a more general, or a more specific subject. Negligence, for instance, is part of the law of torts and there will be a chapter on negligence in all general textbooks on the law of torts.

Many library catalogues also have a subject search. This acts as an index to the classification scheme. If you enter the word "negligence" using a subject search you are shown the classification number (or classmark) for books on negligence. The catalogue then links you to a list of books sharing that classmark. Such a subject search is a more systematic approach to searching the catalogue, as the books listed represent all the books in the library which share a common subject. If you searched on "negligence", you will see a list of the general works on negligence, whether or not they have the word negligence in the title. Using a subject search is of particular help if you want to find books on a specific aspect of a subject, and are not sure where the classification scheme places the books on the library shelves. For medical negligence, for example, a subject search of this kind leads you to a classification which places books on medical negligence with other books on medical law, often some distance away from the general textbooks on negligence.

If your library catalogue does not have a subject search of this kind, an alternative approach is to search for keywords in book titles and note the classmark of a book that matches your subject interest, even if that book might be hopelessly out of date. Most computerised catalogues enable you to search by classmark. You can then find a list of the books on a subject, usually showing the most recent first.

Remember also that footnotes and bibliographies (lists of books) in textbooks and journal articles refer you to other books, journals and cases on a subject. Check in the library catalogue to find out if these are available in your library. Government reports on a subject may not be entered, and you need to make use of other catalogues and indexes to trace these publications (see para.6.15 and para.6.18).

You are not restricted to your own catalogue, if you wish to trace books on a subject. The online catalogues of all of the UK universities, along with the British Library, can be searched. COPAC (at *www.copac.ac.uk*) provides a particularly useful starting point for UK academic research libraries as it provides access to the merged catalogues of the largest research libraries in the UK and Ireland. This means that a single catalogue search can find details of a book held by, among others, the Cambridge University Library, the Bodleian Library, Trinity College

Dublin and the Institute of Advanced Legal Studies. The Institute of Advanced Legal Studies collections can by searched via the Institute's own library pages (at *www.ials.sas.ac.uk/library/ library.htm*). The British Library catalogue (at *www.blpc.bl.uk*) includes both the main reference and document supply collections.

Many universities also have subscriptions to the OCLC FirstSearch service which contains the WorldCat database, the largest online catalogue available. It has records which are based largely, though not exclusively, on US university holdings. The Library of Congress catalogue (at *www.catalog.loc.gov*) provides another starting point for US publications.

## Legal bibliographies

Bibliographies list books that have been published on a subject, both in this country and abroad. A number of possible sources are given below. All of them are print volumes that list books under legal subject headings. Not all of them may be available in your library. However, you will only need one or two of them to trace relevant books.

▶ **7.30**

## D. Raistrick—Lawyer's Law Books

Now somewhat out of date, *Lawyers' Law Books* (3rd edn 1995) is the only convenient single-volume bibliography listing textbooks by subject. However, as many of the textbooks listed can be found in current editions the bibliography is still of some value. At the beginning of each subject heading, there are references to alternative headings and a list of the major legal reference works and journals that contain information on that topic.

▶ **7.31**

## Current Law

At the back of each *Current Law Monthly Digest* is a list of new books published during that month (mainly British, with a few foreign works in English). When the *Monthly Digests* are replaced by the *Current Law Year Book*, a list of books published during the year is printed at the back of the Year Book.

▶ **7.32**

## Current Publications in Legal and Related Fields

*Current Publications in Legal and Related Fields* (published by the American publisher Hein) is issued in looseleaf parts which are replaced by annual volumes. There are entries under authors and titles in the looseleaf volume.

▶ **7.33**

In the annual volume, a detailed subject index at the front of the volume guides you to relevant entries in the main (alphabetically arranged) part of the work. Each item has its own individual number. The bibliography includes UK published works.

## Law Books 1876–1981

The first three volumes of *Law Books 1876–1981* are arranged by subject and cover books published mainly in the US, although some British and other countries' publications are also included. The fourth volume contains some entries under authors, titles and serials. Rather than update the original work, the publishers, Bowker, now publish *Law Books and Serials in Print*.

▶ **7.34**

**Other Legal Bibliographies**

**7.35** ▶ Sweet & Maxwell's *Legal Bibliography of the British Commonwealth* is especially useful for tracing older British Books. C. Szladit's, *Bibliography on Foreign and Comparative Law* is a detailed bibliography covering books and articles on foreign and comparative law published in English.

Many other specialist legal bibliographies have also been published, e.g. P. O'Higgens and M. Partington, *Social Security Law in Britain and Ireland: a Bibliography* (1986); E. Beyerly, *Public International Law: a Guide to Information Sources* (1991); and R.W.M. Dias, *Bibliography of Jurisprudence* (1979). As you can see from their publication dates, such bibliographies do not always provide a guide to recent publications, but this does not exhaust their usefulness. Raistrick's *Lawyers' Law Books* (para.7.31) contains list of more specialised legal bibliographies, under the heading "Bibliographies".

Library staff will help you to trace recent bibliographies. Remember too, that many textbooks will also contain a bibliography on their subject.

**The British National Bibliography**

**7.36** ▶ The main source of information for British books which have been published since 1950 is the *British National Bibliography* (BNB). This is published weekly and the last issue of each month contains an index to books published that month. At the end of the year, an annual volume is produced containing details of British books published that year. Entries are arranged by subject in a classification scheme. You will first need to look up your subject in the Subject Index, which refers you to the classification number under which the books can be found. Entries for law books are at the numbers 340–349.

**Sources for books in print**

**7.37** ▶ A number of sources enable you to search for the titles of books in print. Among the electronic sources, the commercial books in print databases allow subject searching using keywords, and these have been supplemented by the catalogues of the internet booksellers. Publishers' websites also list current and forthcoming publications and many organise their titles by subject.

The Amazon website (at *www.amazon.co.uk*) should not be overlooked as a useful source for information for books in print, as most publishers supply the site with title information. The American site (at *www.amazon.com*) is also worth searching. Contents pages are often available for viewing online. Some libraries may be able to check titles for you, using the BookWise service from Nielson BookData, the major commercial source for information on UK books in print. Access may also be offered to book supplier databases, such as *www.enterBooks.com* from Dawson Books.

# THESES

**7.38** ▶ If you are undertaking a comprehensive piece of research, you may need to find out if any theses have already been written on that subject. The *Index to Theses*, more fully, the *Index to Theses Accepted for Higher Degrees by the Universities of Great Britain and Ireland*, is, as the title suggests, the major source for tracing British and Irish theses. Coverage is extensive, but it does rely on universities to submit theses information. The *Index* is available online but this is a subscription database, so you will need to check if your library can provide access. Online coverage begins in 1970. The print version dates back to 1950. Another print source of information for UK law theses, *Legal Research in the United Kingdom, 1905–1984*, was published by the Institute of Advanced Legal Studies, and updated until 1988 by the *List of Current Legal Research Topics*. Publication has now ceased.

Details of the vast majority of North American theses can be found in Dissertation Abstracts International, which also includes some non-North American theses. Abstracts are available from 1980. The publishers, UMI, have made the Dissertation Abstracts International database available to a number of online database providers.

Theses which have been completed at your own institution are normally available for consultation in the library. It is usually possible for the library staff to borrow, on inter-library loan, copies of theses completed in other universities in this country and abroad. The British Library began in 2008 to place UK theses online via the EThOS (Electronic Thesis Online System) project (at *www.ethos.ac.uk*).

# 8
# European Union law

## INTRODUCTION

**8.1** European Union law is as much part of the law of the UK as the laws passed by the UK Parliament. For this reason, UK legal sources should, and often will, include references to relevant EU law. However, because this is not always so, and because EU law is organised in a different way from English law, students also need to become familiar with the sources of EU law.

The sources of EU law, along with a great deal of other information, are made available both online and in print by the EU itself. Online access is provided from the Europa website (para.8.2), the main source for official EU information. Treaties, legislation and case law are available from the EUR-Lex web pages (para.8.3). There is no subscription charge for access.

Most, if not all, of the printed sources will also be available in your law library, especially if it is a designated European Documentation Centre (E.D.C.). E.D.C.'s are part of the European Information Relay Network and receive copies of publicly available documents from the European Commission. Details of the UK E.D.C.s and other sources of EU information are found on the website of the European Commission Representation office in the UK (at ec.europa.eu/unitedkingdom).

## THE EUROPA WEBSITE

**8.2** The Europa website (at *www.europa.eu*) is the main EU website, providing a wealth of information from the EU institutions. The home page carries recent news items from the EU and links can be followed under "All the news" to press releases from the Europa Press Room (para.8.27). Further information is grouped under four major headings: "Activities", "Institutions", "Documents" and "Services". All four headings provide useful approaches to finding legal information.

A subject approach to legal information is possible using the "Activities" heading on the website. A number of major subject areas are listed, e.g. "Employment and Social Affairs", "Enlargement", and "Environment". Within each heading, links are then available to summaries of key legislation in that area. Further links go to the relevant full text. The "Key sites" section for each subject area provides links to important bodies within the major institutions. If the "Environment" heading is selected, for example, a link is provided to the Committee on the Environment, Public Health and Food Safety page within the European Parliament site. Additional links are provided for subject-specific entries in the *Bulletin of the European Union*

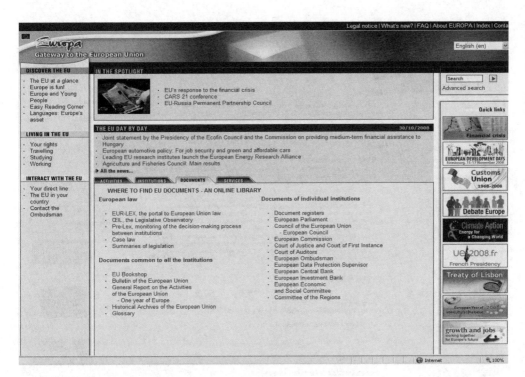

**Fig 8.1**
'The Europa website (documents section selected)

and the *General Report on the Activities of the European Union* (para.8.26). Press releases can also be viewed for the subject area chosen.

The "Institutions" heading is useful if you wish to find further information on the activities of any of the major institutions: the European Parliament, the Council of the European Union, the European Commission and the Court of Justice of the European Communities. There are also links to other significant bodies, such as the Office for Official Publications of the European Communities (the Publications Office), the EU's official publisher.

The "Documents" heading of the Europa site provides a direct link to the EUR-Lex site (para.8.3), along with additional links for preparatory legislation and case law. This is the site to use if you wish to search the primary sources of EU law in their entirety.

Europa's "Services" heading provides a link to Eurostat, the EU's statistical informa-tion service, under the "Statistics" heading, also a link to the European Commission's Central Library and its catalogue (ECLAS), a useful source of information for books and journal articles relevant to the EU (para.8.25).

The "Advanced Search" page of the Europa website's search engine allows searches to be restricted by subject area. However, if you are searching for legislation or case law by subject, a better approach is to use the keyword search facilities provided in the EUR-Lex web pages.

## EUR-LEX

The EUR-Lex website (at *www.eur-lex.europa.eu*), provides access to both legislation and case law. It contains the full text of the following:

▶ **8.3**

**Fig 8.2**
'The EUR-Lex
website'

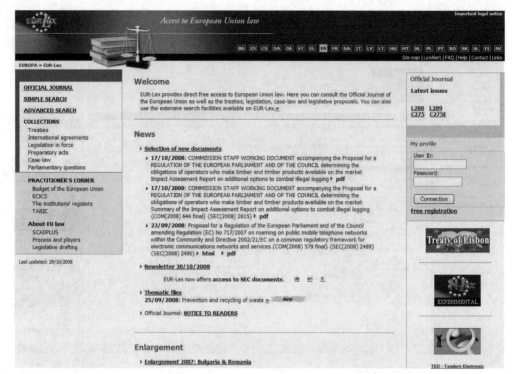

Treaties as currently amended;

Legislation in force (including consolidated texts);

Proposed legislation;

Case-law;

Parliamentary questions.

The full text of the *Official Journal C* and *L* Series is also available (para.8.4).

In 2005 the information on the EUR-Lex site was merged with information from the EU's CELEX database. Until the end of 2004, CELEX had been the EU's official legal database. An accompanying redesign of the EUR-Lex web pages was carried out to ensure that the full range of database searches available on CELEX was also available when searching for legislation and case law on EUR-Lex.

## THE OFFICIAL JOURNAL

**8.4** ▶ The *Official Journal of the European Communities* is issued in print and online by the Publications Office of the European Union and is the official and authoritative source of legislation. It carries the text of proposed and enacted legislation, as well as official announcements and information on the activities of the EU's institutions.

Print editions of the *Official Journal* are published about six times a week carrying the latest legislation and announcements. The issues are also placed online in the same format

ISSN 1725-2555

# Official Journal
# of the European Union

L 278
Volume 51
21 October 2008

**English edition**     **Legislation**

Contents

*I Acts adopted under the EC Treaty/Euratom Treaty whose publication is obligatory*

**REGULATIONS**

(1)   Text with EEA relevance

**EN**     Acts whose titles are printed in light type are those relating to day-to-day management of agricultural matters, and are generally valid for a limited period. The titles of all other acts are printed in bold type and preceded by an asterisk.

**Fig 8.3**
'Example contents page of the Official Journal'

on the EUR-Lex site (at *www.eur-lex.europa.eu*). Your library may no longer take the print issues. The Journal is published in two sequences:

1. *L series (Legislation)*: this consists of the texts of enacted legislation, divided into a further two sequences.
   (a) acts whose publication is obligatory (primarily regulations, directives addressed to all member states);
   (b) acts whose publication is not obligatory (all other legislation).
2. *C series (Information and Notices)*: this is arranged in five parts, as follows:
   Part I, Resolutions, recommendations and opinions, including, e.g Council resolutions and recommendations; recommendations from the European Central Bank;

   Part II, Information, including:
      Information from European Institutions and Bodies, e.g. Commission decisions on competition cases or state aid, opinions from the Court of Auditors;
    Part III, Preparatory Acts: proposed legislation;
   Part IV, Notices, including:
      Notices from European Institutions and Bodies, e.g. Euro exchange rates, opinions and reports from the Commission; European Parliament minutes of proceedings and texts adopted;
   Part V, Announcements, including:
      Administrative procedures, e.g. Commission calls for research, Procedures relating to the implementation of competition policy, Court proceedings: notes of new cases.

Usually only two or three parts of the C series are present in any one issue.

The *Official Journal* web pages also link to public procurement notices, which form a supplement to the *Official Journal*, sometimes referred to as the *S Supplement*. The notices are presented online in the form of the Tenders Electronic Daily (TED) database (at *www.ted. europa.eu*), which provides details of current business tender opportunities.

The Publications Office has issued a monthly CD-ROM version of the *Official Journal C* and *L series* since 1999 which should be available in E.D.C. libraries. An *Official Journal C E* edition was also launched in 1999. It is only available on the EUR-Lex website or as part of the monthly *Official Journal* CD-ROM.

The citation of references to the *Official Journal* is not standardised. The most common forms are O.J. no.L271 11.10.2008, p.3; [2008] O.J. L271/3; and O.J. 2008, L271/3.

## TREATIES

8.5 ▶  The treaties page of the Eur-Lex website (para.8–3) displays links to the founding treaties of the European Union and the European Communities. These are:

   The Treaty establishing the European Economic Community, 1957
   The Treaty establishing the European Atomic Energy Community, 1957
   The Treaty establishing the European Coal and Steel Community, 1951 (expired 2002)
   The Treaty on European Union, 1992

The Treaty on European Union, revised not just the content, but also the name of the original EEC Treaty, so that it became the Treaty establishing the European Community (EC Treaty). Further revisions to the EC Treaty were subsequently introduced by:

The Treaty of Amsterdam, 1997
The Treaty of Nice, 2001

Fortunately, a consolidated version of the Treaty on European Union and of the Treaty establishing the European Community is available on the Eur-Lex treaties page. As a result there is no need to trace the specific changes introduced by these treaties. This consolidated version incorporates all the changes which have been made to the EC Treaty. The EC Treaty performs two main tasks. The first is that it represents a system of sub-stantive rules which are binding on the member states, and whose aim is to foster social and economic integration among the member states. Secondly, and equally importantly, the treaty creates a set of institutions and a procedural framework through which these institutions can create secondary legislation and take other measures which have a legally binding effect.

The Treaty of Lisbon, if ratified by all member states, will introduce further changes to the founding treaties of the European Union and the European Communities. It can be found on the treaties web page under its full title:

Treaty of Lisbon amending the Treaty on European Union and the Treaty establishing the European Community, 2007

A consolidated treaty statement incorporating the revisions of the Treaty of Lisbon is available as a consolidated version of:

The Treaty on European Union and the Treaty on the Functioning of the European Union

The Treaty of Lisbon has the effect of significantly renumbering the articles of the current EC Treaty (The Treaty of Amsterdam had a similar effect). The name of the treaty is also changed, so that it becomes the Treaty on the Functioning of the European Union. A schedule listing the changes can be found at the end of the Treaty of Lisbon itself.

Treaty texts are published in the Official Journal, so that the Treaty of Lisbon, for example, was published in the *Official Journal C* Series, in issue 306, of December 17, 2007. The Treaty was also published as a UK Command Paper, Cm. 7294, on the same day.

In addition to these official sources, many of the important texts of primary materials are published in student textbooks. *Blackstone's Statutes on EU Treaties and Legislation*, for example, edited by Nigel Foster, and currently revised annually (19th edition 2008–2009). The *Encyclopedia of European Union Laws*, a loose-leaf publication, also contains the texts of the treaties.

## SECONDARY LEGISLATION

Secondary legislation is that which is created by the institutions of the European Union in implementing the powers granted to them in the relevant treaties. There are different types of legislative acts, and these are given different names depending on whether they are made

▌8.6

under the EC and EURATOM Treaties, or the former ECSC Treaty. You will be most concerned with the different kinds of act made under the EC Treaty. These are explained in Article 249 of the Treaty and are as follows:

Regulations
Directives
Decisions
Recommendations
Opinions

The legislative process of the EU is very different from that of the UK. Draft legislation or proposals are put forward by the Commission and the final versions are published as *Commission Documents* (known as *COM Docs*). They are also published in the *Official Journal C Series*. Proposals are then considered by the European Parliament and the European Economic and Social Committee (EESC) or the Committee of the Regions (CoR), which publish *Reports* or *Opinions*. The European Parliament may also initiate proposals for legislation.

Consultative documents from the relevant bodies are available online from EU sources, though the websites involved are not always easy to navigate. *COM Docs* are included on EUR-Lex under "Preparatory Acts". EESC and CoR Opinions are published in the *Official Journal C Series*. Recent EESC Opinions are available on their website (at *www.eesc.europa.eu*). Committee of the Regions Opinions are available from the Committee website (at *www.cor.europa.eu*). Resolutions of the European Parliament (but not the full report) are published in the *Official Journal C Series*. The full text of the *Reports of Proceedings*, along with Committee opinions and other relevant documents, is available on the European Parliament website (at *www.europarl.europa.eu*).

Once the various suggestions from these bodies have been considered, and the original proposals amended if necessary, the Council will adopt a directive or regulation and the text is published in the *Official Journal L Series*. Directives must then be implemented in the law of the Member States.

### Citation of legislative acts

8.7 ▶  The formal citation of a legislative act is made up of the following elements:

1. The institutional origin of the act (Commission, European Parliament and Council).
2. The form of the act (regulation, directive, decision, etc.).
3. An act number.
4. The year of the enactment.
5. The institutional treaty basis (EC, ECSC, EURATOM).
6. The date the act was passed.

Regulation numbers are written with the number first and the year following. Decisions and directives are written the other way round, with the year first and the number following. All indexes will therefore always list regulations first and decisions and directives afterwards. Two examples follow:

**Fig 8.4**
'Text of Directive
2003/88/EC'

# DIRECTIVE 2003/88/EC OF THE EUROPEAN PARLIAMENT AND OF THE COUNCIL
## of 4 November 2003
### concerning certain aspects of the organisation of working time

THE EUROPEAN PARLIAMENT AND THE COUNCIL OF THE EUROPEAN UNION,

Having regard to the Treaty establishing the European Community, and in particular Article 137(2) thereof,

Having regard to the proposal from the Commission,

Having regard to the opinion of the European Economic and Social Committee ([1]),

Having consulted the Committee of the Regions,

Acting in accordance with the procedure referred to in Article 251 of the Treaty ([2]),

Whereas:

(1) Council Directive 93/104/EC of 23 November 1993, concerning certain aspects of the organisation of working time ([3]), which lays down minimum safety and health requirements for the organisation of working time, in respect of periods of daily rest, breaks, weekly rest, maximum weekly working time, annual leave and aspects of night work, shift work and patterns of work, has been significantly amended. In order to clarify matters, a codification of the provisions in question should be drawn up.

(2) Article 137 of the Treaty provides that the Community is to support and complement the activities of the Member States with a view to improving the working environment to protect workers' health and safety. Directives adopted on the basis of that Article are to avoid imposing administrative, financial and legal constraints in a way which would hold back the creation and development of small and medium-sized undertakings.

(3) The provisions of Council Directive 89/391/EEC of 12 June 1989 on the introduction of measures to encourage improvements in the safety and health of workers at work ([4]) remain fully applicable to the areas covered by this Directive without prejudice to more stringent and/or specific provisions contained herein.

(4) The improvement of workers' safety, hygiene and health at work is an objective which should not be subordinated to purely economic considerations.

(5) All workers should have adequate rest periods. The concept of 'rest' must be expressed in units of time, i.e. in days, hours and/or fractions thereof. Community workers must be granted minimum daily, weekly and annual periods of rest and adequate breaks. It is also necessary in this context to place a maximum limit on weekly working hours.

(6) Account should be taken of the principles of the International Labour Organisation with regard to the organisation of working time, including those relating to night work.

(7) Research has shown that the human body is more sensitive at night to environmental disturbances and also to certain burdensome forms of work organisation and that long periods of night work can be detrimental to the health of workers and can endanger safety at the workplace.

(8) There is a need to limit the duration of periods of night work, including overtime, and to provide for employers who regularly use night workers to bring this information to the attention of the competent authorities if they so request.

(9) It is important that night workers should be entitled to a free health assessment prior to their assignment and thereafter at regular intervals and that whenever possible they should be transferred to day work for which they are suited if they suffer from health problems.

(10) The situation of night and shift workers requires that the level of safety and health protection should be adapted to the nature of their work and that the organisation and functioning of protection and prevention services and resources should be efficient.

(11) Specific working conditions may have detrimental effects on the safety and health of workers. The organisation of work according to a certain pattern must take account of the general principle of adapting work to the worker.

(12) A European Agreement in respect of the working time of seafarers has been put into effect by means of Council Directive 1999/63/EC of 21 June 1999 concerning the Agreement on the organisation of working time of seafarers concluded by the European Community Shipowners' Association (ECSA) and the Federation of Transport Workers' Unions in the European Union (FST) ([5]) based on Article 139(2) of the Treaty. Accordingly, the provisions of this Directive should not apply to seafarers.

---

([1]) OJ C 61, 14.3.2003, p. 123.
([2]) Opinion of the European Parliament of 17 December 2002 (not yet published in the Official Journal) and Council Decision of 22 September 2003.
([3]) OJ L 307, 13.12.1993, p. 18. Directive as amended by Directive 2000/34/EC of the European Parliament and of the Council (OJ L 195, 1.8.2000, p. 41).
([4]) OJ L 183, 29.6.1989, p. 1.

---

([5]) OJ L 167, 2.7.1999, p. 33.

1. Commission Regulation (EC) No. 994/2008 of October 10, 2008 for a standardised and secured system of registries pursuant to Directive 2003/87/EC (This can be abbreviated to reg.(EC) 994/2008.)
2. Directive 2003/88/EC of the European Parliament and of the Council of November 4 concerning certain aspects of the organisation of working time. (This can be abbreviated to Dir. 2003/88/EC.)

Between 1958 and 1967, this citation form varied. The variations are laid out in *Halsbury's Statutes* (4th edn), Vol.50. From 1992, directives and decisions were given separate numerical sequences, with the consequence that a directive and a decision can both be given the same number. Thus there exist both Dir. 2008/12/EC and Dec. 2008/12/EC.

A legislative act is given a date of enactment but this does not indicate the date when the act is published in the Official Journal: this can be up to several months later.

### How to find the text of a regulation or directive

**8.8** ▶ Suppose you wish to look for the current text of Directive 2003/88/EC on the organisation of working time. How should you set about finding it? The best approach is to use the EUR-Lex website (at *www.eur-lex.europa.eu*).

To begin, select the "Simple Search" from the EUR-Lex home page. Then select the "Natural number" search option under the "Search by document number" heading. A search form can then be used to specify that you wish to search for a directive ("Regulation" or "Decision" could also be specified at this point). A year and document number also need to be entered for the directive. The year is derived from the start of the standard abbreviation and is entered as a 4 digit number (i.e. 2003). The document number is 88. Once these details have been entered, your search will display a results screen with the full title and *Official Journal* reference for the directive. Select the "Bibliographic notice + Text" option to see all the available text.

The bibliographic notice lists any amendments or repeals for a directive and provides links to the full text of the related legislation. For Directive 2003/88/EC, which repeals an earlier working time directive (93/104/EC), the bibliographic notice lists the directive repealed. If a directive has been amended a number of times, the bibliographic notice provides a link to a consolidated version of the text, incorporating all the amendments made. The full text displayed in your search result is the original text of the directive.

The bibliographic information associated with the text of Directives, showing related documents, can also be found using the "EU" search in Westlaw UK (para.2.5). To find a directive, use the standard abbreviation for a directive in the "Case or Document No." search box, e.g. "2003/88/EC". A search by publication reference is also possible. The "Related information" Section displays links to documents related to a particular Directive.

> **TIPS** • *Always check the "bibliographic notice" when tracing the text of a directive on the EUR-Lex site. Links are provided to amending legislation, consolidated texts and important cases.*

### How to trace legislation on a subject without a reference

**8.9** ▶ If you have been told, for example, that there is a directive on part-time working or parental leave, but you do not have a number or a date, you will need to use a subject approach. In most cases, choosing the correct terminology is the first problem you will encounter. Directives are commonly given colloquial titles such as the "Part-Time Working Directive" or the "Parental Leave Directive", but these are not official titles. The "Parental Leave Directive" has the official title "Council Directive 96/34/EC of 3 June 1996 on the framework agreement on parental leave concluded by UNICE, CEEP and the ETUC". However, the colloquial titles used for directives usually contain the keywords needed to search an online database. A search for directives containing the words "parental leave" using EUR-Lex, or Westlaw UK finds the relevant directive.

Because of the advantages provided by the bibliographic notices for legislation noted in para.8.8, the EUR-Lex website provides a good starting point for searching for a directive using keywords. Use the "Simple Search" option and select "Legislation" under "Search by file category". This means that your keyword searches will only find legislation and not all categories of material found on EUR-Lex. "Directives" can be specified as legislation type on the next screen with "search terms" as the search option. A search on "parental leave" then finds two directives: Directive 96/34/EC on parental leave and Directive 97/34/EC amending the original directive and extending it to the UK. The bibliographic note for 96/34/EC includes a link to a consolidated text for 96/34/EC incorporating the amending directive.

More complex searches can be carried out using search terms such as "with" or "except". These are explained on the "Search using search terms" screen. Searches can also be extended to include the full text of legislation, along with the title.

The "EU" search page of Westlaw UK provides a useful alternative for finding legislation by keyword. To use Westlaw UK, enter "parental leave" in the "Parties or title" search box. It is not, unfortunately, possible to restrict the search to legislation, which means that entries for the two relevant directives are accompanied by links to European Court of Justice cases and earlier proposed legislation, though all these, may, of course, be of interest. There is no consolidated version of the parental leave Directive 96/34/EC, incorporating later amendments. This is only available in the EUR-Lex website.

If you are not sure of the keywords to use in searching for a directive, another approach is to use the "Classification headings" search available under the EUR-Lex "Simple Search". A standard EU analytical table of headings is displayed, enabling the Parental Leave directive to be found, for example, under the following string of headings: "05 Freedom of movement for workers and social policy"; "Social Policy"; "Employment and unemployment"; and "Protection of workers". As can be seen from this example, some familiarity with the analytical structure of the headings is required before you can find the most likely path to legislation that might interest you.

The loose-leaf service, Vaughan, Law of the European Union (*Richmond Law & Tax*) provides a print approach to finding EU legislation by subject.

## How to check if legislation is in force

▶ **8.10**

If you have used EUR-Lex to find a directive or regulation as described in para.8.8, the accompanying bibliographic note will confirm whether it is still in force. If you used Westlaw UK, any Directive no longer in force is accompanied by a "no entry" icon indicating that the Directive has been suspended or repealed.

If you are searching EUR-Lex by subject keyword (see para.8.9) a tick box can be used when specifying the type of search you wish to make, restricting the search to legislation in force. This can save possible confusion. If you search for directives using the keywords "working time" and tick the "Restrict your search to acts in force" box, only the current in-force directives are retrieved. You do not see Directive 93/104/EC and its various amending directives. Both the older Directive 93/104/EC and the current Directive 2003/88/EC are directives "concerning certain aspects of the organisation of working time".

An analytical overview of all legislation in force can also be found if you select the "Legislation in force" link from the EUR-Lex home page (at *www.eur-lex.europa.eu*). The over-view uses the standard EU classification scheme noted in para.8.9 and links are provided to the full text of legislation listed under each heading. Consolidated versions of legislation are provided where relevant.

### How to trace proposals for legislation

**8.11** In the UK, draft legislation is introduced into Parliament and becomes law during the same parliamentary session. This is not the case with EU legislation, which may take years to either become law or ultimately fail to become law. How would you know if legislation has been proposed on a particular subject?

The *Bulletin of the European Union* is a useful starting point for updates on recent pro-posals. This can be accessed by subject area if you start from the "Activities" section of the EUROPA website (see para.8.2). Searching under "Activities" and "Environment" in 2008 finds an entry in the *Bulletin*, for example, on a proposed directive on amending and improving existing legislation on the greenhouse gas emission allowance trading system COM (2008) 16. Links are provided from the *Bulletin* entry to the *Official Journal* entry using the Prelex database (see below). Prelex also contains links to the relevant opinions from the Committee of the Regions, the Economic and Social Committee and the European Parliament.

A more systematic search for proposals can be undertaken from the EUR-Lex website. The "Simple search" on the EUR-Lex home page can be used to select a search for prepara-tory acts, rather than legislation or case law. Searches can then be made using keywords, date limits or classification headings. A keyword search for "greenhouse gas emission", for example, finds the COM document mentioned above, along with a Commission Opinion, and a European Parliament and Council Decision. The full text is provided and links are provided in the bibliographic notice to the relevant entries in Prelex and OEIL Legislative Observatory (OEIL) database of the European Parliament.

The PreLex database (at *www.ec.europa.eu/prelex*) was launched by the European Commission in 2000. It provides database entries following all Commission proposals and communications from the Council or European Parliament through to adoption or rejection. It provides detailed tracking of a proposal through all the stages at which it is considered and provides links to the relevant full text. Document numbers can be used to trace the EU texts relevant to a specific COM document, for example. Keyword searches can also be used. A menu choice on the site enables English to be selected, rather than the default French language choice.

The Legislative Observatory (OEIL) database (at *www.europarl.europa.eu/oeil*) is a database provided by the European Parliament which contains the details of all procedures or proposals still ongoing, along with those concluded since the beginning of the fourth legislative term in July 1994. The OEIL entry for proposed legislation provides access to

Legislative Opinions of the European Parliament and the full text of relevant committee reports.

The loose-leaf print service, *Vaughan, Law of the European Union*, also includes proposed legislation.

### How to trace whether a directive has been implemented in the United Kingdom

▶ 8.12

Directives, once adopted by the Council of the European Union, must be implemented by Member States by the most appropriate method for each country. In the UK, this is generally done by passing an Act of Parliament or issuing a statutory instrument. Member States are given a set period of time in which to do this. Tracing UK legislation implementing a directive can be problematic.

The European Commission has developed a web gateway, N-Lex, to help solve the problem of tracing implementing legislation. It provides a common search page which can be used to search national databases of legislation for member states. If the UK is selected, the search page searches the OPSI web pages. Unfortunately, this is less than ideal. UK legislation is best searched directly using the various sources described earlier in this book. The legislation searches of Westlaw UK or LexisNexis Butterworths provide the best approach: to use these databases, follow the approach outlined for searching for legislation by subject in para.7.21.

To search for legislation implementing the Parental Leave directive, for example, use a keyword search to find references to "96/34/EC". An explanatory paragraph is found for the Maternity and Parental Leave etc. Regulations 1999/3312 which includes the statement that "provisions relating to parental leave implement Council Directive 96/34/EC on the framework agreement on parental leave (OJ No.L145, 19.6.96, p.4)". The Maternity and Parental Leave (Amendment) Regulations 2001/4010 and the Maternity and Parental Leave (Amendment) Regulations 2002/2789 are also found.

A convenient print alternative for tracing implementing legislation is provided by the *EC Legislation Implementator* volume of *Halsbury's Statutory Instruments* (para.7–28). If you have already discovered the reference for a directive, a chronological listing of directives enables you to look up the implementing UK legislation. All three statutory instruments noted above for Directive 96/34/EC can be traced from the entry for the directive. The *EC Legislation Implementator* is revised annually.

> **TIPS** • *The EC Legislation Implementor volume of Halsbury's Statutory Instruments provides a convenient quick reference source for UK implementing legislation. The full text can then be found online using UK legislation databases.*

## CASE LAW

▶ 8.13

There are two courts which interpret and enforce law of the European Union. The first, the European Court of Justice (ECJ), has been in existence since the European Communities were founded. The second, the Court of the First Instance (CFI), gave its first judgments in 1990. The ECJ hears all types of cases, including appeals from the CFI, but the CFI only hears competition, anti-dumping and staff cases. The case law of both courts has assumed a position of great importance.

The *Official Journal C Series* carries notices of cases pending before the courts. Brief details only of the nature of the proceedings and the judgment are provided.

### European Court Reports

**8.14 ▶** The official source of European Court judgments is the *Reports of Cases before the Court*. These are more commonly known as the *European Court Reports* (abbreviated to E.C.R.). In this series, the opinion of the Advocate General is given alongside the judgment. This is an important stage in the proceedings before the European Court of Justice. The Advocate General's opinion is not binding on the court, but it is of great use to students of EU law in that it will include a thorough analysis of the facts and legal arguments in the case. There is an English language set of the *Reports* covering the judgments of the courts since 1954. Since 1990, the *Reports* have been split into two parts in each issue. Part I contains ECJ cases and Part II contains CFI cases. Since 1994 staff cases are being published in a separate series known as *Reports of European Community Staff Cases* (ECS-SC), and are not all translated into other languages.

Although the E.C.R. is the official series, it suffers from major delays in publication. Precise and accurate translation into the various EU languages results in delays of up to two years which makes it impossible to use it for recent cases. However, both opinions of the Advocate General and judgments of the European Court of Justice are available online from the Court website (at *www.curia.europa.eu*). Opinions and judgments for 1989 onwards can also be searched from the EUR-Lex website (at *www.eur-lex.europa.eu*). These sites provide the official online source of all opinions and judgments from the European Court of Justice. As with all EU websites, there is no subscription charge for access. (See para.8.18 to para.8.22 for more on searching using these sites).

### Citation of European Court of Justice and Court of First Instance cases

**8.15 ▶** The case citation is made up as follows:

1. case number;
2. year;
3. name of parties;
4. citation: indicating where the case can be found in the European Court Reports (E.C.R.):

> E.g. Case C–59/89 *Commission v Germany* [1991] E.C.R. I–2607; Case T–12/90 *Bayer v Commission* [1991] E.C.R. II–219.

Alternatively the citations for the European Court Reports can be written as follows:

> [1991] I E.C.R. 2067 and [1991] II E.C.R. 219.

Note that each case after 1990 is preceded by the letter C (European Court of Justice) or the letter T (Court of First Instance). Also note that a case with a reference . . . /07, for example, means that the application or reference to the court was made in 2007. The judgment was not given in that year. This means that you cannot automatically go to the E.C.R. for the year 2007 to find the judgment.

## Other sources of case law

A number of UK published law reports publish reports of European Court of Justice cases. The    **8.16**
*Common Market Law Reports* (C.M.L.R) provides the main alternative to the European Court
Reports. It is published by Sweet & Maxwell and also covers the cases with an EU dimension in
national courts. C.M.L.R. appears sooner than the *European Court Reports* with a full, if not
official, report. Both the Advocate General's opinion and the judgment made in a case are
included in the reports. Whilst it does not report all cases, it does report all cases of significance. The reports are available online from Westlaw UK (para.2.4).

The *All England Reporter (European Cases)*—All E.R. (EC)—has published decisions from
the Court of Justice and the Court of First Instance since 1995. The reports are available online
from LexisNexis Butterworths (para.2.3). *European Community Cases* (C.E.C) is another source
of case law. Only very important cases are covered. Specialist law report series such as *Fleet
Street Reports* or *Industrial Relations Law Reports* also include relevant EC case law.

Both Westlaw UK and LexisNexis Butterworths can also be used to search for judgments
online as noted in the following sections.

## How to find a Court of Justice judgment or opinion if you have the reference

Suppose you are given the following case reference: Case C-196/04 *Cadbury Schweppes Plc v*    **8.17**
*Inland Revenue Commissioners*. How do you find it?

Both the Court of Justice website (at curia.europa.eu) and the EUR-Lex website (at
*www.eur-lex-europa.eu*) provide free public access to the full text of judgments and opinions.
Whichever route you choose, the final text is the same. Direct access to judgments from the
Court of Justice site is possible using the "Numerical access to case-law" link under the Case-
law heading. Coverage is from 1953 onwards and pending cases are also listed. Recent judgments and opinions (from 1997 onwards) can be found using the site's search form. The *Cadbury
Schweppes* case can then be found using either the case number or the "Names of parties"
search. The Advocate General's opinion and the judgment are found as separate entries in the
database along with links to the *Official Journal* notices for the case.

Numerical access to case law is also possible under the "Case-law" link on the EUR-Lex
home page. Links for the most recent judgment or opinions are provided at the top of the page,
followed by a menu which allows either judgments or opinions to be selected by year and case
number. For the period 1954 to 1997 access is by year only. Database searching for cases is
possible (for 1997 onwards) using the "Simple Search" link from the home page. The search by
"Natural number" option can then be chosen and a case law search specified.

An alternative route to Court of Justice cases is provided by Westlaw UK (para.2.4)
and LexisNexis Butterworths (para.2.3). There are some advantages to using Westlaw UK in
particular.

All Court of Justice cases can be found in Westlaw UK using the EU search page. A
search using "C-196/04" in the "Case or Document No" search box finds both the opinion and
judgment for the case. The "Commentary" section at the end of the judgment text in Westlaw
UK includes, in addition, brief notes of articles on the case in European journals.

The *Common Market Law Reports* are also included in Westlaw UK. As noted in
para.8.16, these report all significant Court of Justice cases. To check for a reported version
of the *Cadbury Schweppes* case, use the "Cases" search page in Westlaw UK. The "Citation"

**Fig 8.5**

Example page from the *Common Market Law Reports*, [2007] 1 C.M.L.R. 2

## *43  Cadbury Schweppes Plc and Another v Commissioners of Inland Revenue

(Case C-196/04)

Before the Court of Justice of the European Communities (Grand Chamber)

12 September 2006

## [2007] 1 C.M.L.R. 2

Presiding , Skouris P.; Jann and Rosas P.C.; Cunha Rodrigues , Silva de Lapuerta , Lenaerts ( Rapporteur ), Juhász , Arestis and Borg Barthet JJ.; Léger A.G.

September 12, 2006

Abuse of rights; Controlled foreign companies; Corporation tax; Freedom of establishment; Proportionality; Tax advantage

H1 Establishment— national legislation including profits of controlled foreign companies in tax base of parent company— scope of Arts 43 and 48 EC— applicable to national provisions affecting shareholdings giving definite influence on company decisions— establishment in Member State offering tax advantages— not of itself constituting abuse of rights— direct tax measures— capable of restricting freedom of establishment— obstacles to that freedom encompassing measures hindering establishment in another Member State— legislation at issue involving difference in treatment of resident companies based on level of taxation of controlled foreign company— dissuasive effect in relation to acquisition of controlling interest— restriction on freedom of establishment— public interest— prevention of reduction in tax revenue not valid justification— no presumption of tax avoidance— objective of freedom of establishment— economic and social interpenetration— legitimate to restrict artificial arrangements not reflecting economic reality— legislation at issue suitable to prevent abusive practices— lack of proportionality— motive test— consideration given only to subjective consideration of avoiding higher taxes— necessary to take account of objective considerations— whether incorporation of controlled company reflecting actual establishment carrying out genuine economic activities.

H2 Reference from the United Kingdom by the Special Commissioners of Income Tax, London, under Art.234 EC.

H3 According to legislation in the United Kingdom on corporation tax (the legislation on CFCs), where a company resident in the United Kingdom (resident company) had a holding of more than 50 per cent in a controlled foreign company (CFC) in a State in which the CFC was subject to a " lower level of taxation" within the meaning of that legislation, the profits made by such a controlled company **\*44** were attributed to the resident company, which was taxed on them. Where, on the other hand, the controlled company was incorporated and taxed in the United Kingdom or in a State in which it was not subject to a " lower level of taxation" within the meaning of the legislation on CFCs, the resident company was not taxed on the profits of the controlled company. CS, a company in the United Kingdom, was the parent company of CS. That group included, inter alia, two subsidiaries in Ireland, which CS owned indirectly through a chain of subsidiaries at the head of which was CSO. The Irish subsidiaries were established in the IFSC in Dublin to benefit from its favourable tax regime, and were subject to a " lower level of taxation" at the time of the facts at issue. Their business was to raise finance and to provide that finance to subsidiaries in the CS group. The UK tax authorities took the view that, for the 1996 financial year, none of the conditions for exemption from taxation provided for by the legislation on CFCs applied to those subsidiaries and, therefore, claimed corporation tax from CSO on the profits made by the Irish subsidiaries in that financial year. On appeal against the tax notice issued by the tax authorities, CS and CSO argued that the legislation on CFCs was contrary to Arts 43, 49 and 56 EC. The referring court sought a preliminary ruling from the Court of Justice as to whether Arts 43, 49 and 56 EC precluded national tax legislation such search on the page only recognises the *European Court Reports* citation for the case, [2006] ECR I–7995, not the case number, so you may need to search by party name. However a search finds the case reported in the *Common Market Law Reports*, [2007] 1 C.M.L.R. 2. The importance of the case for UK law also meant that it was reported in the *Law Reports* and the *Weekly Law Reports*. Citations and links to full text are available to these reports from the Westlaw UK results page. The "Case Analysis" entry for the case in Westlaw UK also provides references for the considerable number of UK journals that have commented on the case.

> **TIPS** • *Use "Free text" or party name searches to find Court of Justice cases in UK law reports. Case numbers are not recognised in the "Cases" citation search of either Westlaw UK or LexisNexis Butterworths.*

EU cases in LexisNexis Butterworths are currently (misleadingly) found under the "International Cases" heading within the "Cases" search. Searching is limited to a single search box, with no specific provision for citation or party name searching.

### How to find a judgment of the Court of Justice on a subject

What can you do if you want to find cases on, for instance, the Common Customs Tariff? ▶ **8.18**

Both the Court of Justice website and the EUR-Lex websites allow the full text of judgments and opinions to be searched from 1997 onwards. Keywords can be entered using the Court of Justice search form found under "Case-law" (at *www.curia.europa.eu*). Using EUR-Lex, select the "Simple Search" option from the home page (at *www.europa.eu.int/eur-lex/en*) and choose the Case-law file category, before selecting the option enabling a search using search terms. The phrase "Common Customs Tariff" can then be entered to find relevant cases.

Searches can also be made using the "EU" search page in Westlaw UK or in the "Cases" search in LexisNexis Butterworths. The advice given in para.7.10 on searching full-text databases of UK case law holds equally well for searches of EU case law. Unless you are only interested in very recent cases, for example, your first concern, if searching for cases on the Common Customs Tariff, will be to find a way of further restricting your search so that a manageable list of results can be found. Are you for instance interested in cases where issues of nomenclature are important? Or is it another aspect of cases discussing the Commons Customs Tariff that interests you?

The print volumes of *The Digest* (para.7.14) provide a more selective approach to finding Court of Justice cases by subject.

### How to trace further information on a case

If a case has been reported in a UK published law report, the Westlaw UK "Cases" search ▶ **8.19** (para.3–15), is a useful source of case summaries and further information. As noted in para.8.17, the "Case Analysis" entry for *Cadbury Schweppes Plc v Inland Revenue Commissioners*, for example, displays references to journal articles discussing the case. Later cases citing the case are also noted.

The Westlaw UK "Cases" search can be particularly useful for tracing information on key cases that have had a significant impact on EC law. A search for "Factortame", for example, under "Cases Cited" in the "Advanced Search" finds a number of UK cases for which the

*Factortame* case has been significant. The results page lists cases which have applied, followed, or considered *Factortame*, both in the European Court of Justice and in UK domestic courts. Citations for case comment in journal articles are also given in the relevant "Case Analysis" entries.

### How to trace cases which have interpreted EU legislation

8.20 ▶ Commonly in research, there is a need to trace cases which are concerned with the interpretation of the provisions of EU law. For example, how do you find Court of Justice cases which have interpreted Directive 93/104/EC on the organisation of working time?

The best approach is to search for the directive using EUR-Lex as described in para.8.8. Once the directive has been found, the accompanying bibliographic notice provides links to any EU cases providing interpretation. A number of cases are listed for Directive 93/104/EC, including C–84/94 *United Kingdom v Council of the European Union*, which declared the directive void.

An alternative approach is to use the Westlaw UK "Cases" search (para.3.15) to search for UK reported cases which have interpreted the directive. Results will include Court of Justice cases reported in reports such as the *Common Market Law Reports* along with UK domestic reported cases. Search using "93/104" as a search term.

### How to trace recent judgments

8.21 ▶ If you wish to go directly to the full text of a judgment (or opinion) which you know to be very recent, the EUR-Lex website (at *www.eur-lex.europa.eu*) provides a convenient list of recent judgments under the "Case-law" section of the website.

A complete listing of judicial proceedings is available from the "News" section of the European Court of Justice website (at *www.curia.europa.eu*). Brief notes of recent judgments are available along with notes of opinions and new cases brought before the court. A link is provided for each case to the Court's case law database.

The Court press releases on cases can also be found in the "News" section of the website. These can often help identify the key issues considered in recent judgments.

## LEGAL ENCYCLOPEDIAS

8.22 ▶ *Vaughan: Law of the European Union* provides coverage of EU Law by subject. The *Encyclopedia of European Union Laws* also provides coverage of all EU constitutional texts. There are four sections: the Treaties, the Institutions, Ancillary texts, and the Union Pillars.

*Halsbury's Laws of England* (para.7.3) is also a potential source of information on EU Law. If you are using the online version from LexisNexis Butterworths, a search on Directive 2003/88 on working time, for example, finds a section summarising EU requirements and noting UK implementation. Relevant Court of Justice cases are also noted and the update section cites a relatively recent judgment relating to the directive (C–124/05), *Federatie Nederlandse Vakbeweging v Netherlands* [2006] All E.R. (EC) 913.

## BOOKS

The European Commission publishes a wide range of material providing introductions, overviews and summaries of topics. All these will be available to you if your library is a European Documentation Centre (see para.8.1). The library catalogue will help you locate them.

⬤ **8.23**

The library catalogue can also help you find relevant textbooks. These may include books on political and economic aspects of European integration found outside the law section of your library. Remember that books in almost any area of law can provide discussion of EU law. Though there will be a specific section on EU law within your library, the textbooks found there are not the only ones that can help you understand EU law.

ECLAS, the European Commission's own library catalogue can provide an effective means of tracing details of books of all kinds of EU law and wider EU related issues. The Central Library page of the European Commission site provides a link to the catalogue search page (at *http://ec.europa.eu/eclas/F*). Limit the language choice to "English" and the format choice to "Books" to find books in English on a subject, e.g. competition law.

## JOURNALS

Many legal journals cover EU topics in a selective manner. Major English language journals that specialise in the subject include the *Common Market Law Review*, the *European Law Review*, the *European Business Law Review*, the *European Competition Law Review*, *International and Comparative Law Quarterly* and the *Yearbook of European Law*. Your library may be able to provide access to recent issues both online and in print (see para.5.2).

⬤ **8.24**

### How to find articles on EU law

If you are looking for recent articles on EU law the best source for coverage in UK law journals is the *Legal Journals Index*. See para.5–6 for further information on searching the index using keywords. Citations for Court of Justice cases and EC legislation can also be used to trace articles.

⬤ **8.25**

The European Commission's ECLAS catalogue (at *www.ec.europa.eu/eclas/F*) can also help trace journal articles on EC law. Limit the format choice to "Article" and the language to "English" to find details of English language journal articles on a subject, e.g. "Common Customs Tariff".

### The Bulletin of the European Union and General Report

The "Documents" section of the Europa website (at *europa.eu*) provides a link to the current issue of the *Bulletin of the European Union*, a monthly review of the Union's work. The EU's standard headings are used and news items are listed for each subject area. These include notes of new legislation. Earlier issues can also be accessed.

⬤ **8.26**

The *General Report on the Activities of the European Union* can also be accessed from Europa's "Documents" page. The *General Review* is an annual review, summarising key developments in particular areas. EU actions can be reviewed under standard subject headings, e.g. "Environment", for the previous year. If you turn to previous issues of the *General Review* a picture can be built up of the development of EU policy in an area.

## CURRENT INFORMATION

**8.27** ▶ Recent EU developments can be traced using the "Press room" section of the Europa website. Access is provided from the "Services" section of the home page (at *www.europa.eu*). The latest press releases are available along with a list of upcoming events. A link to the RAPID database at the end of the current press releases, allows press releases to be searched from 1985 onwards. The database search (at *www.europa.eu/rapid*) can be restricted to search for press releases from particular EU institutions, e.g. the Court of Justice, or particular topics.

If your library has a subscription to the Nexis news service (see para.5.22), you can also access the full-text news coverage of many European newspapers.

# Appendix I  Online Sources of Scots and Northern Ireland Law

## SCOTS LAW

▶ A1.1

### Case Law

▶ A1.2

Westlaw UK (para.2.4) provides access to the two major series of Scottish law reports:

*Session Cases*

cited, e.g. *Billig v Council of the Law Society of Scotland* 2008 S.C. 150

*Scots Law Times*

cited, e.g. *A v Scottish Ministers* 2008 S.L.T. 412

LexisNexis Butterworths (para.2.3) provides access to the Law Society of Scotland's *Scottish Criminal Case Reports* and *Scottish Civil Law Reports*. Access is also provided to *Butterworths Scottish Case Digests*.

Judgments are available from the Scottish Court Service (at *www.scotcourts.gov.uk*); also from the BAILII website (at *www.bailii.org*).

### Acts of the Scottish Parliament

▶ A1.3

Acts of the Scottish Parliament (ASPs) are cited, e.g. as

Abolition of Bridge Tolls (Scotland) Act 2008 asp 1

The official version of the text is provided by Queen's Printer for Scotland (at *www.oqps.gov.uk*). BAILII (at *www.bailii.org*) provides alternative non-subscription access. Justis UK Statutes (para.2.6) and Lawtel (para.2.5) also provide access to the original unamended text. Links are provided to amending legislation.

LexisNexis Butterworths (para.2.3) and Westlaw UK (para.2.4) and the Statute Law Database (para.2.13) provide access to the amended text of Acts in force.

### Scottish Statutory Instruments

▶ A1.4

Scottish Statutory Instruments are cited, e.g. as

The Police (Special Constables) (Scotland) Regulations 2008 S.S.I. 2008/117

The official version of the text is provided by Queen's Printer for Scotland (at *www.oqps.gov.uk*). The Statute Law Database (para.2.13) and BAILII (para.2.15) provide alternative non-subscription access.

LexisNexis Butterworths (para.2.3) and Westlaw UK (para.2.4) and the Statute Law Database (para.2.13) provide subscription access.

### The Scottish Parliament

**A1.5** ▶ The *Official Report* of the Scottish Parliament can be found on the Parliament website (*www.scottish.parliament.uk*). The "Current Business" section of the website provides links to the full text of Bills, Committee web pages, research briefings and the Official Report of Proceedings.

### The Scottish Executive

**A1.6** ▶ Papers from the Scottish Executive can be found on its website (at *www.scotland.gov.uk*).

### Official Publications

**A1.7** ▶ Official Publications can be traced using the TSO Scotland section of the TSO bookshop Parliamentary and Legal pages (at *www.tso.co.uk/parliament*); other official publications can be traced using the UKOP database (para.6.16).

### Encyclopedias

**A1.8** ▶ The *Laws of Scotland: Stair Memorial Encyclopedia* is available from LexisNexis Butterworths (para.2.3). *Laws of Scotland* provides a comprehensive statement of the law of Scotland, comparable to that provided for England and Wales by *Halsbury's Laws of England* (para.7.3).

Westlaw UK (para.2.4) provides access to the full text of *Renton and Brown Criminal Procedure* and *Renton and Brown Criminal Procedure Legislation*.

## NORTHERN IRELAND LAW

### Case law

**A1.9** ▶ LexisNexis Professional (para.2.3) provides full text access to the major series of Northern Ireland law reports:
*Northern Ireland Reports*
cited, e.g. *Re Duffy* [2008] N.I. 152
The *Northern Ireland Judgments Bulletin* is not available online. It is cited,
e.g. *Belfast Fashions v Wellworth Properties Ltd* [2005] N.I.J.B. 95
Judgments reported in the N.I.J.B. (along with other "unreported" judgments) can be found for the mid–1980s onwards using the LexisNexis Butterworths "Cases" search. Judgments from 2000 onwards are available from the Northern Ireland Court Service (at *www.courtsni.gov.uk*); also the BAILII website (para.2.15).

### Northern Ireland Statutes

**A1.10** ▶ The updated text of Northern Ireland Statutes from 1922 onwards can be found using the Statute Law Database (para.2.13). Updates currently lag three years behind the current date. Pre-1988 revised legislation can be found on the Northern Ireland Legislation page of the OPSI legislation website (at *www.opsi.gov.uk/legislation*), along with original versions of Northern Ireland legislation from 1987 onwards. Northern Ireland primary legislation includes:
Acts of the Northern Ireland Assembly cited:
e.g. Charities Act (Northern Ireland) 2008 c.12

Orders in Council cited: e.g. Criminal Justice (Northern Ireland) Order 2008
Orders in council are also cited as UK statutory instruments, cited, e.g. S.I. 2005/255 (N.I. 1).

## Statutory Rules of Northern Ireland

The unamended text of all secondary legislation for Northern Ireland from 1996 onwards can be found on both the OPSI legislation website (at *www.opsi.gov.uk/legislation*), the BAILII website (para.2.15) and the Statute Law Database (para.2–13). A selection of Statutory Rules is available for 1991–1995.

▶ A1.11

## Northern Ireland Assembly

The *Official Report* of debates for the Assembly is available from the Northern Ireland Assembly website (at *www.niassembly.gov.uk*). Assembly and Committee Reports (published as Northern Ireland Assembly Papers) are also available.

▶ A1.12

## Northern Ireland Executive

The Northern Ireland Executive website (at *www.northernireland.gov.uk*) provides links to Executive publications and to the websites of Northern Ireland government departments. Policing and criminal justice currently remains the responsibility of the Northern Ireland Office (NIO). Its website (at *www.nio.gov.uk*) has links for publications and statistics and research.

▶ A1.13

## Official Publications

Official Publications can be traced using the TSO Ireland section of the TSO bookshop Parliamentary and Legal pages (at *www.tsoshop.co.uk/parliament*); other official publications can be traced using the UKOP database (para.6.16).

▶ A1.14

## Bulletin of Northern Ireland Law

The *Bulletin of Northern Ireland Law* provides updates on legal developments in Northern Ireland. Online access is available from SLS Legal Publications (at *www.sls.qub.ac.uk*). This is a subscription service.

▶ A1.15

# Appendix II  Abbreviations of Reports, Series and Journals

This alphabetical list contains a selection of the more commonly used abbreviations in the UK, the EU and the Commonwealth. It is not exhaustive and further information can be found in D. Raistrick, *Index to Legal Citations and Abbreviations* and in the I.A.L.S. *Manual of Legal Citations*, Vols. I and II, the *Index to Legal Periodicals*, the *Legal Journals Index*. *The Digest* (Cumulative Supplement) and the *Current Law Citators* also contain lists of abbreviations, at the front.

A.C.—Law Reports Appeal Cases 1891—
A.J.—Acts Juridica
A.J.I.L.—American Journal of International Law
A.L.J.—Australian Law Journal
A.L.R.—American Law Reports Annotated
A.L.R.—Australian Law Reports, formerly Argus Law Reports
All E.R.—All England Law Reports 1936—
All E.R. Rep.—All England Law Reports Reprint 1558–1935
Am. J. Comp. L.—American Journal of Comparative Law
Anglo-Am. L.R.—Anglo-American Law Review
Ann. Dig.—Annual Digest of Public International Law Cases (1919–1949). (From 1950 this series has been published as the International Law Reports—I.L.R.)
App. Cas.—Law Reports Appeal Cases 1875–1890
B.C.L.C.—Butterworths Company Law Cases
B.D.I.L.—British Digest of International Law
B.F.S.P.—British and Foreign State Papers
B.I.L.C.—British International Law Cases
B.J.A.L.—British Journal of Administrative Law
B.J. Crim.—British Journal of Criminology
B.J.L.S.—British Journal of Law and Society
B.L.R.—Building Law Reports
B.L.R.—Business Law Review
B.N.I.L.—Bulletin of Northern Ireland Law
B.T.R.—British Tax Review
B.Y.I.L.—British Yearbook of International Law
Bull. E.C.—Bulletin of the European Communities
Business L.R.—Business Law Review
C.A.R.—Criminal Appeal Reports
C.A.T.—Court of Appeal Transcript (unpublished)
C.B.R.—Canadian Bar Review
C.D.E.—Cahiers de Droit Européen
C.J.Q.—Civil Justice Quarterly

C.L.—Current Law
C.L.J.—Cambridge Law Journal
C.L.P.—Current Legal Problems
C.L.R.—Commonwealth Law Reports (Australia)
C.M.L.R.—Common Market Law Reports
C.M.L. Rev.—Common Market Law Review
C.P.D.—Law Reports Common Pleas Division 1875–1880
C.T.S.—Consolidated Treaty Series
Calif. L. Rev.—California Law Review
Camb. L.J.—Cambridge Law Journal
Can. B.R.—Canadian Bar Review
Ch.—Law Reports Chancery Division 1891–
Ch.D.—Law Reports Chancery Division 1875–1890
Co. Law.—Company Lawyer
Colum. L. Rev.—Columbia Law Review
Com. Cas.—Commercial Cases 1895–1941
Constr. L.J.—Construction Law Journal
Conv.; Conv.—N.S.—Conveyancer and Property Lawyer
Cox C.C.—Cox's Criminal Law Cases
Cr. App. R.; Cr. App. Rep.—Criminal Appeal Reports
Cr.App.R.S.—Criminal Appeal Reports (Sentencing)
Crim. L.R.—Criminal Law Review
D.L.R.—Dominion Law Reports (Canada)
D.U.L.J.—Dublin University Law Journal
E.C.R.—European Court Reports
E.G.—Estates Gazette
E.G.L.R.—Estates Gazette Law Reports
E.H.R.R.—European Human Rights Reports
E.I.P.R.—European Intellectual Property Review
E.L. Rev.—European Law Review
E.R.—*English Reports*
Eng. Rep.—*English Reports*
Eur. Comm. H.R. D.R.—European Commission for Human Rights Decisions and
    Reports
Eur. Court H.R. Series A/Series B—European Court of Human Rights Series A & B
Euro C.L.—European Current Law
Ex.D.—Law Reports Exchequer Division 1875–1880
F.L.R.—Family Law Reports
F.L.R.—Federal Law Reports
F.S.R.—Fleet Street Reports
F.T.—Financial Times
Fam.—Law Reports Family Division 1972–
Fam. Law—Family Law
Grotius Trans.—Transactions of the Grotius Society

H.L.R.—Housing Law Reports
Harv. L. Rev.—Harvard Law Review
I.C.J. Rep.—International Court of Justice Reports
I.C.J.Y.B.—International Court of Justice Yearbook
I.C.L.Q.—International and Comparative Law Quarterly
I.C.R.—Industrial Cases Reports 1975–
I.C.R.—Industrial Court Reports 1972–1974
I.J.; Ir. Jur.—Irish Jurist
I.L.J.—Industrial Law Journal
I.L.M.—International Legal Materials
I.L.Q.—International Law Quarterly
I.L.R.—International Law Reports
I.L.R.M.—Irish Law Reports Monthly
I.L.T.; Ir.L.T.—Irish Law Times
I.R.—Irish Reports
I.R.L.R.—Industrial Relations Law Reports
I.R.R.R.—Industrial Relations Review & Reports
Imm.A.R.—Immigration Appeal Reports
Ir. Jur.—Irish Jurist
I.T.R.—Industrial Tribunal Reports
J.B.L.—Journal of Business Law
J.C.—Session Cases: Justiciary Cases (Scotland)
J.C.L.—Journal of Criminal Law
J.C.M.S.—Journal of Common Market Studies
J.I.S.E.L.—Journal of the Irish Society for European Law
J.I.S.L.L.—Journal of the Irish Society for Labour Law
J.L.S.—Journal of Law and Society
J.L.S.—Journal of the Law Society of Scotland
J. Legal Ed.—Journal of Legal Education
J.O.—Journal Officiel des Communautés Européennes
J.P.—Justice of the Peace Reports (also Justice of the Peace (journal))
J.P.I.L.—Journal of Personal Injury Litigation
J.P.L.—Journal of Planning and Environment Law
J.R.—Juridical Review
J.S.P.T.L.—Journal of the Society of Public Teachers of Law
J.S.W.L.—Journal of Social Welfare Law
K.B.—Law Reports: King's Bench Division 1901–1952
K.I.R.—Knight's Industrial Reports
L.A.G. Bul.—Legal Action Group Bulletin
L.G.C.—Local Government Chronicle
L.G.R.—Knight's Local Government Reports
L.J.—Law Journal 1866–1965 (newspaper)
L.J. Adm.—Law Journal: Admiralty N.S. 1865–1875
L.J. Bcy.—Law Journal: Bankruptcy N.S. 1832–1880

L.J.C.C.R.—Law Journal: County Courts Reports 1912–1933

L.J.C.P.—Law Journal: Common Pleas N.S. 1831–1875

L.J. Ch.—Law Journal: Chancery N.S. 1831–1946

L.J. Eccl.—Law Journal: Ecclesiastical Cases N.S. 1866–1875

L.J. Eq.—Law Journal: Equity N.S. 1831–1946

L.J. Ex.—Law Journal: Exchequer N.S. 1831–1875

L.J. Ex. Eq.—Law Journal: Exchequer in Equity 1835–1841

L.J.K.B. (or Q.B.)—Law Journal: King's (or Queen's) Bench N.S. 1831–1946

L.J.M.C.—Law Journal: Magistrates' Cases N.S. 1831–1896

L.J.N.C.—Law Journal: Notes of Cases 1866–1892

L.J.N.C.C.R.—Law Journal Newspaper: County Court Reports 1934–1947

L.J.O.S.—Law Journal (Old Series) 1822–1831

L.J.P.—Law Journal: Probate, Divorce and Admiralty N.S. 1875–1946

L.J.P.D. & A.—Law Journal: Probate, Divorce and Admiralty N.S. 1875–1946

L.J.P. & M.—Law Journal: Probate and Matrimonial Cases N.S. 1858–1859, 1866–1875

L.J.P.C.—Law Journal: Privy Council N.S. 1865–1946

L.J.P.M. & A.—Law Journal: Probate, Matrimonial and Admiralty N.S. 1860–1865

L.J.R.—Law Journal Reports 1947–1949

L. Lib.J.—Law Library Journal

L.M.C.L.Q.—Lloyd's Maritime and Commercial Law Quarterly

L.N.T.S.—League of Nations Treaty Series

L.Q.R.—Law Quarterly Review

L.R.A. & E.—Law Reports: Admiralty and Ecclesiastical Cases 1865–1875

L.R.C.C.R.—Law Reports: Crown Cases Reserved 1865–1875

L.R. C.P.—Law Reports: Common Pleas Cases 1865–1875

L.R. Ch. App.—Law Reports: Chancery Appeal Cases 1865–1875

L.R. Eq.—Law Reports: Equity Cases 1866–1875

L.R. Ex.—Law Reports: Exchequer Cases 1865–1875

L.R.H.L.—Law Reports: English and Irish Appeals 1866–1875

L.R. P. & D.—Law Reports: Probate and Divorce Cases 1865–1875

L.R.P.C.—Law Reports: Privy Council Appeals 1865–1875

L.R.Q.B.—Law Reports: Queen's Bench 1865–1875

L.R.R.P.; L.R. R.P.C.—Law Reports: Restrictive Practices Cases 1957–1973

L.S.—Legal Studies

L.S. Gaz.—Law Society Gazette

L.T.—Law Times

L.T.R.; L.T. Rep.—Law Times Reports (New Series) 1859–1947

L.T.Jo.—Law Times (newspaper) 1843–1965

L.T.O.S.—Law Times Reports (Old Series) 1843–1860

L. Teach.—Law Teacher

Law & Contemp. Prob.—Law and Contemporary Problems

Lit.—Litigation

Liverpool L.R.—Liverpool Law Review

Ll. L.L.R.; Ll.L.R.; LL.L. Rep.—Lloyd's List Law Reports later Lloyd's Law Reports
Lloyd's L.R.; Lloyd's Rep.—Lloyd's List Law Reports later Lloyd's Law Reports
M.L.J.—Malayan Law Journal
M.L.R.—Modern Law Review
Man. Law—Managerial Law
Med. Sci. & Law—Medicine, Science & the Law
Mich. L. Rev.—Michigan Law Review
N.I.—Northern Ireland Law Reports
N.I.J.B.—Northern Ireland Law Reports Bulletin of Judgments
N.I.L.Q.—Northern Ireland Legal Quarterly
N.I.L.R.—Northern Ireland Law Reports
N.L.J.—New Law Journal
N.Y.U.L. Rev.—New York University Law Review
N.Z.L.R.—New Zealand Law Reports
New L.J.—New Law Journal
O.J.—Official Journal of the European Communities
O.J.C.—Official Journal of the European Communities: Information and Notices
O.J.L.—Official Journal of the European Communities: Legislation, e.g. 1972, L139/28
O.J.L.S.—Oxford Journal of Legal Studies
P.—Law Reports: Probate, Divorce and Admiralty 1891–1971
P. & C.R.—Planning (Property from 1968) and Compensation Reports
P.C.I.J.—Permanent Court of International Justice Reports of Judgments
P.D.—Law Reports: Probate Division 1875–1890
P.L.—Public Law
P.N.—Professional Negligence
Q.B.—Law Reports: Queen's Bench Division 1891–1901, 1952–
Q.B.D.—Law Reports: Queen's Bench Division 1875–1890
R.D.E.—Rivista di Diritto Europeo
R.G.D.I.P.—Revue Générale de Droit International Public
R.M.C.—Revue du Marché Commun
R.P.C.—Reports of Patent, Design & Trade Mark Cases
R.R.—*Revised Reports*
R.R.C.—Ryde's Rating Cases
R.T.R.—Road Traffic Reports
R.V.R.—Rating & Valuation Reporter
Rec.—Recueil des Cours
Rec.—Recueil de la Jurisprudence de la Cour (Court of Justice of the European Communities)
S.A.—South African Law Reports
S.C.—Session Cases (Scotland)
S.C. (H.L.)—Session Cases: House of Lords (Scotland)
S.C.(J.)—Session Cases: Justiciary Cases (Scotland)
S.C.C.R.—Scottish Criminal Case Reports
S.I.—Statutory Instruments

S.J.—Solicitors Journal
S.L.R.—Law Reporter/Scottish Law Review
S.L.T.—Scots Law Times
S.R.—Statutory Rules (Northern Ireland)
S.R. & O.—Statutory Rules and Orders
S.T.C.—Simon's Tax Cases
Scolag.—Bulletin of the Scottish Legal Action Group
Sol. Jo.—Solicitors Journal
St. Tr.; State Tr.—State Trials 1163–1820
Stat.L.R.—Statute Law Review
State Tr. N.S.—State Trials (New Series) 1820–1858
T.C.—Reports of Tax Cases
T.L.R.—Times Law Reports
TSO—The Stationery Office, 1996–
Tax Cas.—Reports of Tax Cases
Tul. L. Rev.—Tulane Law Review
U. Chi. L. Rev.—University of Chicago Law Review
U.K.T.S.—United Kingdom Treaty Series
U.N.T.S.—United Nations Treaty Series
U.N.J.Y.—United Nations Juridical Yearbook
U.N.Y.B.—Yearbook of the United Nations
U. Pa. L. Rev.—University of Pennsylvania Law Review
U.S. —United States Supreme Court Reports
U.S.T.S.—United States Treaty Series
V.A.T.T.R.—Value Added Tax Tribunal Reports
V.L.R.—Victorian Law Reports (Australia)
W.I.R.—West Indian Reports
W.L.R.—Weekly Law Reports
W.N.—Weekly Notes
W.W.R.—Western Weekly Reporter
Y.B.—Yearbook (old law report), e.g. (1466) Y.B.Mich. (the term) 6 Edw. 4, pl.18, fol.7
    (plea, folio)
Y.B.W.A.—Yearbook of World Affairs
Yale L.J.—Yale Law Journal
Yearbook E.C.H.R.—Yearbook of the European Convention on Human Rights

# Appendix III  How Do I Find? A Summary of Sources for English Law

## ABBREVIATIONS (para.3.5)

**A3.1** ▶ Cardiff Index to Legal Abbreviations
D. Raistrick, *Index to Legal Citations and Abbreviations*.
The front pages of: *Current Law Case Citator*; *The Digest*, Vol. 1 and the *Cumulative Supplement*; *Halsbury's Laws of England*, Vol.1.

## A3.2 ▶ BOOKS

**A3.3** ▶ **Tracing Books on a Subject**
Use the library catalogue (para.7.29).
Consult bibliographies (see below).

**Tracing Books by Author or Title**
**A3.4** ▶ Use the library catalogue (para.7.29).
Consult bibliographies (see below).

## BIBLIOGRAPHIES

**A3.5** ▶ D. Raistrick, *Lawyers' Law Books* (para.7.31).
*Current Publications in Legal and Related Fields* (authors, titles and subjects) (para.7.33).
*Legal Bibliography of the British Commonwealth* (useful for older books) (para.7.35).
*Bibliography on Foreign and Comparative Law* (para.7.35).
*British National Bibliography* (para.7.36).
*Law Books 1876–1981* (para.7.34).
Specialist legal bibliographies (para.7.35)—ask the library staff for advice.
The catalogues of large specialist and national libraries (para.7.29).
Sources for books in print (para.7.37).

## FINDING CASES

**A3.6** ▶ **If you Know the Name of the Case**
(Summary: after para.3.20)
Westlaw UK "Cases" search (para.3.15).

*Current Law Case Citators* (para.3.16).
Online databases of case law (para.2.2, para.3.8).
*The Digest* (para.3.15).
*English Reports* (for English cases before 1865) (para.3.10).

**For Recent Law Reports**
Westlaw UK "Cases" search (para.3.15).
*Current Law* (para.3.16).
Cases in recent issues of *The Times* and other newspapers (para.5.22).

▶ **A3.7**

**For Very Recent Unreported Cases (para.3.17)**
Online updates on recent cases (para.3.22).
*Daily Law Notes* (para.3.22).
Full-text databases of judgments (para.3.19 and para.3.20).

▶ **A3.8**

**Tracing Cases on a Subject**
Westlaw UK "Cases" search (para.7.9).
*Current Law* (para.7.12 and para.7.13).
*The Digest* (para.7.14).
Full-text case law databases (para.7.10).
*Halsbury's Laws of England* (para.7.4).
Databases providing updates to recent cases (para.3.22).

▶ **A3.9**

**Tracing the Subsequent Judicial History of a Case (para.7.18)**
Westlaw UK "Case Analysis" (para.7.9).
*Current Law* (para.7.12 and para.7.13).
*The Digest* (para.7.14).
Full-text case law databases (para.7.10).
*Law Reports Index* (table of cases judicially considered) (para.7.16).

▶ **A3.10**

**Are there any Journal Articles on this Case?**
Latest issue of *Current Law Monthly* (entries in the Cumulative Table of Cases).
Lawtel "Articles Index" (para.5.8).
*Legal Journals Index* (para.5.6).
Indexes to individual journals, e.g. *Modern Law Review; Law Quarterly Review*.

▶ **A3.11**

## GENERAL STATEMENTS OF THE LAW

Textbooks (para.7.29).
*Halsbury's Laws of England* (para.7.3).
Specialised legal encyclopedias (para.7.6).

▶ **A3.12**

## OFFICIAL PUBLICATIONS

### Tracing Official Publications

**A3.13** ▶ BOPCRIS database (pre–1995 publications) (para.6.16).
*General Index to Accounts and Papers* (para.6.16).
Proquest House of Commons Papers (para.6.16).
Printed indexes to the House of Commons Parliamentary Papers (para.6.16).
TSO *Daily Lists* and catalogues (HMSO pre-1996) (6–15).
UKOP database (para.6.16).

## A3.14 ▶ JOURNAL ARTICLES

### A3.15 ▶ Articles on a Subject

*Legal Journals Index* (para.5.6).
Lawtel "Articles Index" (para.5.8).
*Index to Legal Periodicals* (para.5.7).
*Index to Foreign Legal Periodicals* (para.5.9).
*Current Law Monthly Digests* (under appropriate subject heading) (para.7.12) and *Current Law Year Books* (at the back of the volumes) (para.7.13).
Other non-legal journal indexes (para.5.12 et seq.)

### Articles on a Case

**A3.16** ▶ Latest issue of *Current Law Monthly* (entries in the Cumulative Table of Cases).
*Legal Journals Index* (para.5.6).
Lawtel "Articles Index" (para.5.8).
Indexes to individual journals, e.g. *Modern Law Review; Law Quarterly Review*.

### Articles on an Act

**A3.17** ▶ *Legal Journals Index* (para.5.6).
Westlaw UK "Legislation Analysis" (para.4.18).
*Current Law Legislation Citators* (para.4.19).
Indexes to journals (under the appropriate subject heading).

### Tracing Journals

**A3.18** ▶ Consult the library's periodicals catalogue (para.1–9).
If the journal is not available in your library, use other catalogues, as for books (para.7–29)—ask the library staff for advice.

## A3.19 ▶ STATUTES

**A3.20** ▶ **Collections of the Statutes**
**A3.21** ▶ **Older statutes**
*Statutes of the Realm* (para.4–22).
*Statutes at Large* (various editions) (para.4–23).
*Acts and Ordinances of the Interregnum* (para.4–24).

## Modern statutes

BAILII United Kingdom Statutes (para.4–8).
Justis UK Statutes (para.4–9).
*Current Law Statutes* (para.4–11).
LexisNexis Butterworths "Legislation" search (para.4–13).
Westlaw UK "Legislation" search (para.4.14).
Statute Law Database (para.4.15).
*Halsbury's Statutes* (para.4.16).

▶ A3.22

## Collections of Acts by subject

Halsbury's Statutes (para.4.16, para.7.23).

▶ A3.23

## Annotated editions of statutes

*Current Law Statutes* (para.4.11).
*Halsbury's Statutes* (para.4.16, para.7.23).

## Statutes in force

*Halsbury's Statutes* (para.4.16, para.7.23).
Westlaw UK "Legislation Analysis" (para.4.18).
LexisNexis Butterworths "Legislation" search (para.4.13).
Westlaw UK "Legislation" search (para.4.14).
*Chronological Table of the Statutes* (para.4.20).
*Current Law Legislation Citators* (para.4.19).
*Is It In Force?* (para.4.17).

▶ A3.24

## Tracing Statutes on a Subject

*Halsbury's Statutes* (para.4.17, para.7.23).
Full-text databases of legislation (para.7.21) (other online sources para.7.22).
*Halsbury's Laws* (para.7.3).

▶ A3.25

## Indexes to the Statutes

*Chronological Table of the Statutes* (shows whether Acts of any date are still in force) (para.4.20).
*Is It In Force?* (para.4.17).
*Halsbury's Statutes* (alphabetically arranged by subject. Consult alphabetical list of statutes, then look in the *Cumulative Supplement* and *Noter-Up* service to check if an Act is still in force) (para.7.23).
*Public General Acts: Tables and Index* (annual—brings the information in the Chronological Table of Statutes up to date) (para.4.6).

▶ A3.26

## Local and Personal Acts—Indexes

*Index to Local and Personal Acts 1801–1947* (para.4.25).
*Supplementary Index to the Local and Personal Acts 1948–1966* (para.4.25).
*Local and Personal Acts; Tables and Index* (annual) (para.4.25).

▶ A3.27

### Is this Act Still in Force? Has it Been Amended?

A3.28 ▶ *Is It In Force?* (shows whether Acts passed since 1961 are still in force) (para.4.17).
*Chronological Table of the Statutes* (indicates if an Act of any date is in force) (para.4.20).
Westlaw UK "Legislation Analysis"(para.4.18).
*Current Law Legislation Citators* (para.4.19).
Full-text databases of legislation in force (para.4.12).
*Public General Acts: Tables and Index* (annual—brings the information in the Chronological Table up to date—see the table "Effects of Legislation") (para.4.6).
*Halsbury's Statutes* (consult the main volumes, the Cumulative Supplement and the looseleaf Service volume) (para.4.16).

### What Cases Have there Been on the Interpretation of this Act?

A3.29 ▶ Westlaw UK "Legislation Analysis"(para.4.18).
*Current Law Legislation Citators* (para.4.19).
*Halsbury's Statutes* (para.7.23).

### What Statutory Instruments Have Been Made under this Act?

A3.30 ▶ Westlaw UK "Legislation Analysis"(para.4.18).
*Current Law Legislation Citators* (para.4.19).
*Halsbury's Statutes* (para.4.16).

### Have any Journal Articles Been Written about this Act?

A3.31 ▶ Westlaw UK "Legislation Analysis" (para.4.18).
*Current Law Legislation Citators* (para.4.19).
*Legal Journals Index* (para.5.6).
Other indexes to journal articles (see heading "Journal Articles", above).

### Has this Act Been Brought into Force by a Statutory Instrument?

A3.32 ▶ *Halsbury's Statutes* (para.4.16).
Westlaw UK "Legislation Analysis" (para.4.18).
*Current Law Legislation Citators* (para.4.19).

## STATUTORY INSTRUMENTS

### Collections of Statutory Instruments

A3.33 ▶ *Statutory Rules and Orders and Statutory Instruments Revised* (all statutory instruments in force in 1948) (para.4.26).
*Statutory Instruments* (annual volumes—subject index in last volume of each year) (para.4.26).
*Halsbury's Statutory Instruments* (selective—arranged by subject) (para.4.29).
Justis UK Statutory Instruments database (para.4.26).
Full-text databases of legislation (para.4.12).

### Is this Statutory Instrument in Force? Has it Been Amended?
*Halsbury's Statutory Instruments* (para.4.29).  ▶ **A3.34**
Full-text databases of legislation in force (para.4.12).

### What Statutory Instruments Have been Made under this Act?
Westlaw UK "Legislation Analysis" (para.4.18).  ▶ **A3.35**
*Current Law Legislation Citator* (para.4.19).
*Halsbury's Statutes* (para.4.16).

### Has this Act Been Brought into Force by a Statutory Instrument?
*Is It in Force?* (para.4.17).  ▶ **A3.36**
Westlaw UK "Legislation Analysis"(para.4.18).
*Current Law Legislation Citators* (para.4.19).

### Indexes to Statutory Instruments
*Halsbury's Statutory Instruments* (chronological, alphabetical and by subject) (para.4.29,  ▶ **A3.37**
para.7.27).
TSO *Daily Lists* (includes all new Instruments as they are published) (para.6.15).

## THESES  ▶ **A3.38**
  ▶ **A3.39**
*Index to Theses* (para.7.38).
*Dissertation Abstracts* (para.7.38).

## WORDS AND PHRASES

For the meaning of words and phrases, use legal dictionaries (para.1.10).  ▶ **A3.40**
For Latin phrases, use legal dictionaries and *Broom's Legal Maxims* (para.1.11).

### Judicial and Statutory Definitions of Words and Phrases
*Words and Phrases Legally Defined* (para.7.19).  ▶ **A3.41**
*Stroud's Judicial Dictionary*.
The entry "Words and Phrases" in: *Law Reports: Consolidated Index; Current Law Monthly Digests* and *Current Law Year Books*; and indexes to the *All England Law Reports, Halsbury's Laws,* and *The Digest*.

# Index

This index has been prepared using Sweet and Maxwell's Legal Taxonomy. Main index entries conform to keywords provided by the Legal Taxonomy except where references to specific documents or non-standard terms (denoted by quotation marks) have been included. These keywords provide a means of identifying similar concepts in other Sweet & Maxwell publications and online services to which keywords from the Legal Taxonomy have been applied. Readers may find some minor differences between terms used in the text and those which appear in the index. Suggestions to **sweetandmaxwell.taxonomy@ thomson.com.**

*(all references are to paragraph number)*